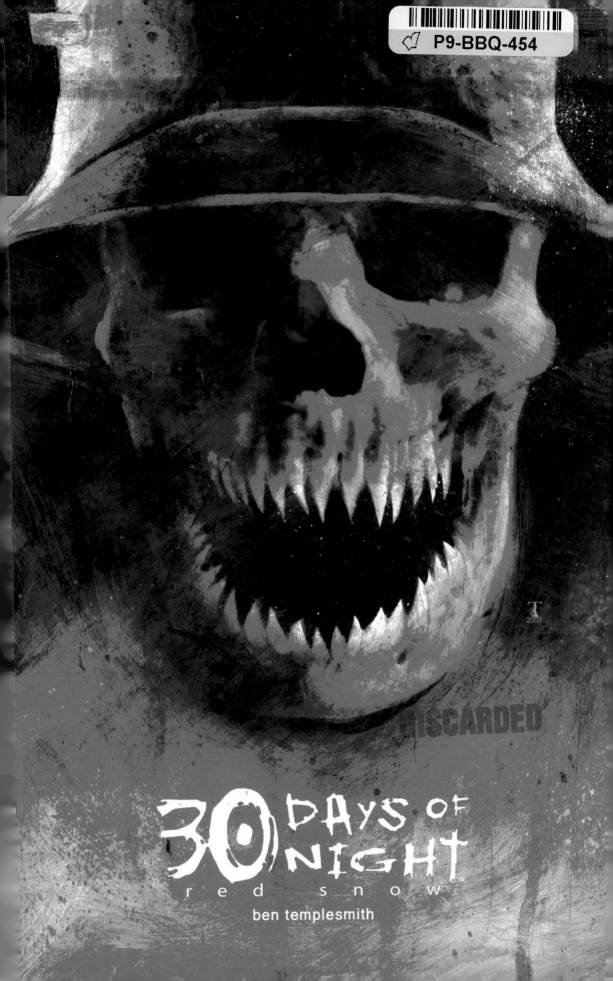

30 DAYS OF NIGHT

red snow

ben templesmith

30 Days of Night: Red Snow

story and art: ben templesmith,
for Singularity Pty Ltd.

letters: neil uyetake & robbie robbins

editor: chris ryall

collection design: chris mowry
collection edits: justin eisinger

IDW Publishing is:
Ted Adams, President
Robbie Robbins, EVP/Sr. Graphic Artist
Clifford Meth, EVP of Strategies/Editorial
Chris Ryall, Publisher/Editor-in-Chief
Alan Payne, VP of Sales
Neil Uyetake, Art Director
Justin Eisinger, Editor
Tom Waltz, Editor
Andrew Steven Harris, Editor
Chris Mowry, Graphic Artist
Amauri Osorio, Graphic Artist
Matthew Ruzicka, CPA, Controller
Alonzo Simon, Shipping Manager
Kris Oprisko, Editor/Foreign Lic. Rep.

ISBN: 978-1-60010-149-6

11 10 09 08   1 2 3 4 5

30 Days of Night created by
Steve Niles & Ben Templesmith

Table of Contents

Chapter One

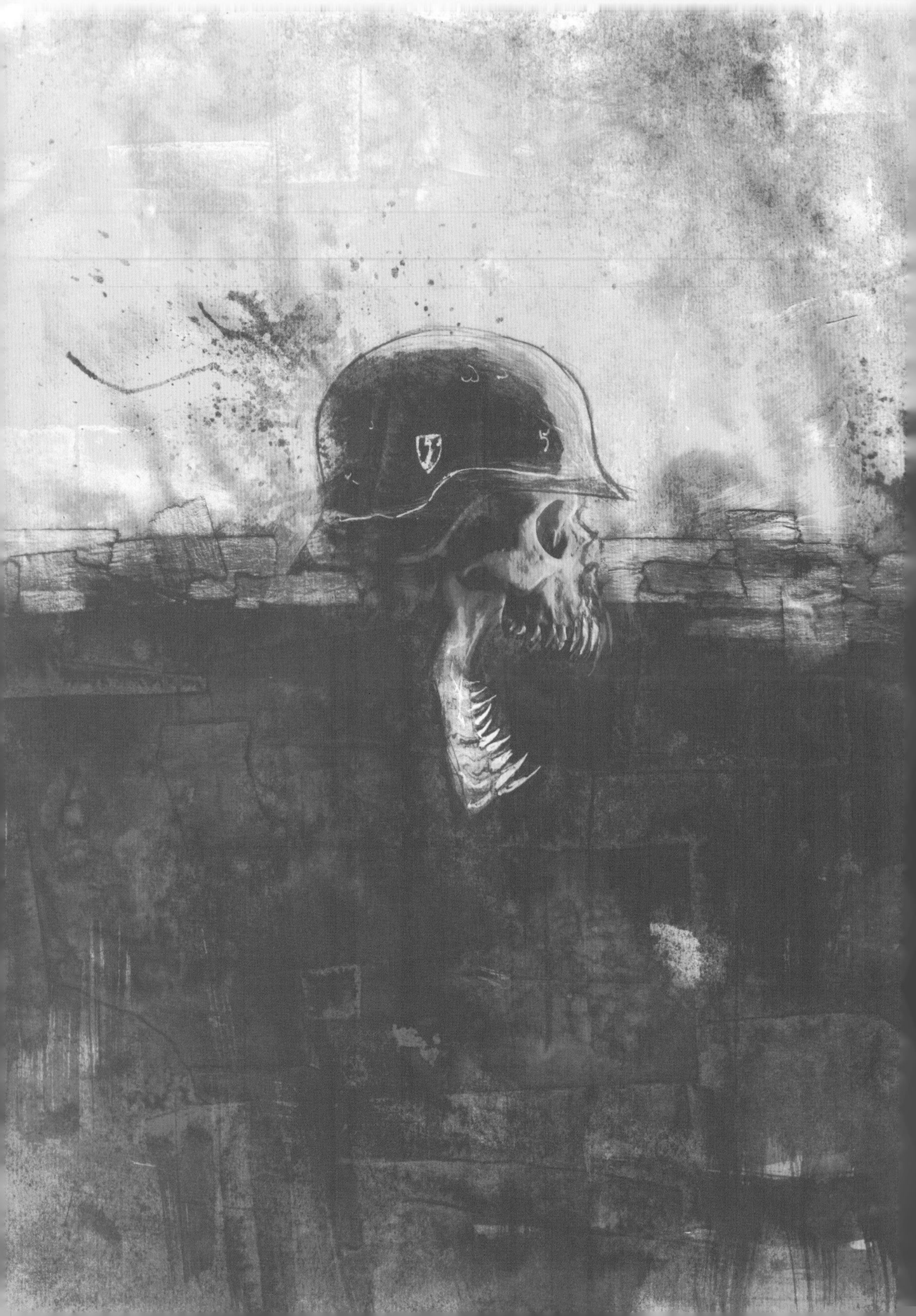

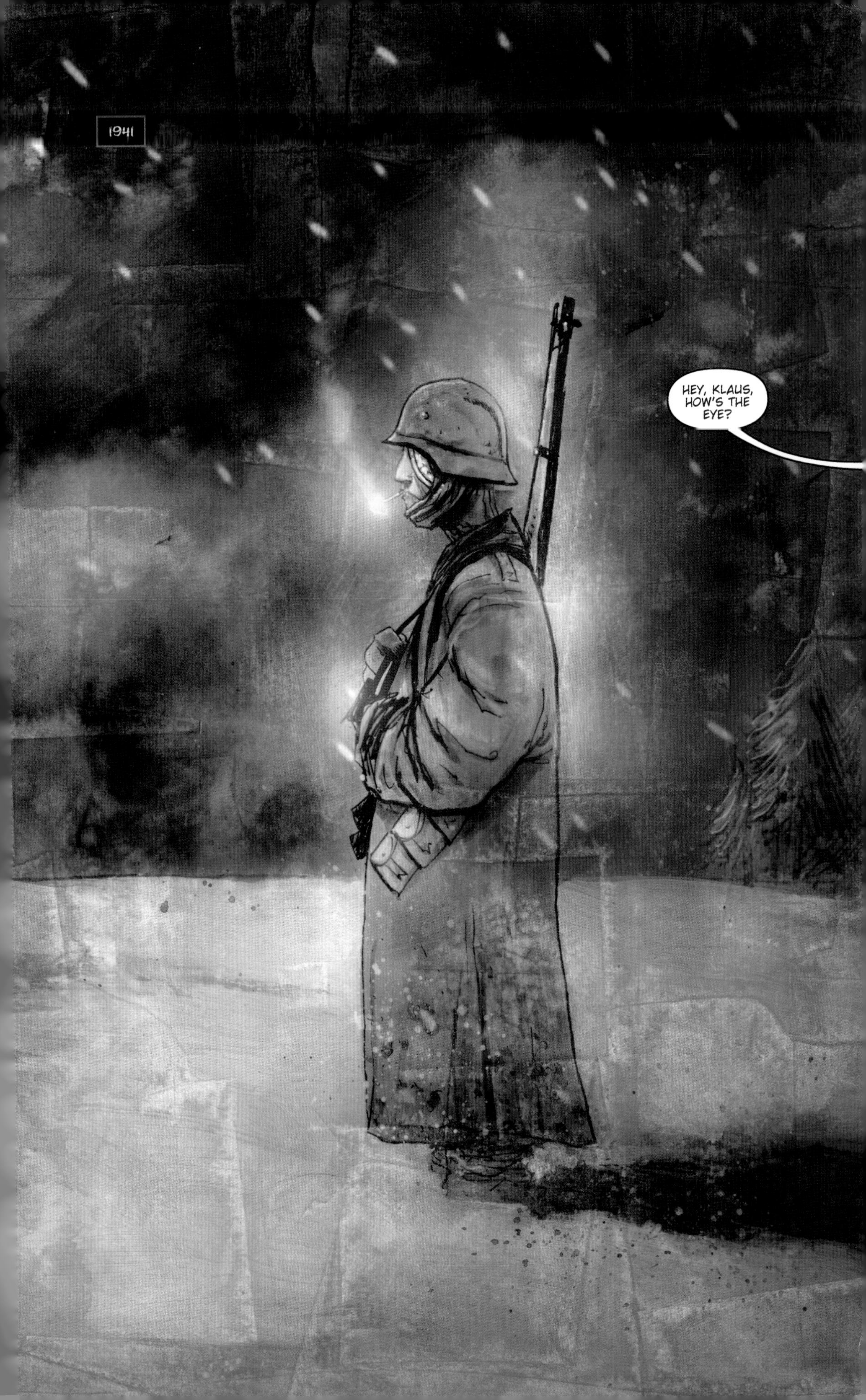
1941
HEY, KLAUS, HOW'S THE EYE?

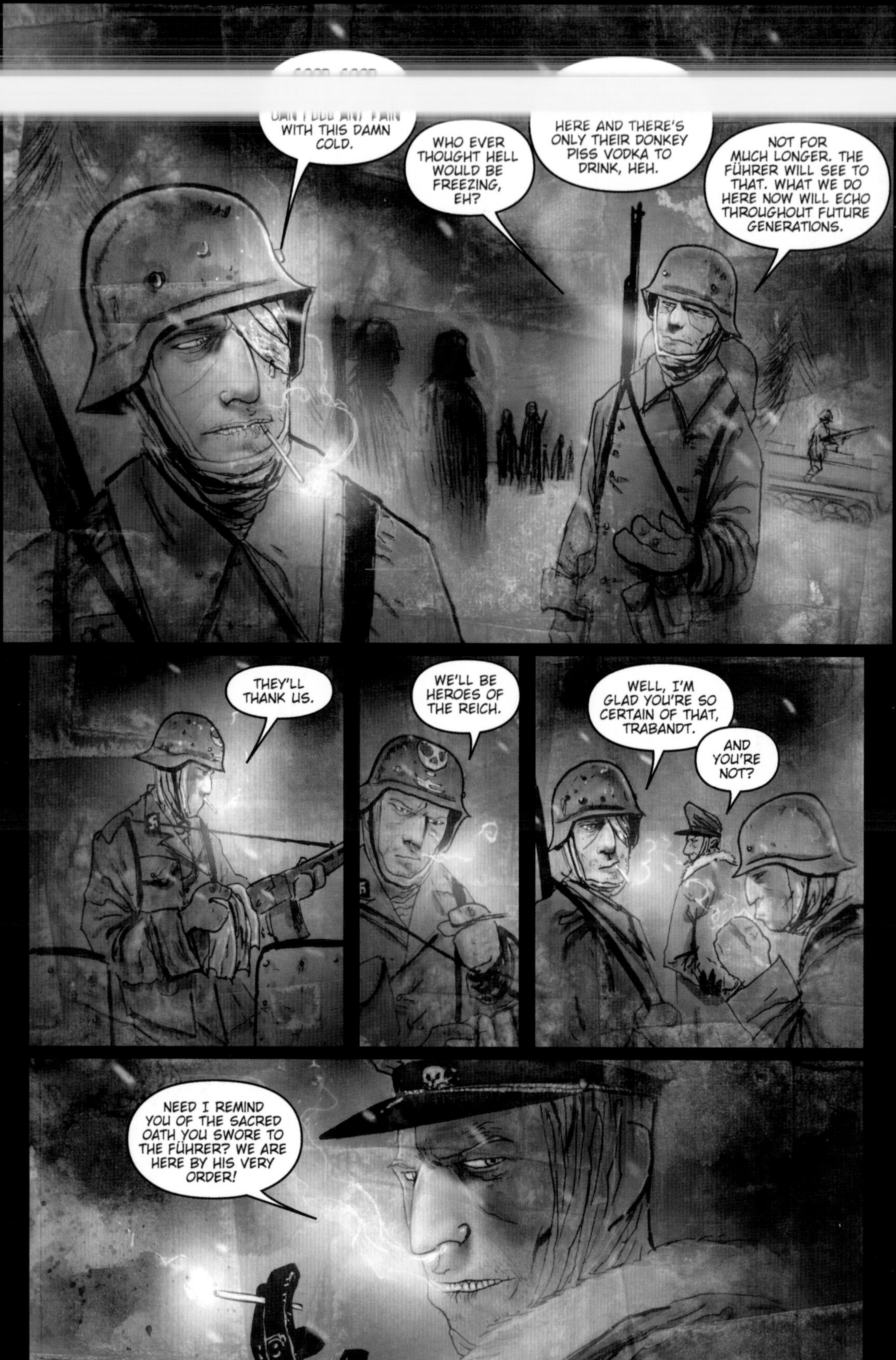
WITH THIS DAMN COLD.
WHO EVER THOUGHT HELL WOULD BE FREEZING, EH?
HERE AND THERE'S ONLY THEIR DONKEY PISS VODKA TO DRINK, HEH.
NOT FOR MUCH LONGER. THE FÜHRER WILL SEE TO THAT. WHAT WE DO HERE NOW WILL ECHO THROUGHOUT FUTURE GENERATIONS.
THEY'LL THANK US.
WE'LL BE HEROES OF THE REICH.
WELL, I'M GLAD YOU'RE SO CERTAIN OF THAT, TRABANDT.
AND YOU'RE NOT?
NEED I REMIND YOU OF THE SACRED OATH YOU SWORE TO THE FÜHRER? WE ARE HERE BY HIS VERY ORDER!

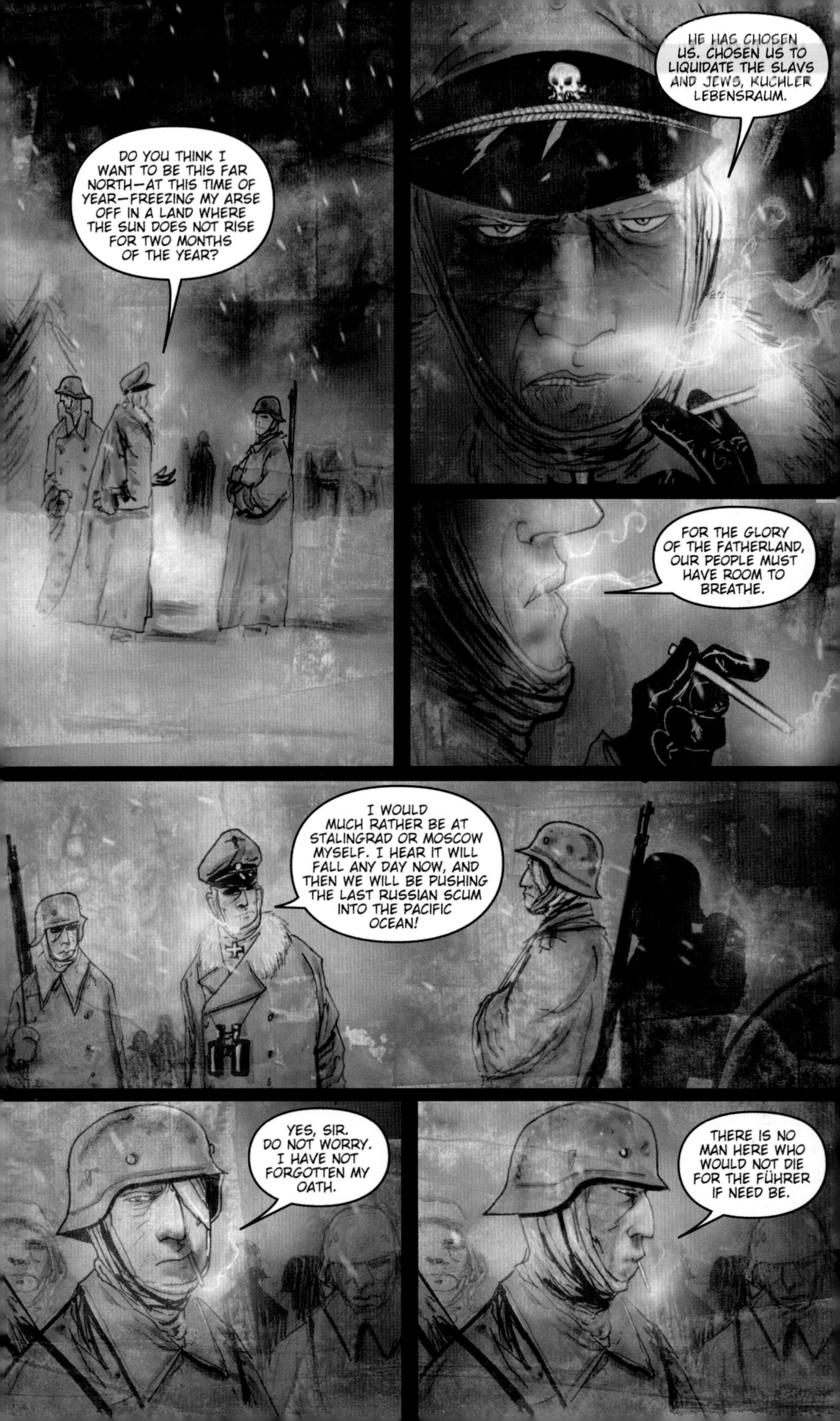
DO YOU THINK I WANT TO BE THIS FAR NORTH—AT THIS TIME OF YEAR—FREEZING MY ARSE OFF IN A LAND WHERE THE SUN DOES NOT RISE FOR TWO MONTHS OF THE YEAR?
HE HAS CHOSEN US. CHOSEN US TO LIQUIDATE THE SLAVS AND JEWS, KUCHLER LEBENSRAUM.
FOR THE GLORY OF THE FATHERLAND, OUR PEOPLE MUST HAVE ROOM TO BREATHE.
I WOULD MUCH RATHER BE AT STALINGRAD OR MOSCOW MYSELF. I HEAR IT WILL FALL ANY DAY NOW, AND THEN WE WILL BE PUSHING THE LAST RUSSIAN SCUM INTO THE PACIFIC OCEAN!
YES, SIR. DO NOT WORRY. I HAVE NOT FORGOTTEN MY OATH.
THERE IS NO MAN HERE WHO WOULD NOT DIE FOR THE FÜHRER IF NEED BE.

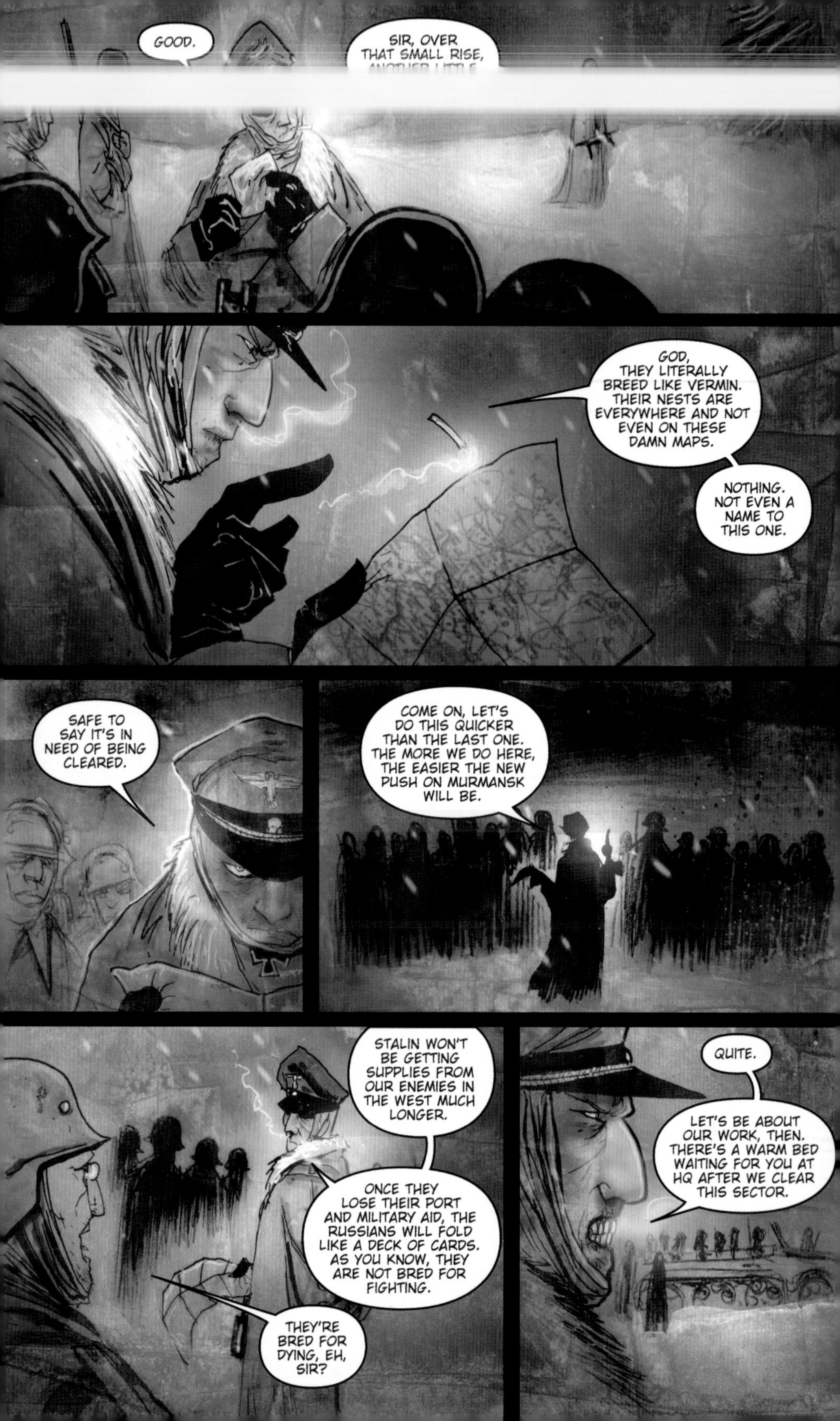
GOOD.
SIR, OVER THAT SMALL RISE,
GOD, THEY LITERALLY BREED LIKE VERMIN. THEIR NESTS ARE EVERYWHERE AND NOT EVEN ON THESE DAMN MAPS.
NOTHING. NOT EVEN A NAME TO THIS ONE.
SAFE TO SAY IT'S IN NEED OF BEING CLEARED.
COME ON, LET'S DO THIS QUICKER THAN THE LAST ONE. THE MORE WE DO HERE, THE EASIER THE NEW PUSH ON MURMANSK WILL BE.
STALIN WON'T BE GETTING SUPPLIES FROM OUR ENEMIES IN THE WEST MUCH LONGER.
ONCE THEY LOSE THEIR PORT AND MILITARY AID, THE RUSSIANS WILL FOLD LIKE A DECK OF CARDS. AS YOU KNOW, THEY ARE NOT BRED FOR FIGHTING.
THEY'RE BRED FOR DYING, EH, SIR?
QUITE.
LET'S BE ABOUT OUR WORK, THEN. THERE'S A WARM BED WAITING FOR YOU AT HQ AFTER WE CLEAR THIS SECTOR.

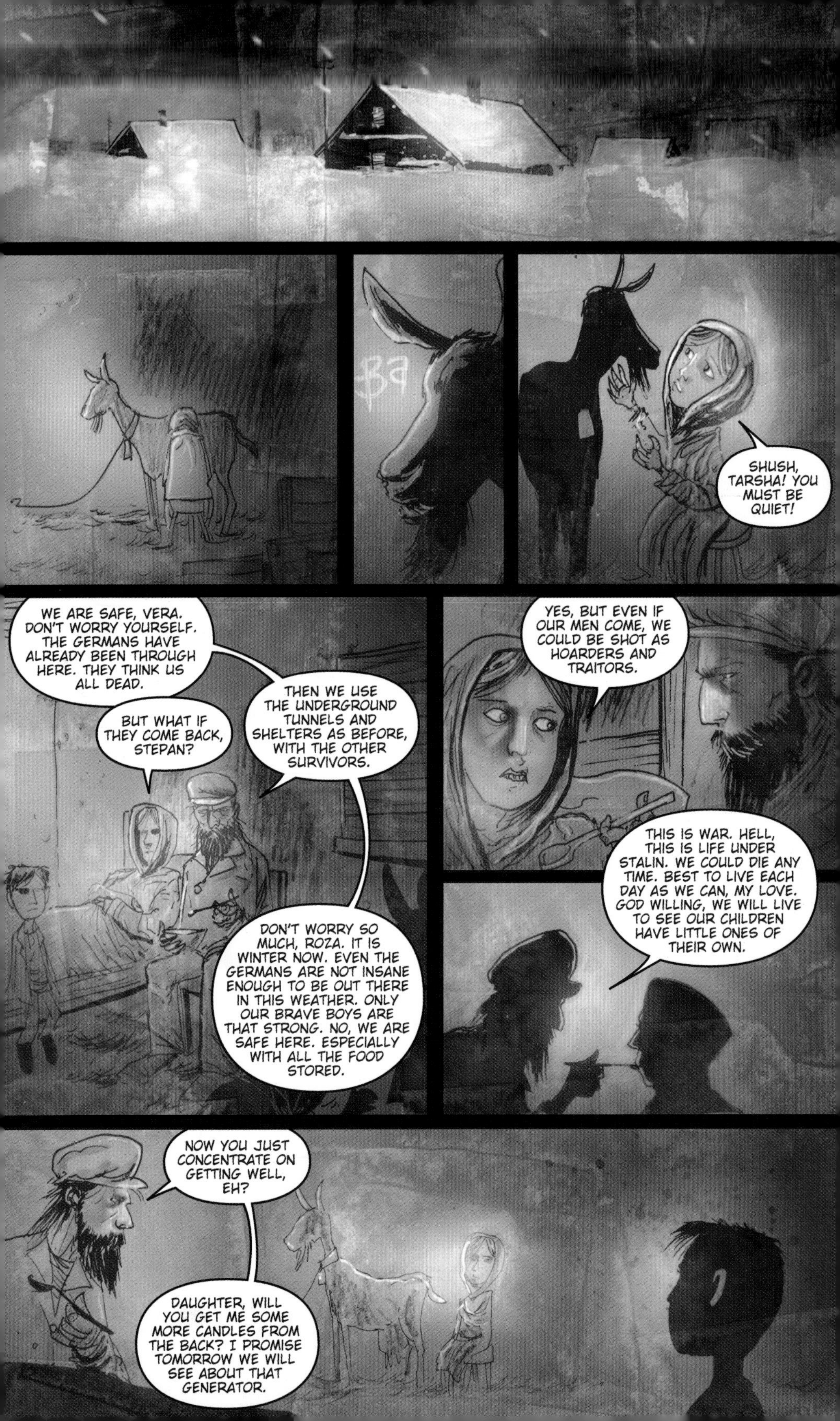
BA
SHUSH, TARSHA! YOU MUST BE QUIET!
WE ARE SAFE, VERA. DON'T WORRY YOURSELF. THE GERMANS HAVE ALREADY BEEN THROUGH HERE. THEY THINK US ALL DEAD.
BUT WHAT IF THEY COME BACK, STEPAN?
THEN WE USE THE UNDERGROUND TUNNELS AND SHELTERS AS BEFORE, WITH THE OTHER SURVIVORS.
DON'T WORRY SO MUCH, ROZA. IT IS WINTER NOW. EVEN THE GERMANS ARE NOT INSANE ENOUGH TO BE OUT THERE IN THIS WEATHER. ONLY OUR BRAVE BOYS ARE THAT STRONG. NO, WE ARE SAFE HERE. ESPECIALLY WITH ALL THE FOOD STORED.
YES, BUT EVEN IF OUR MEN COME, WE COULD BE SHOT AS HOARDERS AND TRAITORS.
THIS IS WAR. HELL, THIS IS LIFE UNDER STALIN. WE COULD DIE ANY TIME. BEST TO LIVE EACH DAY AS WE CAN, MY LOVE. GOD WILLING, WE WILL LIVE TO SEE OUR CHILDREN HAVE LITTLE ONES OF THEIR OWN.
NOW YOU JUST CONCENTRATE ON GETTING WELL, EH?
DAUGHTER, WILL YOU GET ME SOME MORE CANDLES FROM THE BACK? I PROMISE TOMORROW WE WILL SEE ABOUT THAT GENERATOR.

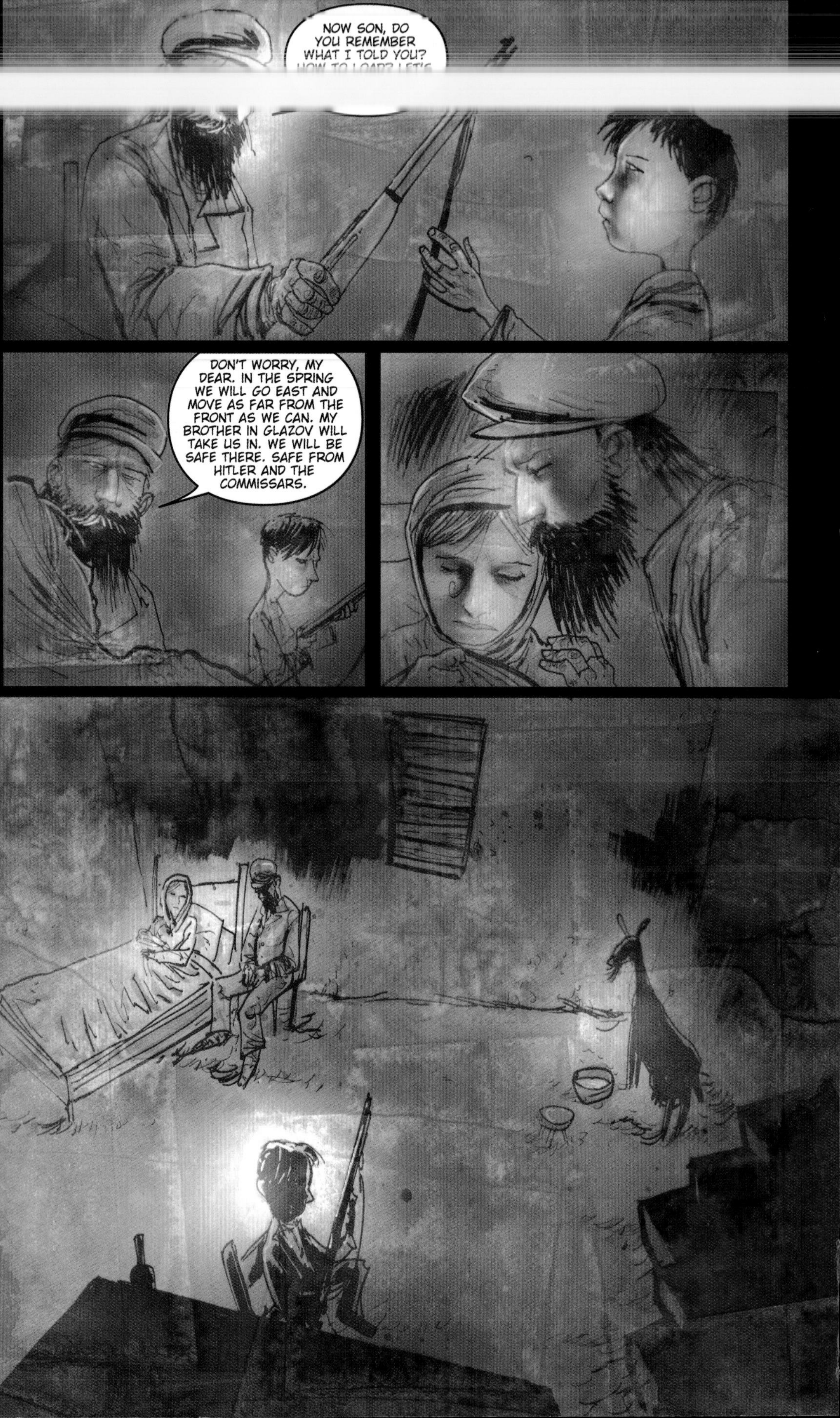
NOW SON, DO YOU REMEMBER WHAT I TOLD YOU?
DON'T WORRY, MY DEAR. IN THE SPRING WE WILL GO EAST AND MOVE AS FAR FROM THE FRONT AS WE CAN. MY BROTHER IN GLAZOV WILL TAKE US IN. WE WILL BE SAFE THERE. SAFE FROM HITLER AND THE COMMISSARS.

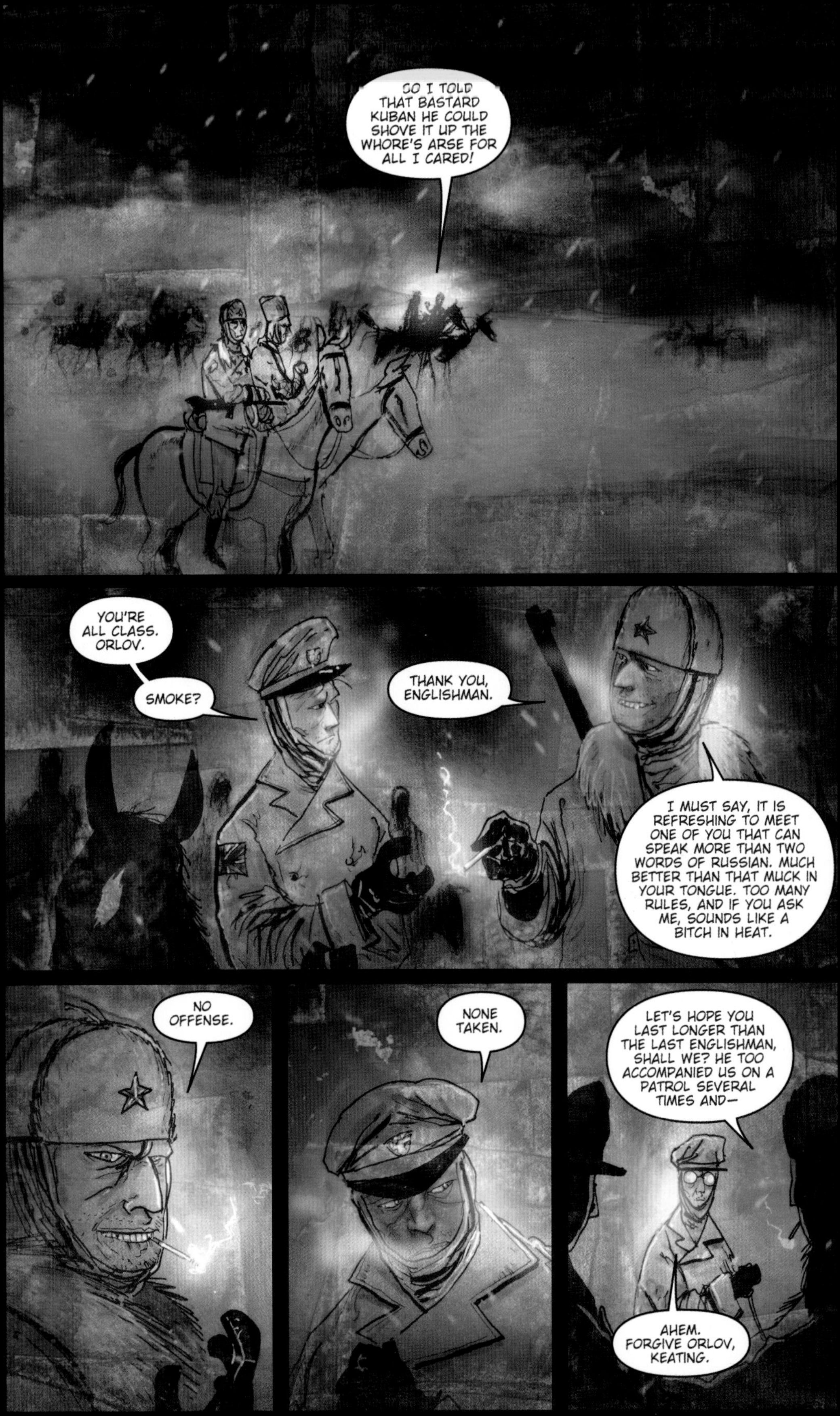
SO I TOLD THAT BASTARD KUBAN HE COULD SHOVE IT UP THE WHORE'S ARSE FOR ALL I CARED!
YOU'RE ALL CLASS. ORLOV.
SMOKE?
THANK YOU, ENGLISHMAN.
I MUST SAY, IT IS REFRESHING TO MEET ONE OF YOU THAT CAN SPEAK MORE THAN TWO WORDS OF RUSSIAN. MUCH BETTER THAN THAT MUCK IN YOUR TONGUE. TOO MANY RULES, AND IF YOU ASK ME, SOUNDS LIKE A BITCH IN HEAT.
NO OFFENSE.
NONE TAKEN.
LET'S HOPE YOU LAST LONGER THAN THE LAST ENGLISHMAN, SHALL WE? HE TOO ACCOMPANIED US ON A PATROL SEVERAL TIMES AND—
AHEM. FORGIVE ORLOV, KEATING.

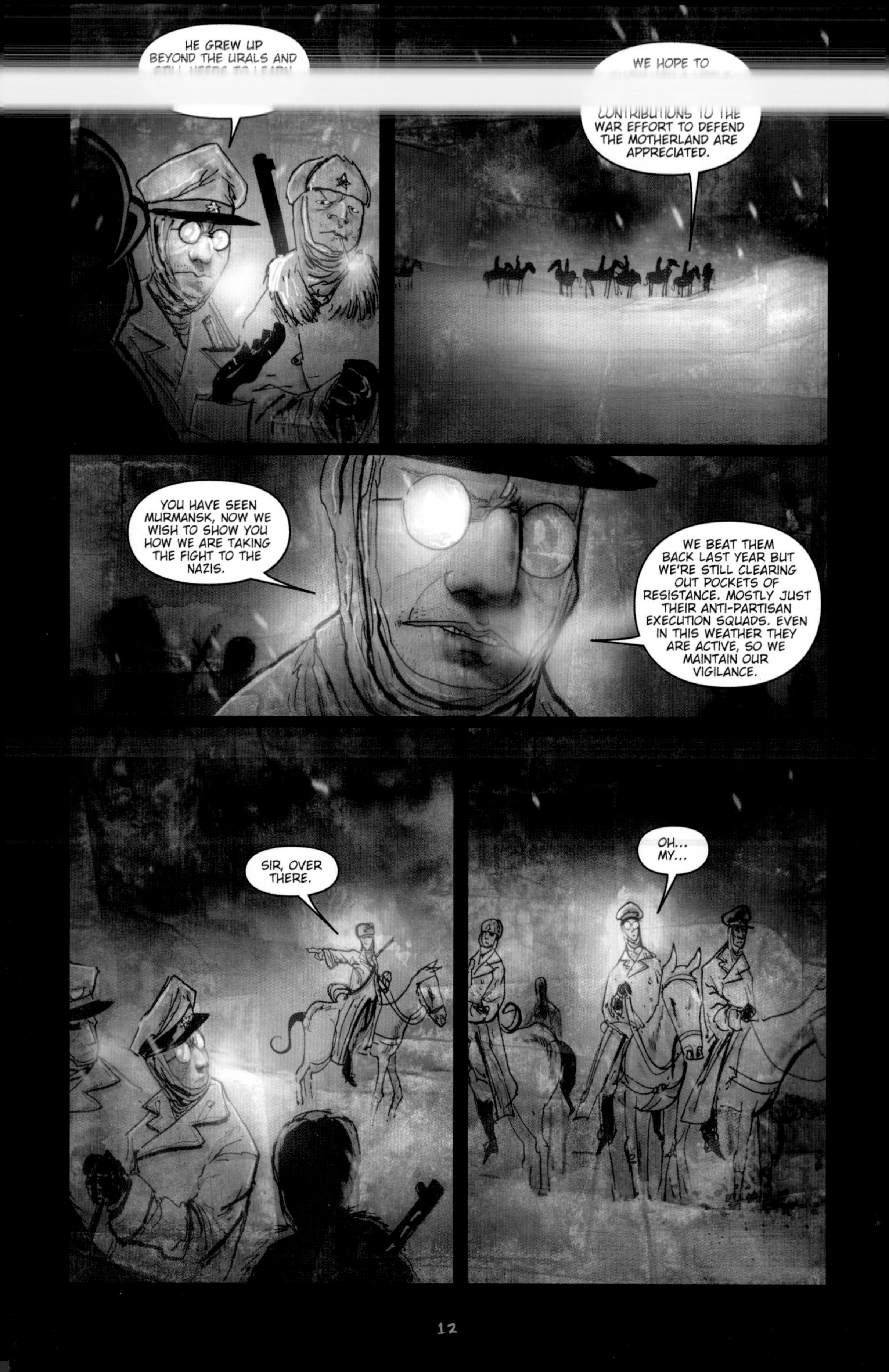
HE GREW UP
BEYOND THE URALS AND
WE HOPE TO
CONTRIBUTIONS TO THE
WAR EFFORT TO DEFEND
THE MOTHERLAND ARE
APPRECIATED.
YOU HAVE SEEN MURMANSK, NOW WE WISH TO SHOW YOU HOW WE ARE TAKING THE FIGHT TO THE NAZIS.
WE BEAT THEM BACK LAST YEAR BUT WE'RE STILL CLEARING OUT POCKETS OF RESISTANCE. MOSTLY JUST THEIR ANTI-PARTISAN EXECUTION SQUADS. EVEN IN THIS WEATHER THEY ARE ACTIVE, SO WE MAINTAIN OUR VIGILANCE.
SIR, OVER THERE.
OH... MY...

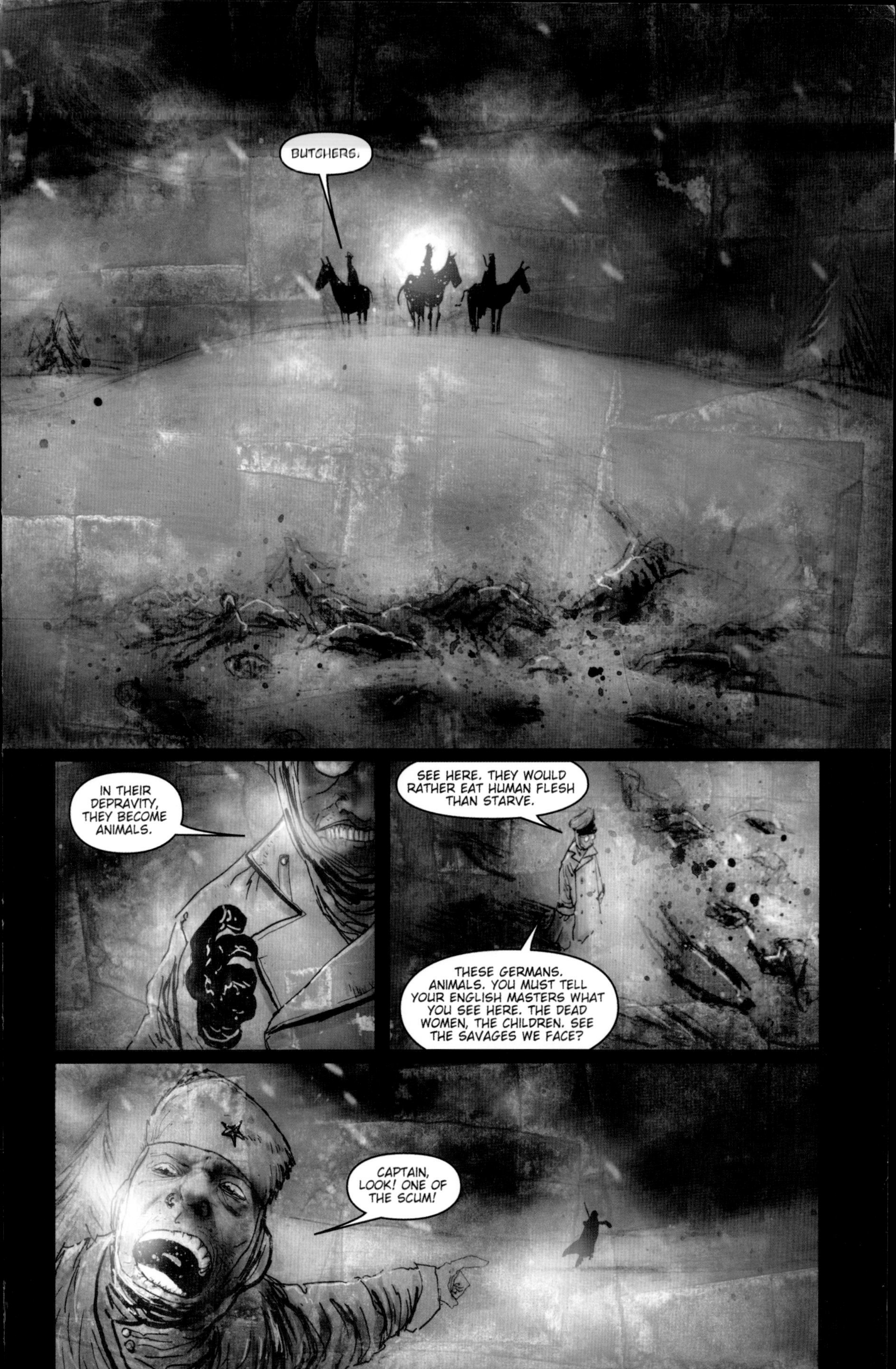
BUTCHERS.
IN THEIR DEPRAVITY, THEY BECOME ANIMALS.
SEE HERE. THEY WOULD RATHER EAT HUMAN FLESH THAN STARVE.
THESE GERMANS. ANIMALS. YOU MUST TELL YOUR ENGLISH MASTERS WHAT YOU SEE HERE. THE DEAD WOMEN, THE CHILDREN. SEE THE SAVAGES WE FACE?
CAPTAIN, LOOK! ONE OF THE SCUM!

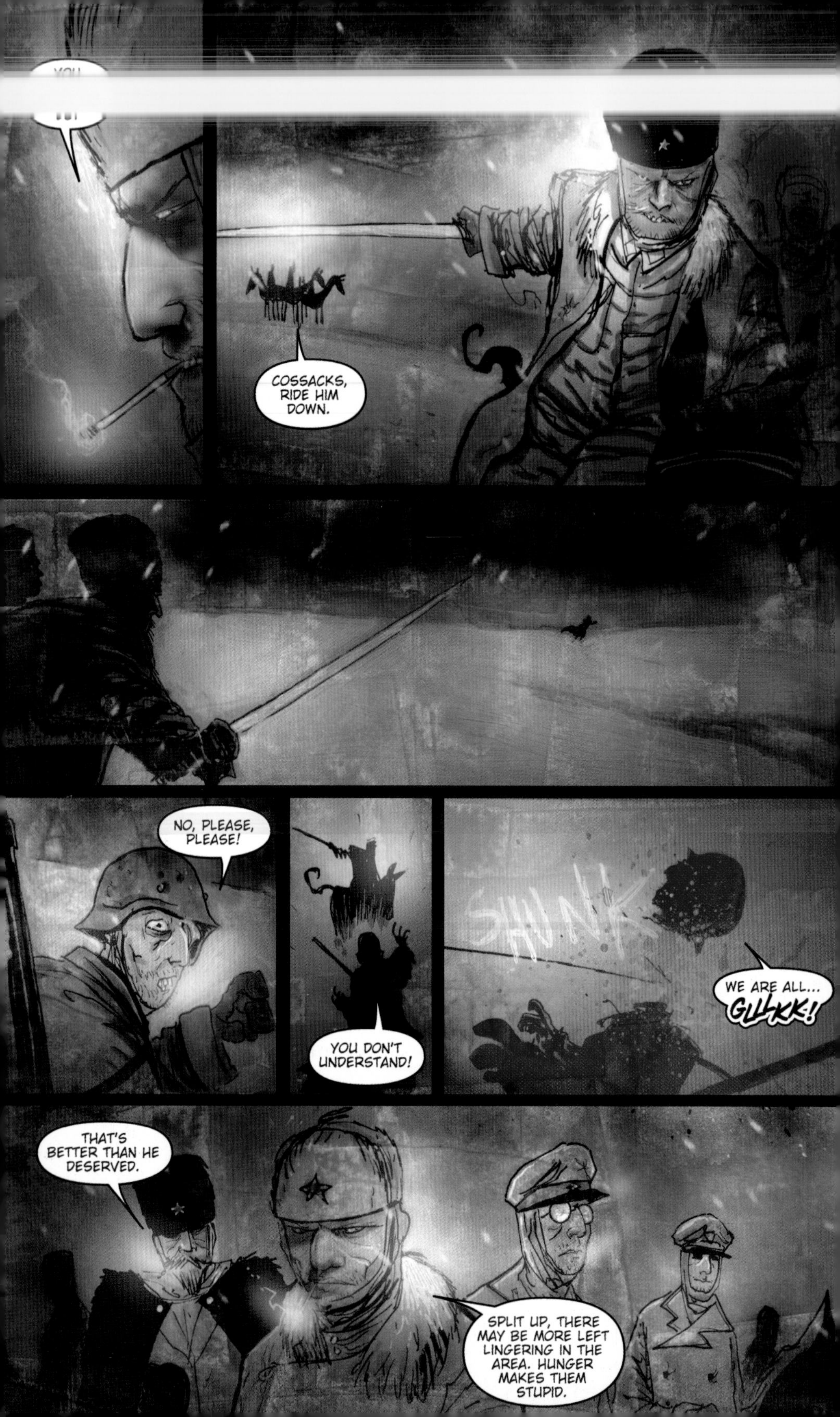
YOU
COSSACKS, RIDE HIM DOWN.
NO, PLEASE, PLEASE!
YOU DON'T UNDERSTAND!
SHUNK
WE ARE ALL... GLLKK!
THAT'S BETTER THAN HE DESERVED.
SPLIT UP, THERE MAY BE MORE LEFT LINGERING IN THE AREA. HUNGER MAKES THEM STUPID.

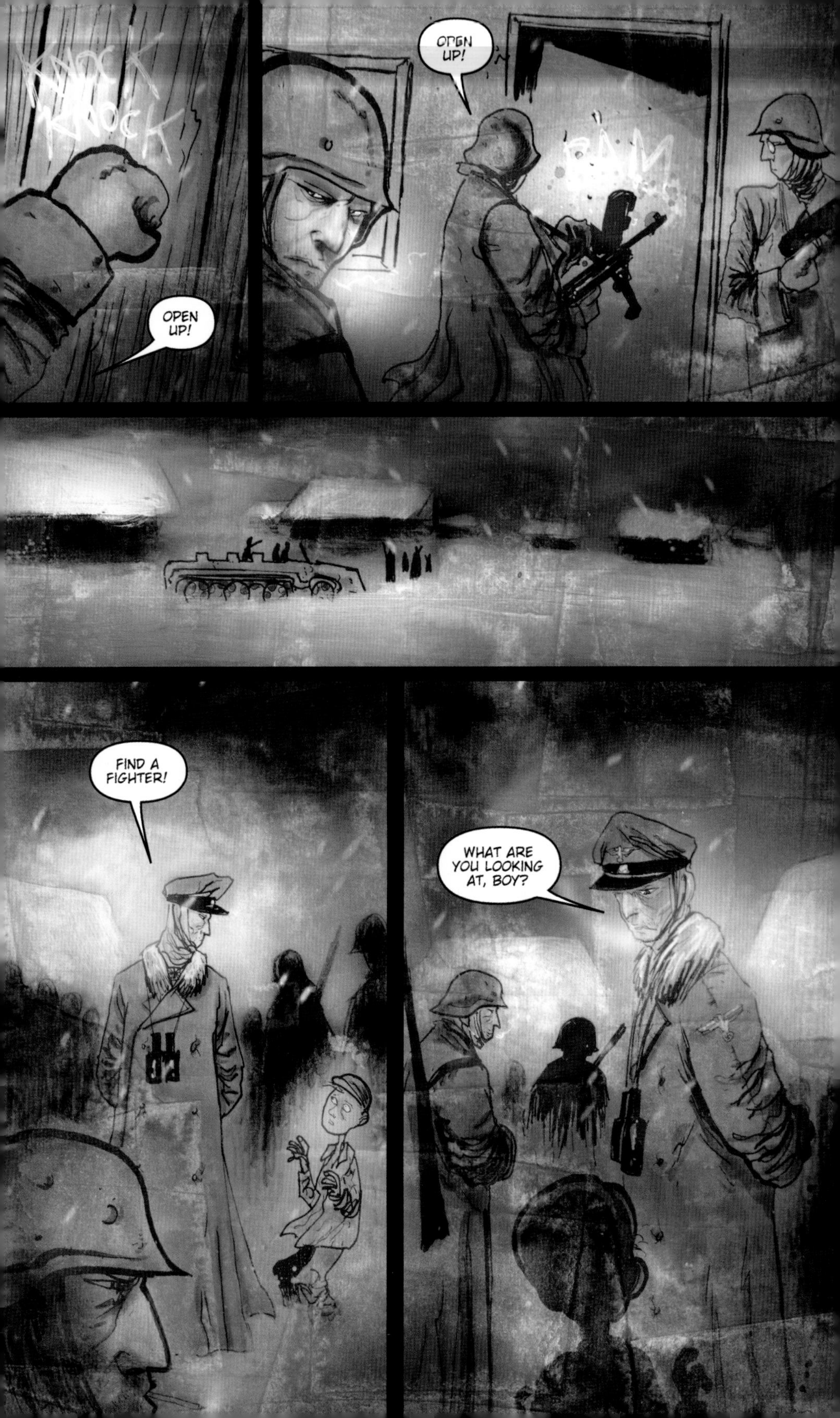
KNOCK KNOCK
OPEN UP!
OPEN UP!
BAM
FIND A FIGHTER!
WHAT ARE YOU LOOKING AT, BOY?

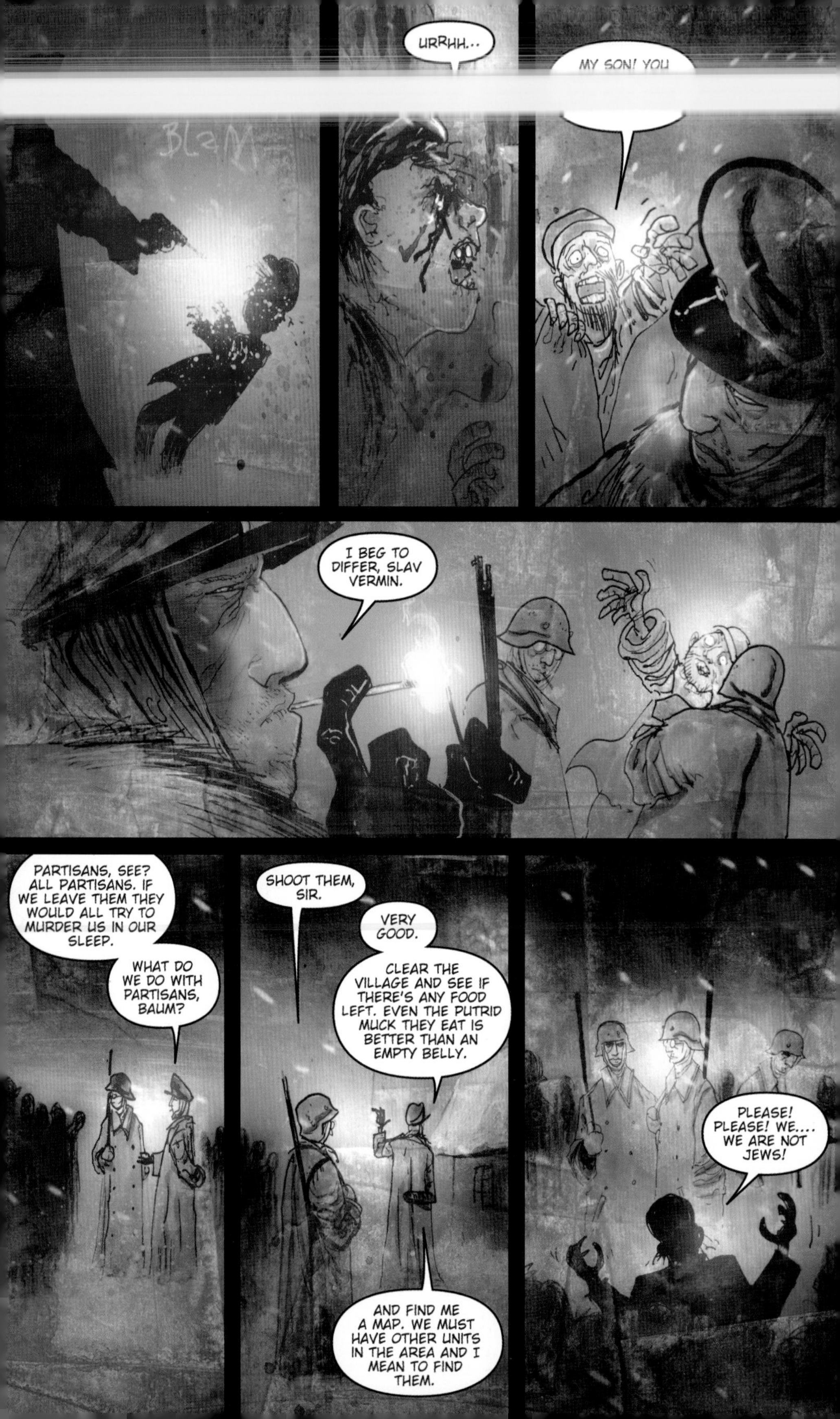

Bl2M
URRHH...
MY SON! YOU
I BEG TO DIFFER, SLAV VERMIN.
PARTISANS, SEE? ALL PARTISANS. IF WE LEAVE THEM THEY WOULD ALL TRY TO MURDER US IN OUR SLEEP.
WHAT DO WE DO WITH PARTISANS, BAUM?
SHOOT THEM, SIR.
VERY GOOD.
CLEAR THE VILLAGE AND SEE IF THERE'S ANY FOOD LEFT. EVEN THE PUTRID MUCK THEY EAT IS BETTER THAN AN EMPTY BELLY.
AND FIND ME A MAP. WE MUST HAVE OTHER UNITS IN THE AREA AND I MEAN TO FIND THEM.
PLEASE! PLEASE! WE.... WE ARE NOT JEWS!

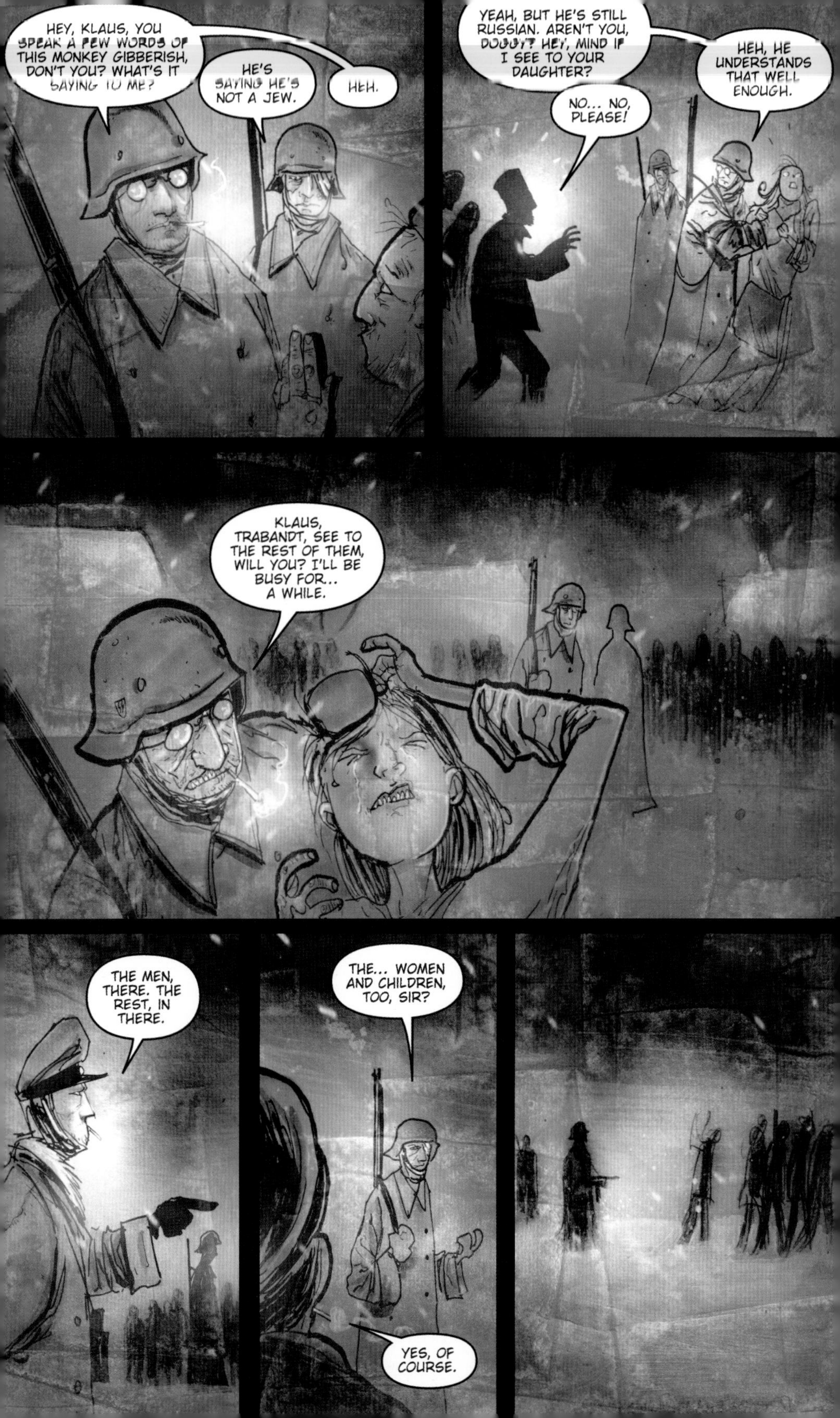
HEY, KLAUS, YOU SPEAK A FEW WORDS OF THIS MONKEY GIBBERISH, DON'T YOU? WHAT'S IT SAYING TO ME?
HE'S SAYING HE'S NOT A JEW.
HEH.
YEAH, BUT HE'S STILL RUSSIAN. AREN'T YOU, DOGGY? HEY, MIND IF I SEE TO YOUR DAUGHTER?
NO... NO, PLEASE!
HEH, HE UNDERSTANDS THAT WELL ENOUGH.
KLAUS, TRABANDT, SEE TO THE REST OF THEM, WILL YOU? I'LL BE BUSY FOR... A WHILE.
THE MEN, THERE. THE REST, IN THERE.
THE... WOMEN AND CHILDREN, TOO, SIR?
YES, OF COURSE.

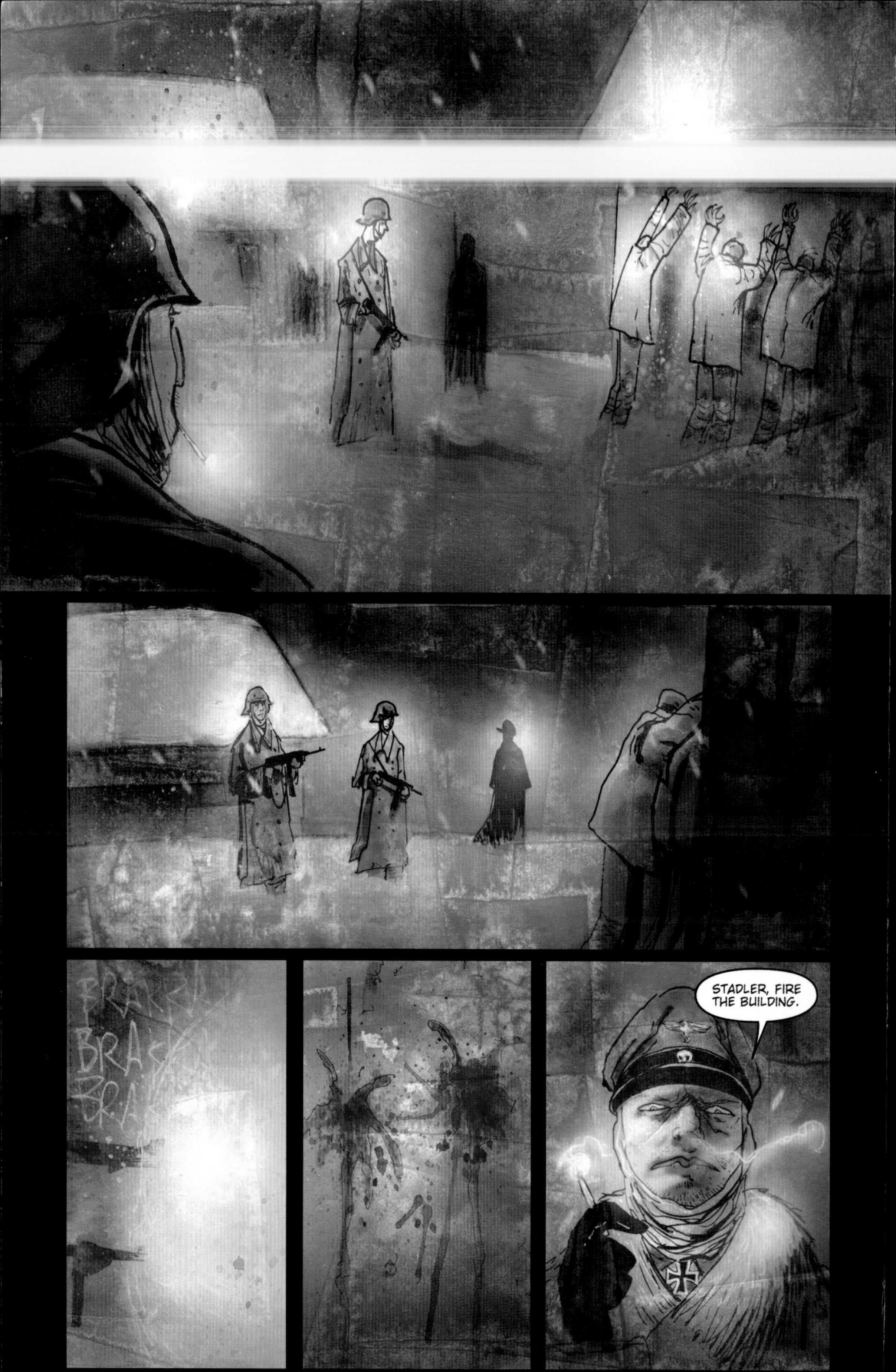
STADLER, FIRE THE BUILDING.

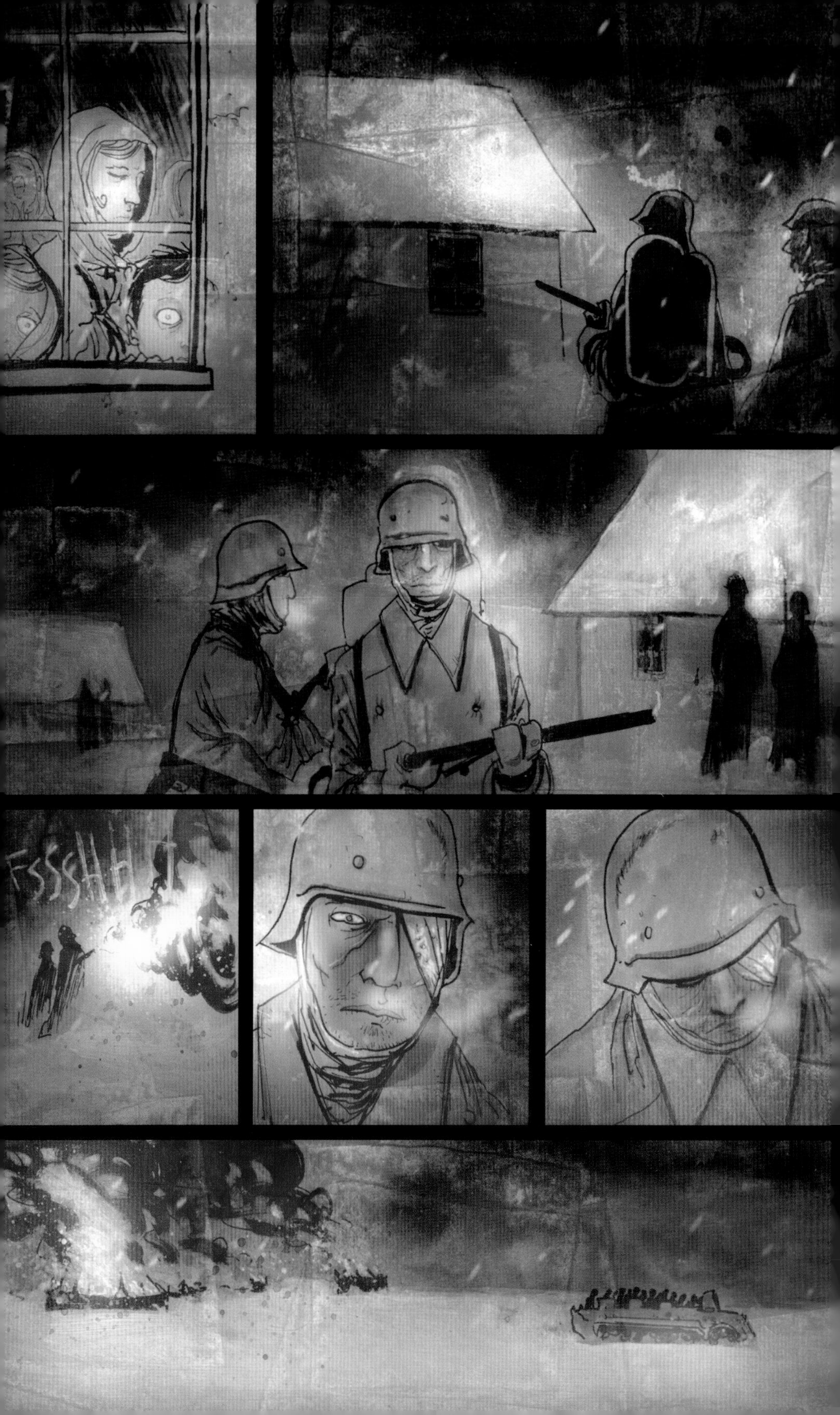
FSSSHHT

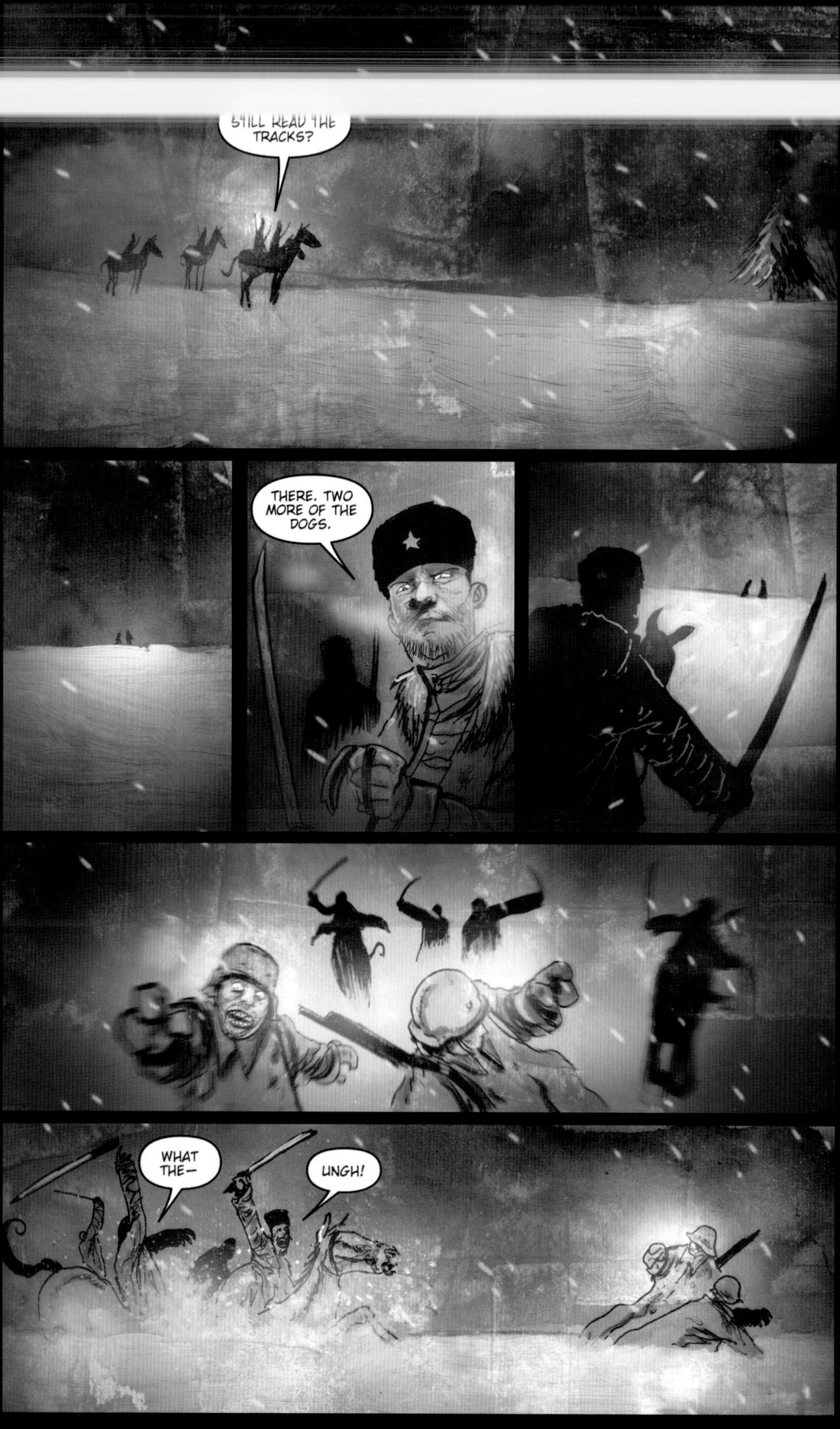
STILL READ THE TRACKS?
THERE. TWO MORE OF THE DOGS.
WHAT THE—
UNGH!

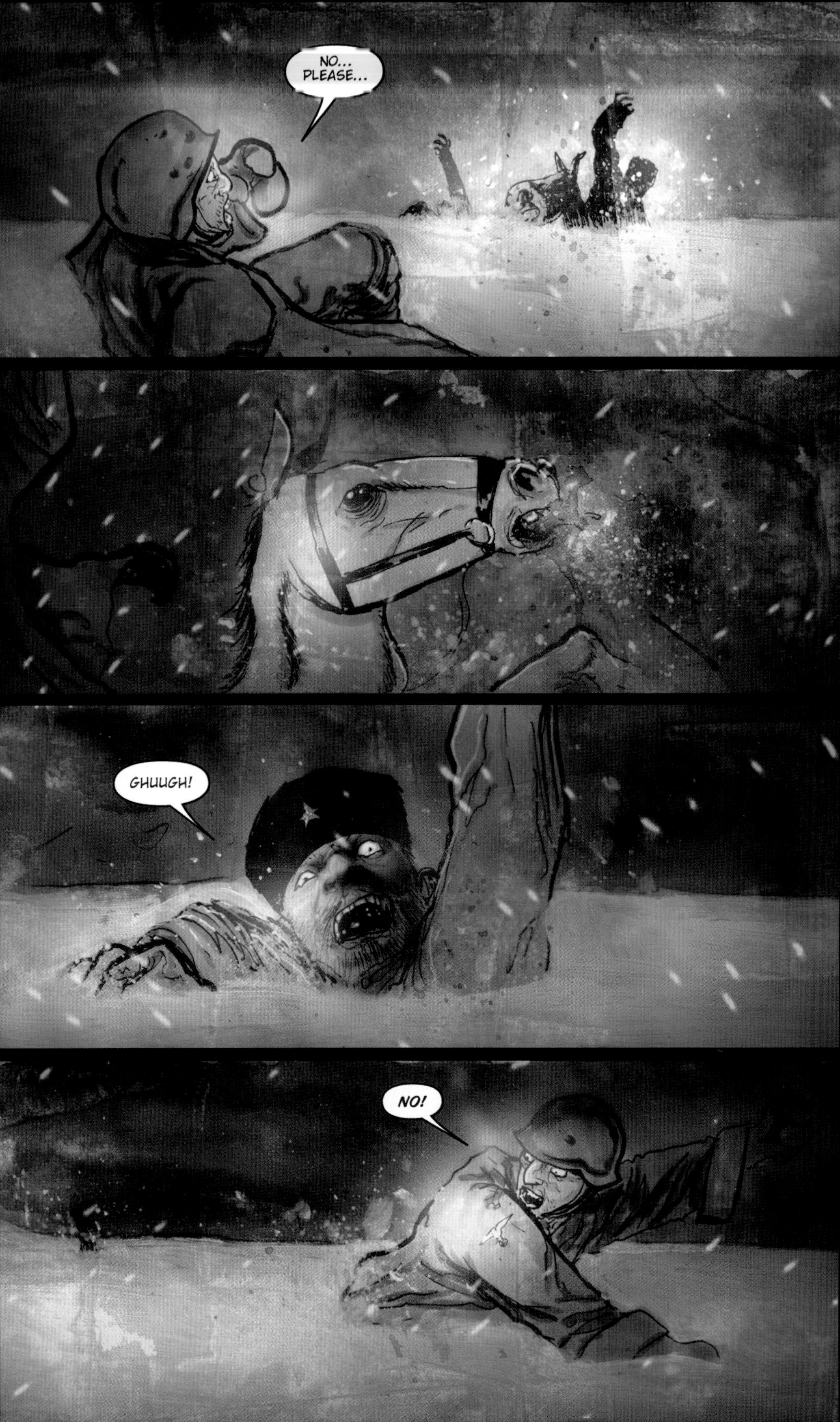
NO... PLEASE...
GHUUGH!
NO!

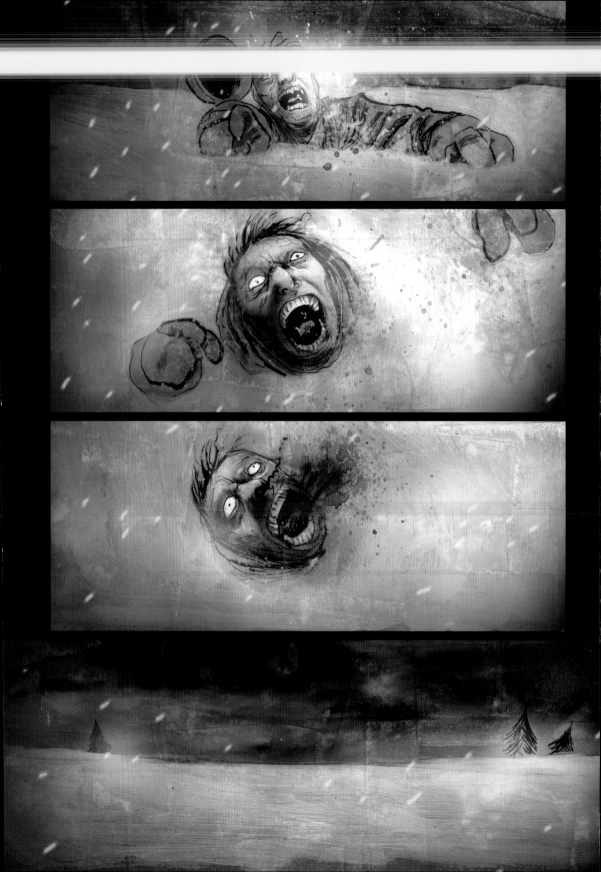

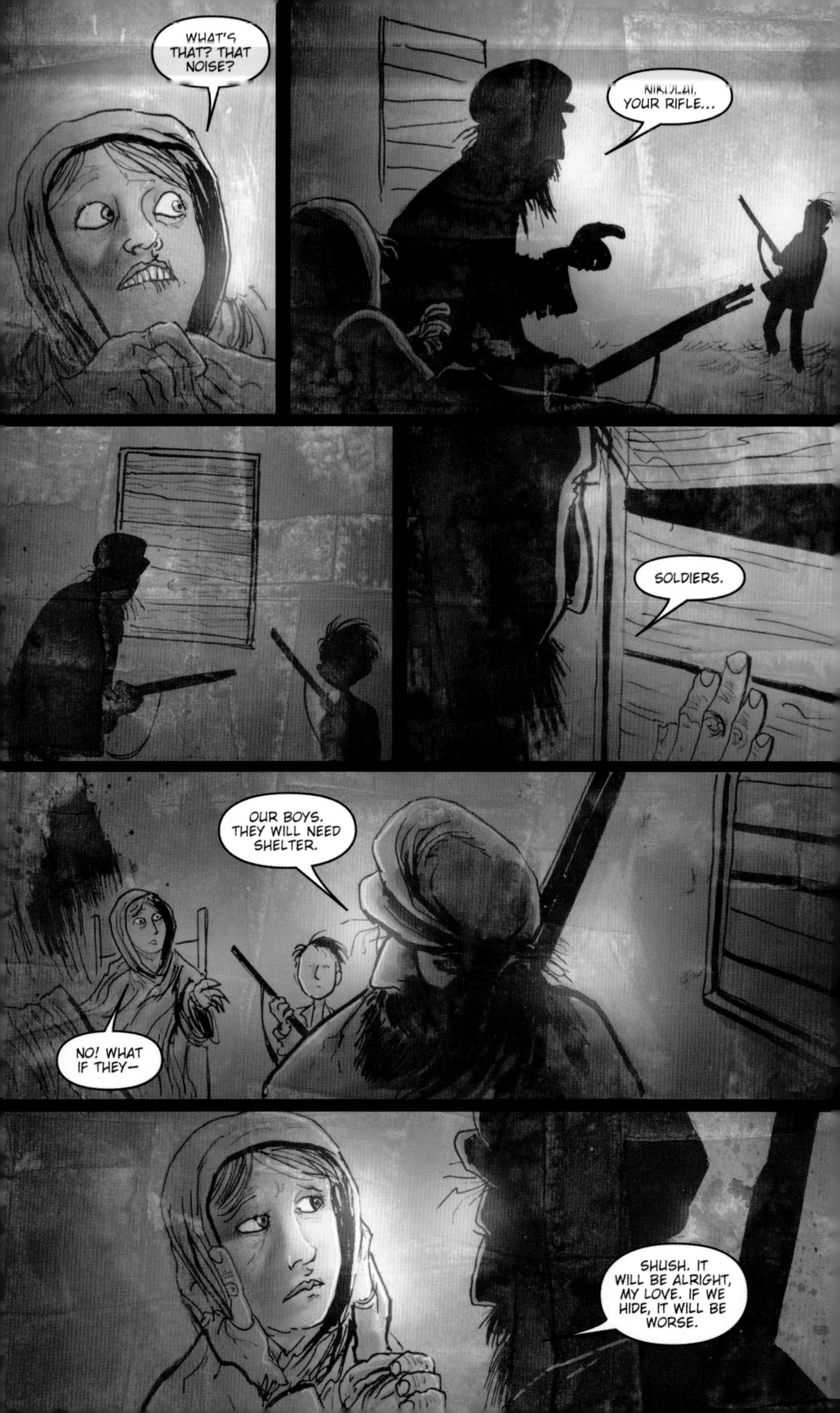
WHAT'S THAT? THAT NOISE?
NIKOLAI, YOUR RIFLE...
SOLDIERS.
OUR BOYS. THEY WILL NEED SHELTER.
NO! WHAT IF THEY—
SHUSH. IT WILL BE ALRIGHT, MY LOVE. IF WE HIDE, IT WILL BE WORSE.

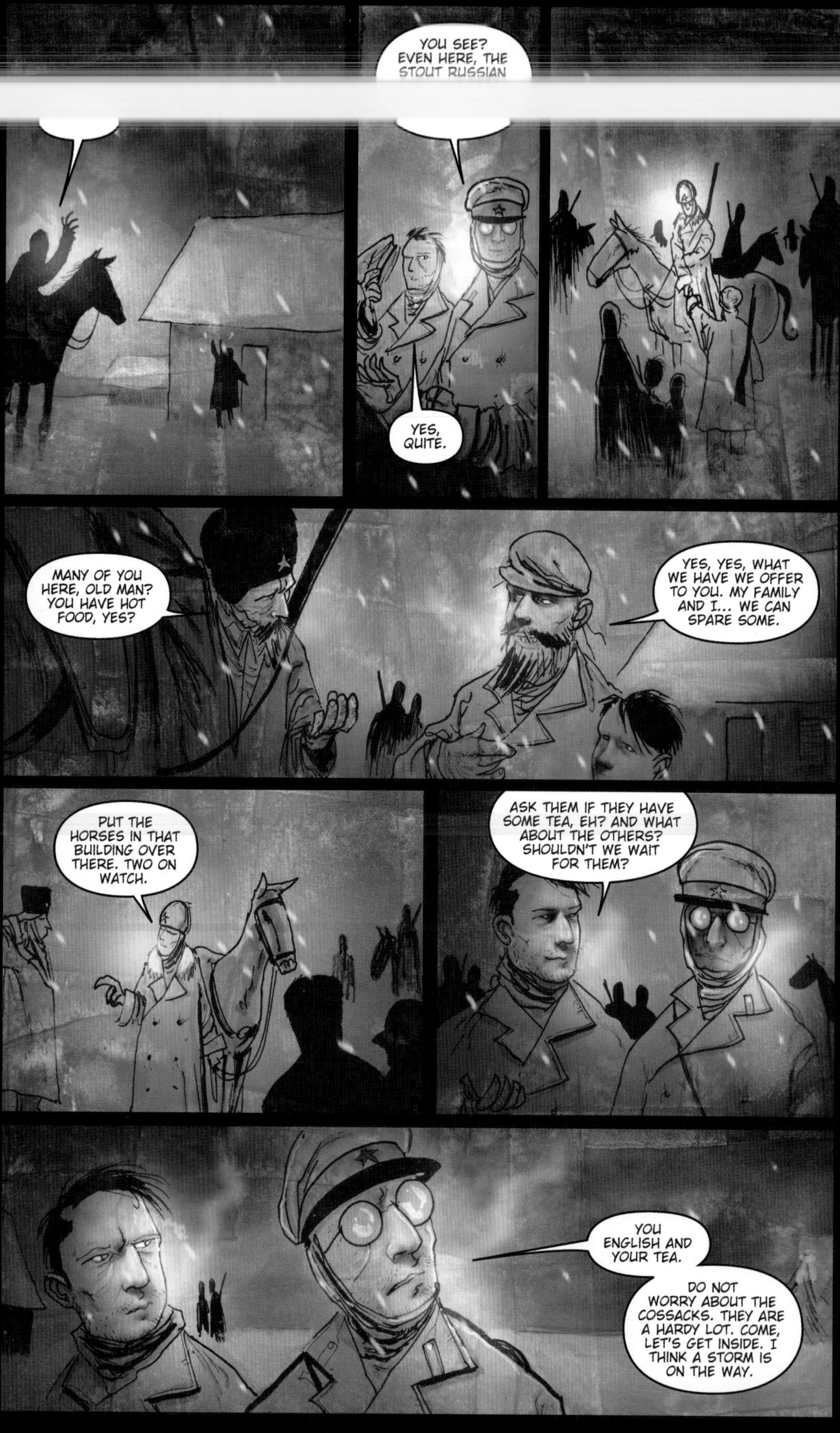
YOU SEE? EVEN HERE, THE STOUT RUSSIAN
YES, QUITE.
MANY OF YOU HERE, OLD MAN? YOU HAVE HOT FOOD, YES?
YES, YES, WHAT WE HAVE WE OFFER TO YOU. MY FAMILY AND I... WE CAN SPARE SOME.
PUT THE HORSES IN THAT BUILDING OVER THERE. TWO ON WATCH.
ASK THEM IF THEY HAVE SOME TEA, EH? AND WHAT ABOUT THE OTHERS? SHOULDN'T WE WAIT FOR THEM?
YOU ENGLISH AND YOUR TEA.
DO NOT WORRY ABOUT THE COSSACKS. THEY ARE A HARDY LOT. COME, LET'S GET INSIDE. I THINK A STORM IS ON THE WAY.

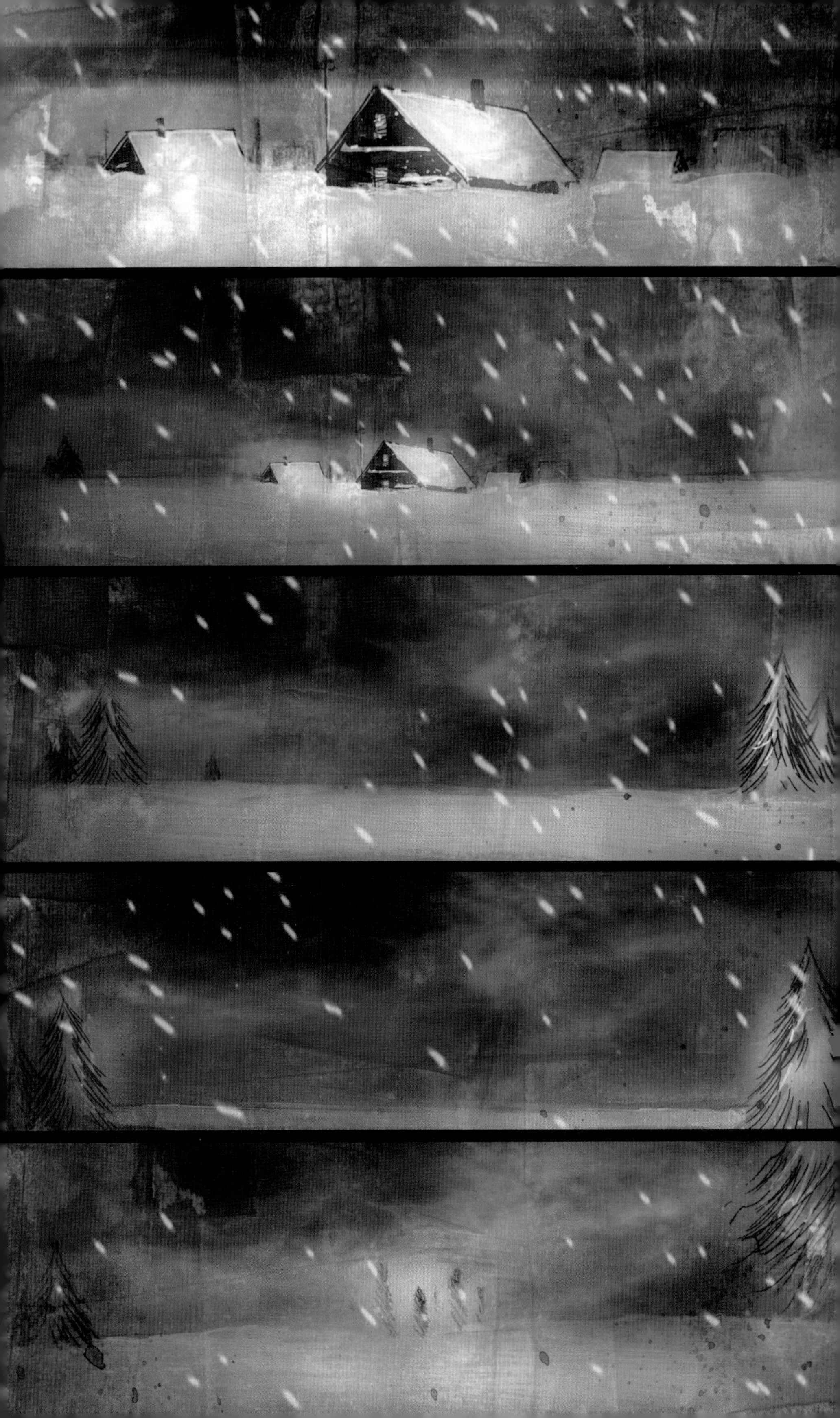

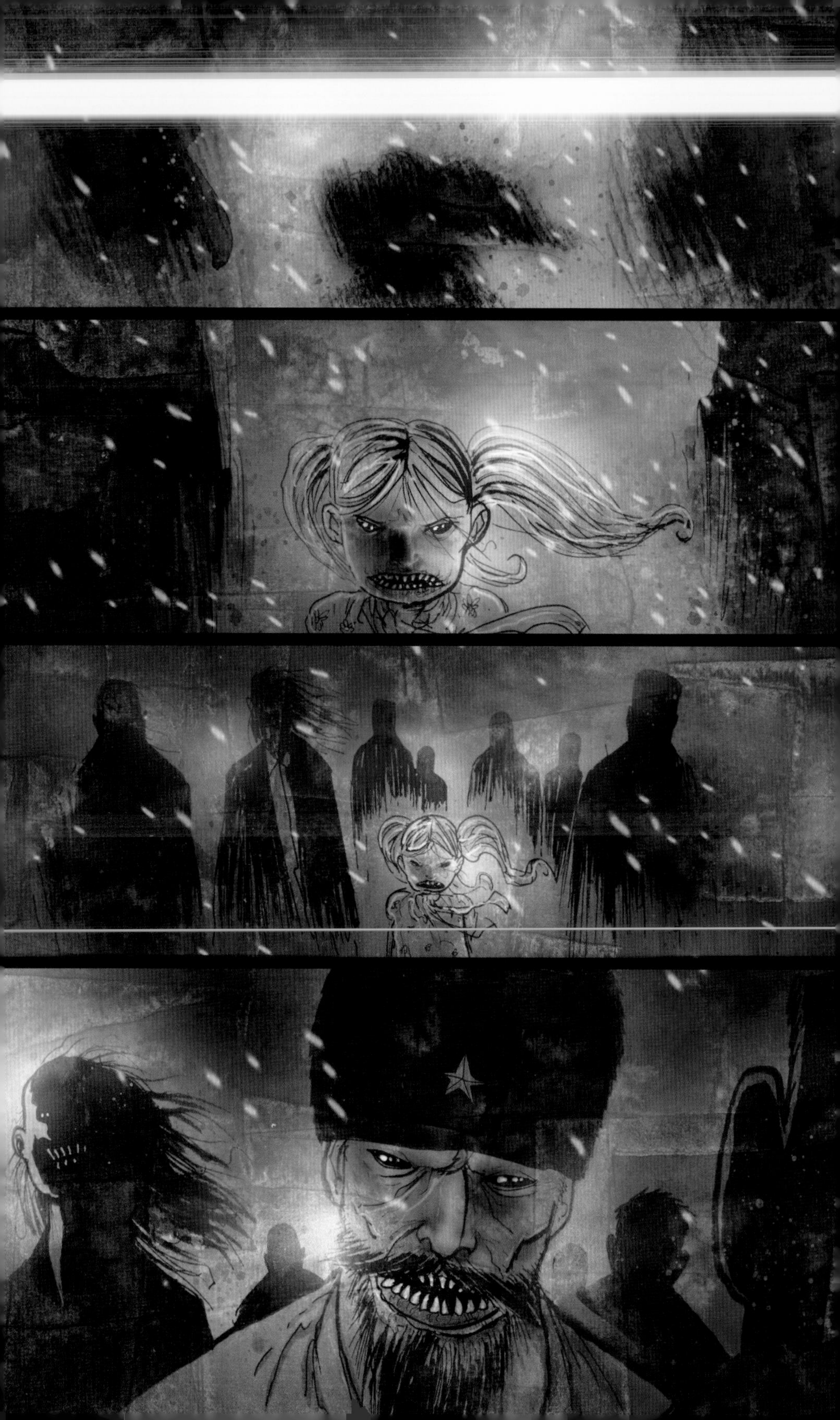

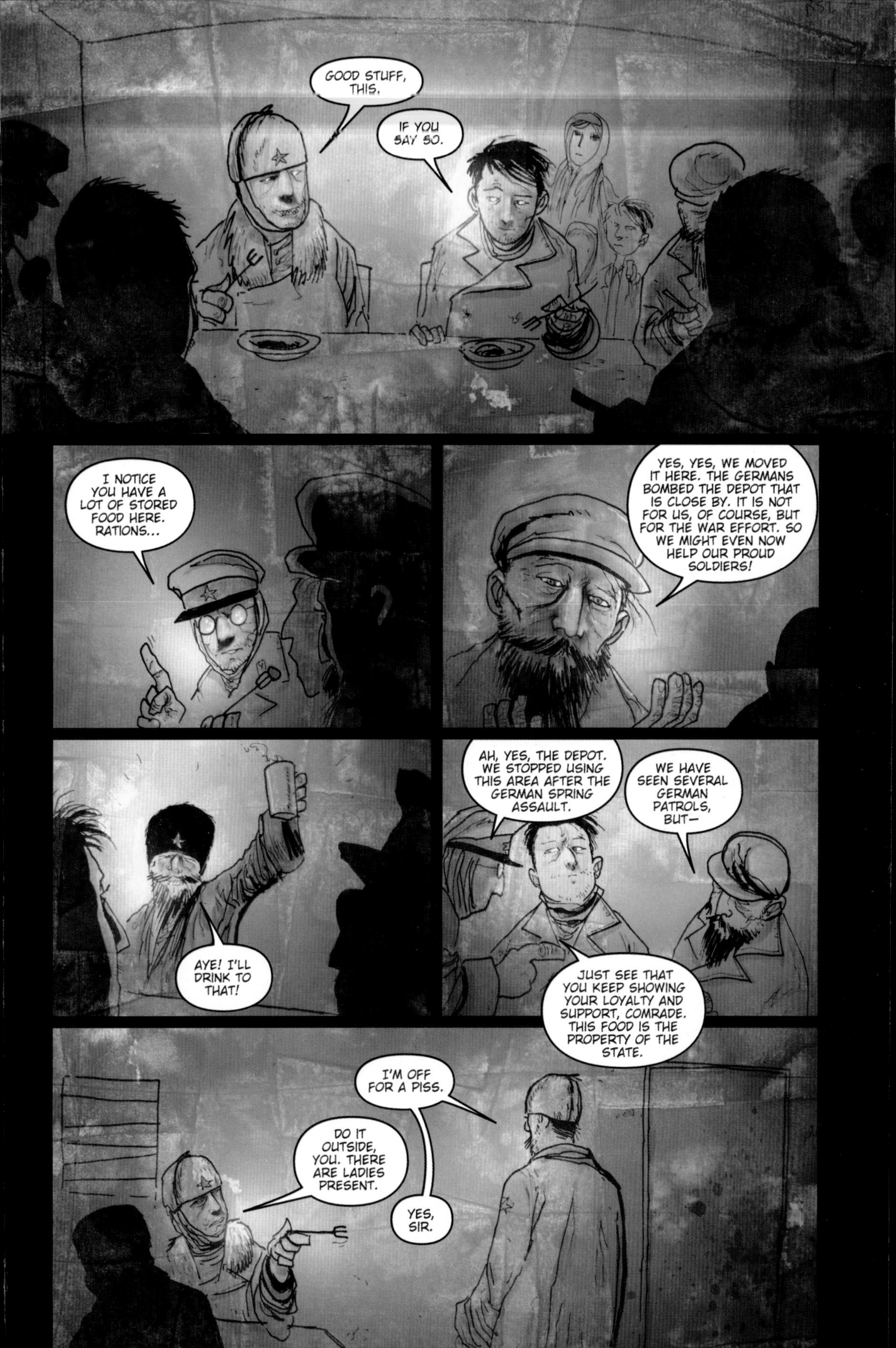
GOOD STUFF, THIS.
IF YOU SAY SO.
I NOTICE YOU HAVE A LOT OF STORED FOOD HERE. RATIONS...
YES, YES, WE MOVED IT HERE. THE GERMANS BOMBED THE DEPOT THAT IS CLOSE BY. IT IS NOT FOR US, OF COURSE, BUT FOR THE WAR EFFORT. SO WE MIGHT EVEN NOW HELP OUR PROUD SOLDIERS!
AYE! I'LL DRINK TO THAT!
AH, YES, THE DEPOT. WE STOPPED USING THIS AREA AFTER THE GERMAN SPRING ASSAULT.
WE HAVE SEEN SEVERAL GERMAN PATROLS, BUT—
JUST SEE THAT YOU KEEP SHOWING YOUR LOYALTY AND SUPPORT, COMRADE. THIS FOOD IS THE PROPERTY OF THE STATE.
I'M OFF FOR A PISS.
DO IT OUTSIDE, YOU. THERE ARE LADIES PRESENT.
YES, SIR.

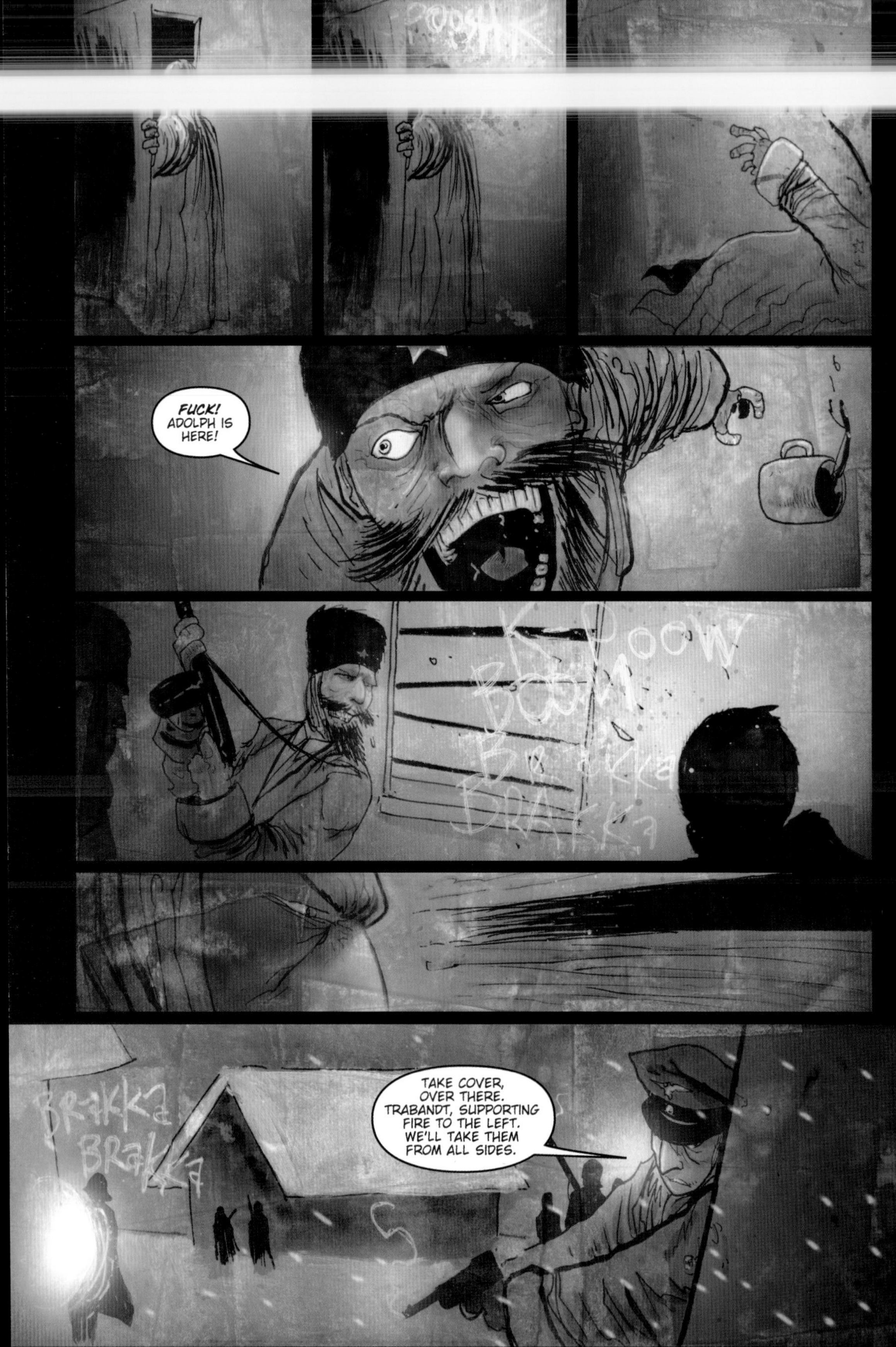
POOSH
FUCK! ADOLPH IS HERE!
K-POOOW
BOOM
BRAKKA
BRAKKA
BRAKKA
BRAKKA
TAKE COVER, OVER THERE. TRABANDT, SUPPORTING FIRE TO THE LEFT. WE'LL TAKE THEM FROM ALL SIDES.

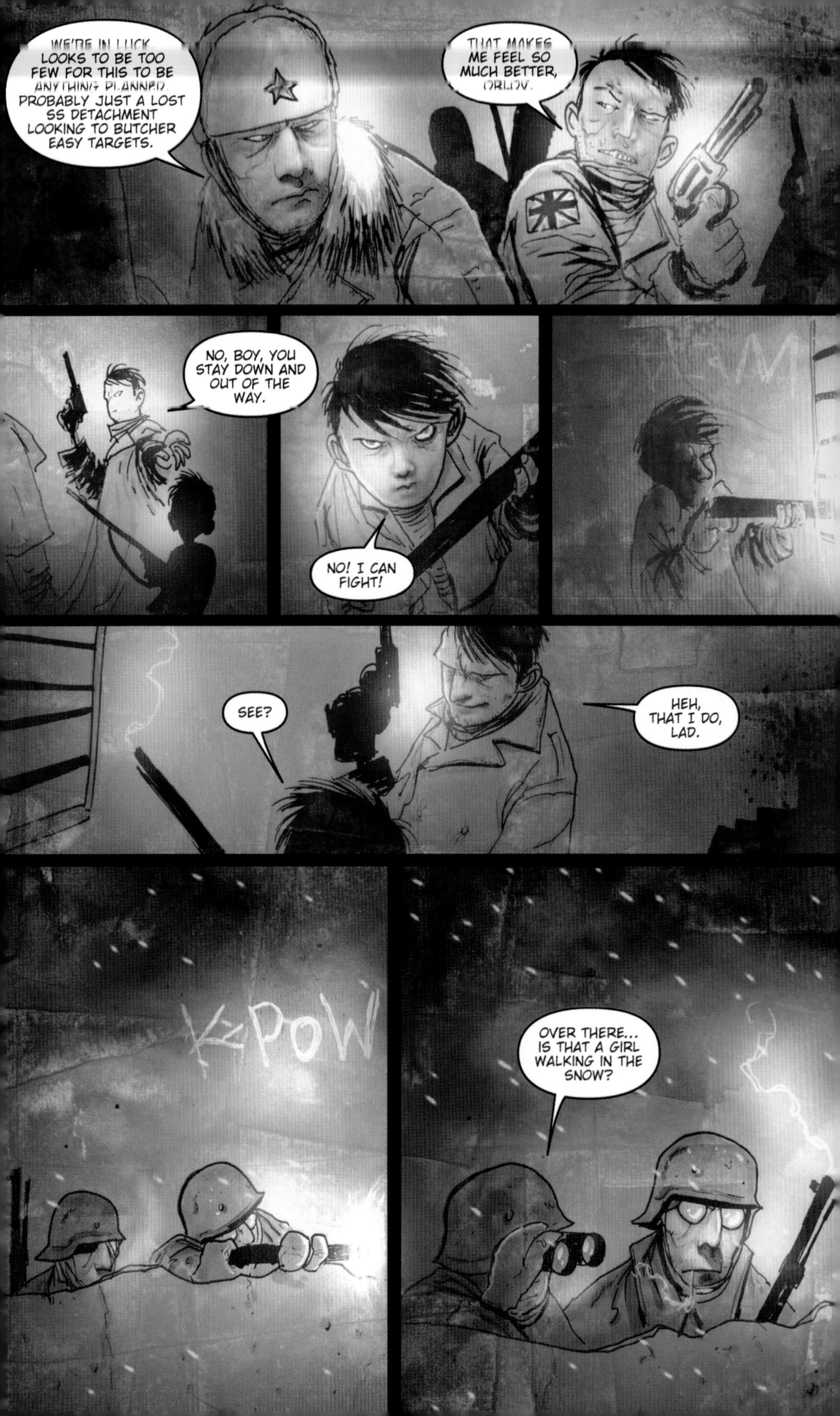
WE'RE IN LUCK. LOOKS TO BE TOO FEW FOR THIS TO BE ANYTHING PLANNED. PROBABLY JUST A LOST SS DETACHMENT LOOKING TO BUTCHER EASY TARGETS.
THAT MAKES ME FEEL SO MUCH BETTER, ORLOV.
NO, BOY, YOU STAY DOWN AND OUT OF THE WAY.
NO! I CAN FIGHT!
SEE?
HEH, THAT I DO, LAD.
KPOW
OVER THERE... IS THAT A GIRL WALKING IN THE SNOW?

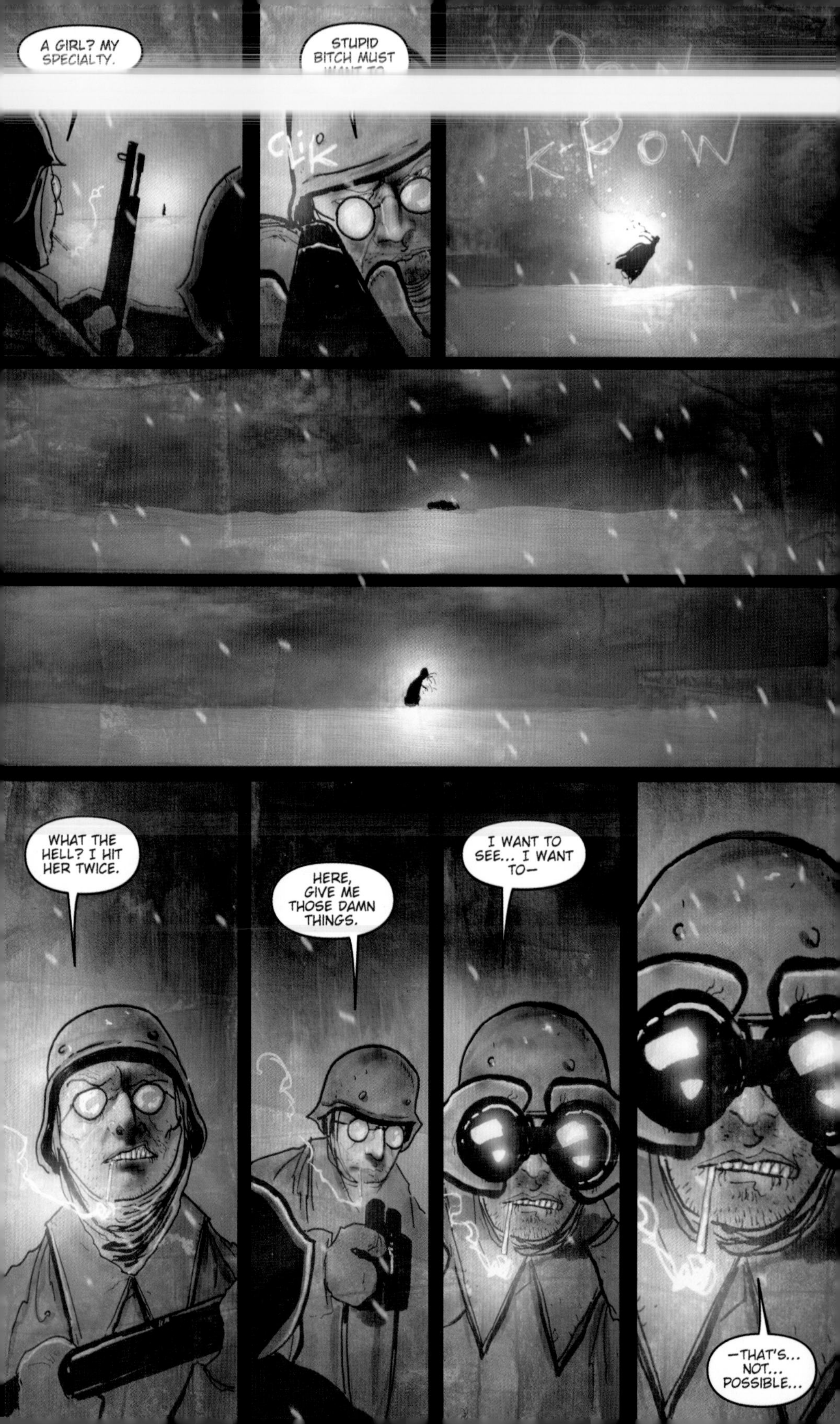
A GIRL? MY SPECIALTY.
STUPID BITCH MUST
CLIK
K-POW
WHAT THE HELL? I HIT HER TWICE.
HERE, GIVE ME THOSE DAMN THINGS.
I WANT TO SEE... I WANT TO—
—THAT'S... NOT... POSSIBLE...

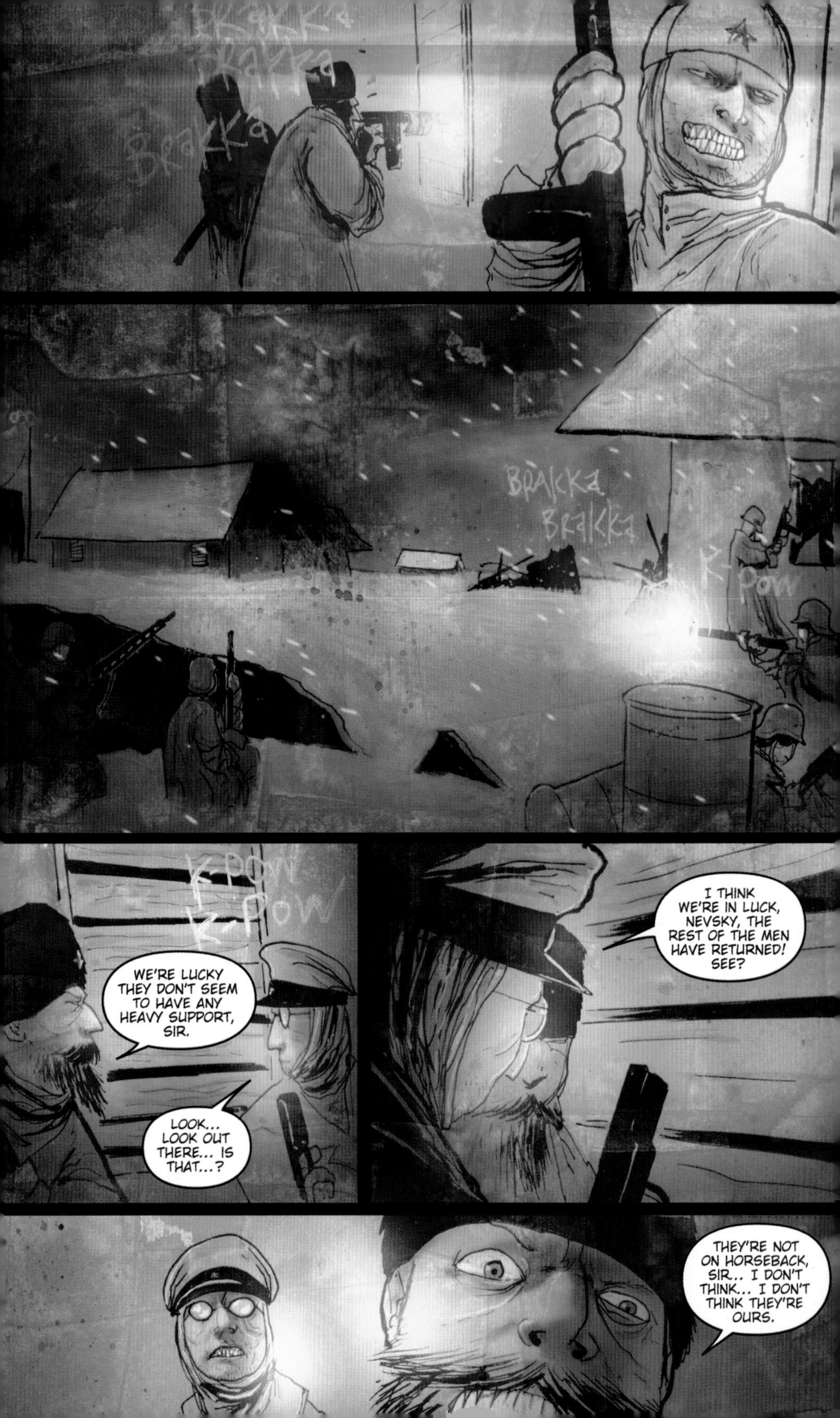
BRAKKA
BRAKKA
BRAKKA
BRAKKA
BRAKKA
K-POW
K-POW
K-POW
WE'RE LUCKY THEY DON'T SEEM TO HAVE ANY HEAVY SUPPORT, SIR.
LOOK... LOOK OUT THERE... IS THAT...?
I THINK WE'RE IN LUCK, NEVSKY, THE REST OF THE MEN HAVE RETURNED! SEE?
THEY'RE NOT ON HORSEBACK, SIR... I DON'T THINK... I DON'T THINK THEY'RE OURS.

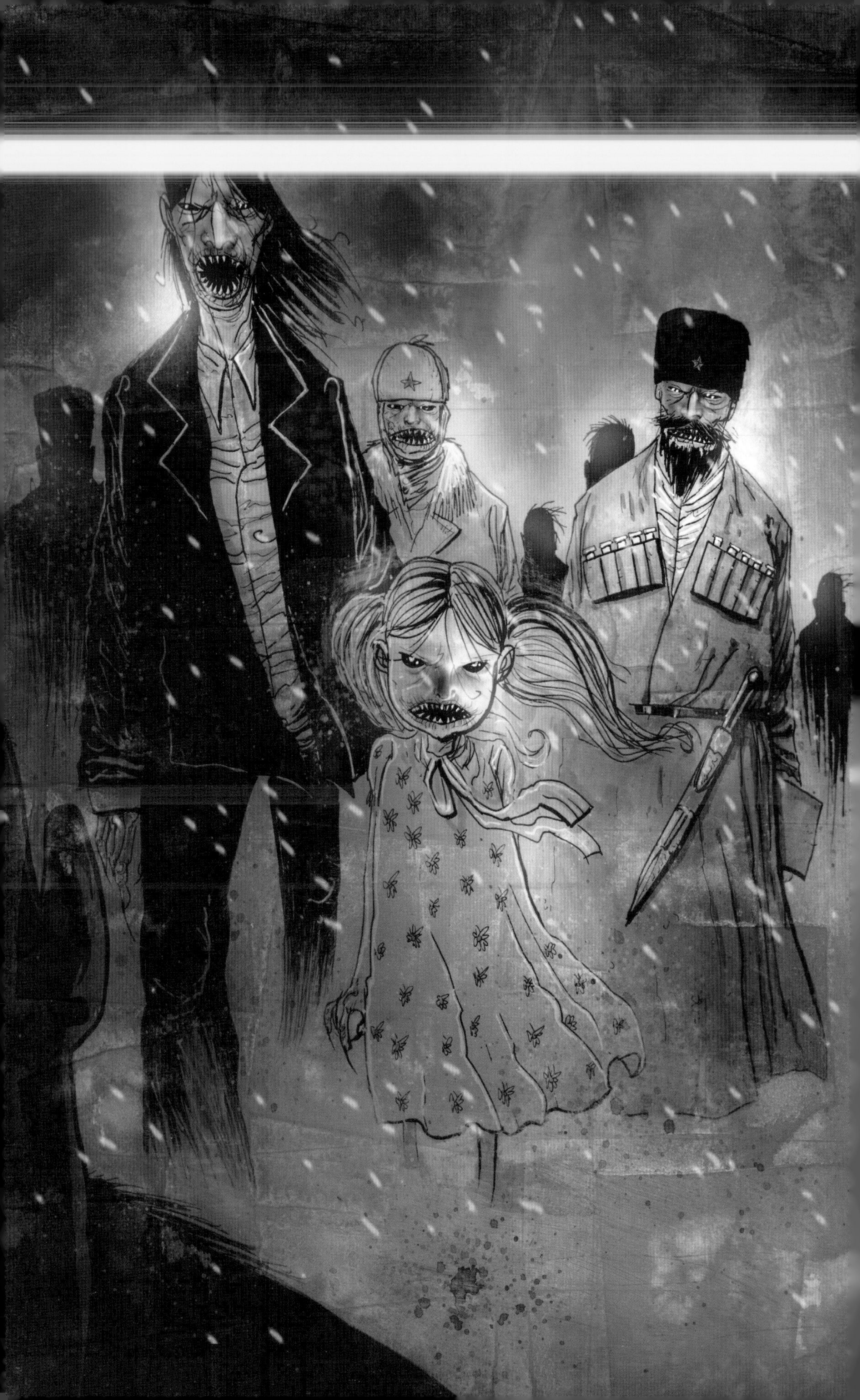

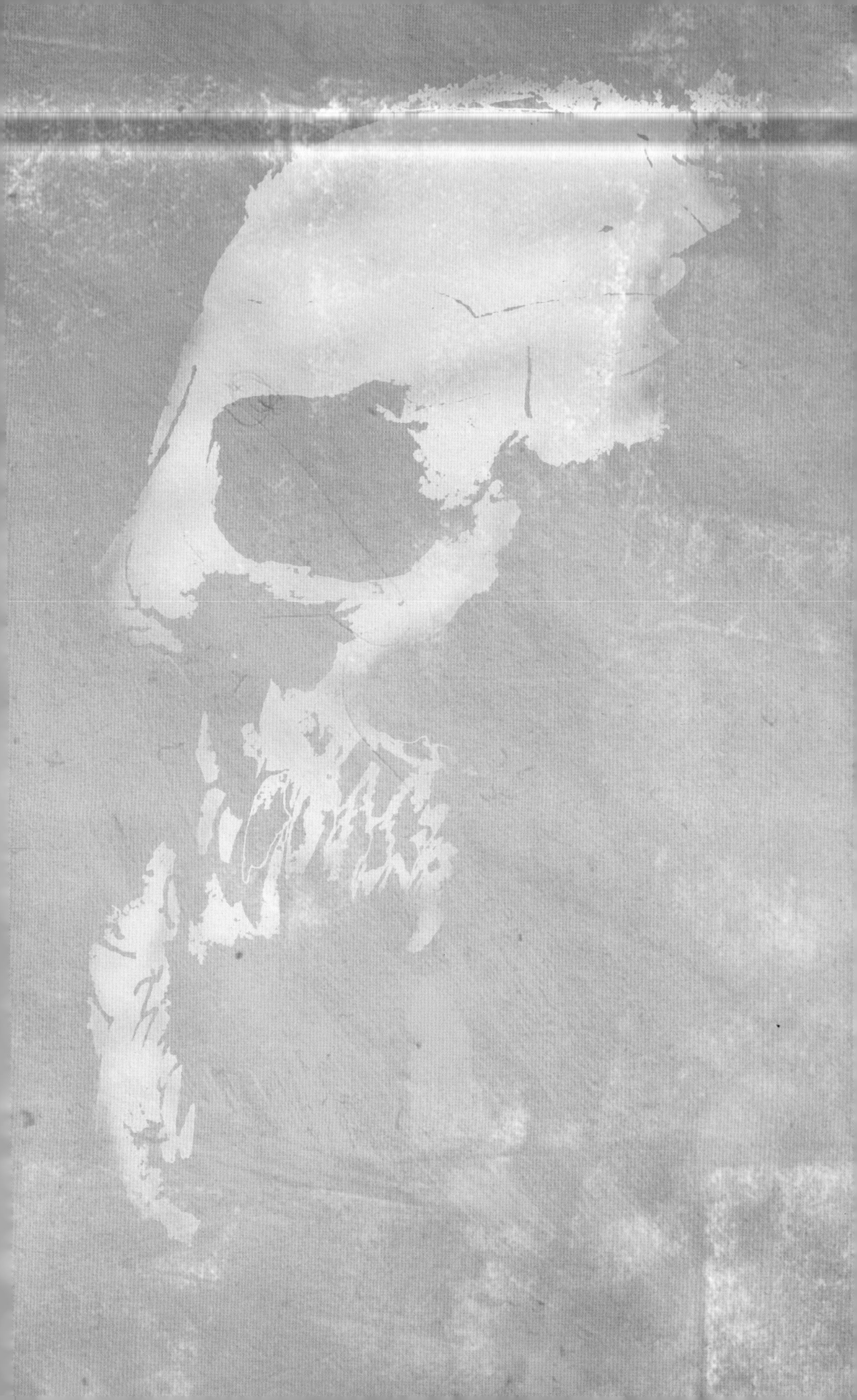

Chapter Two

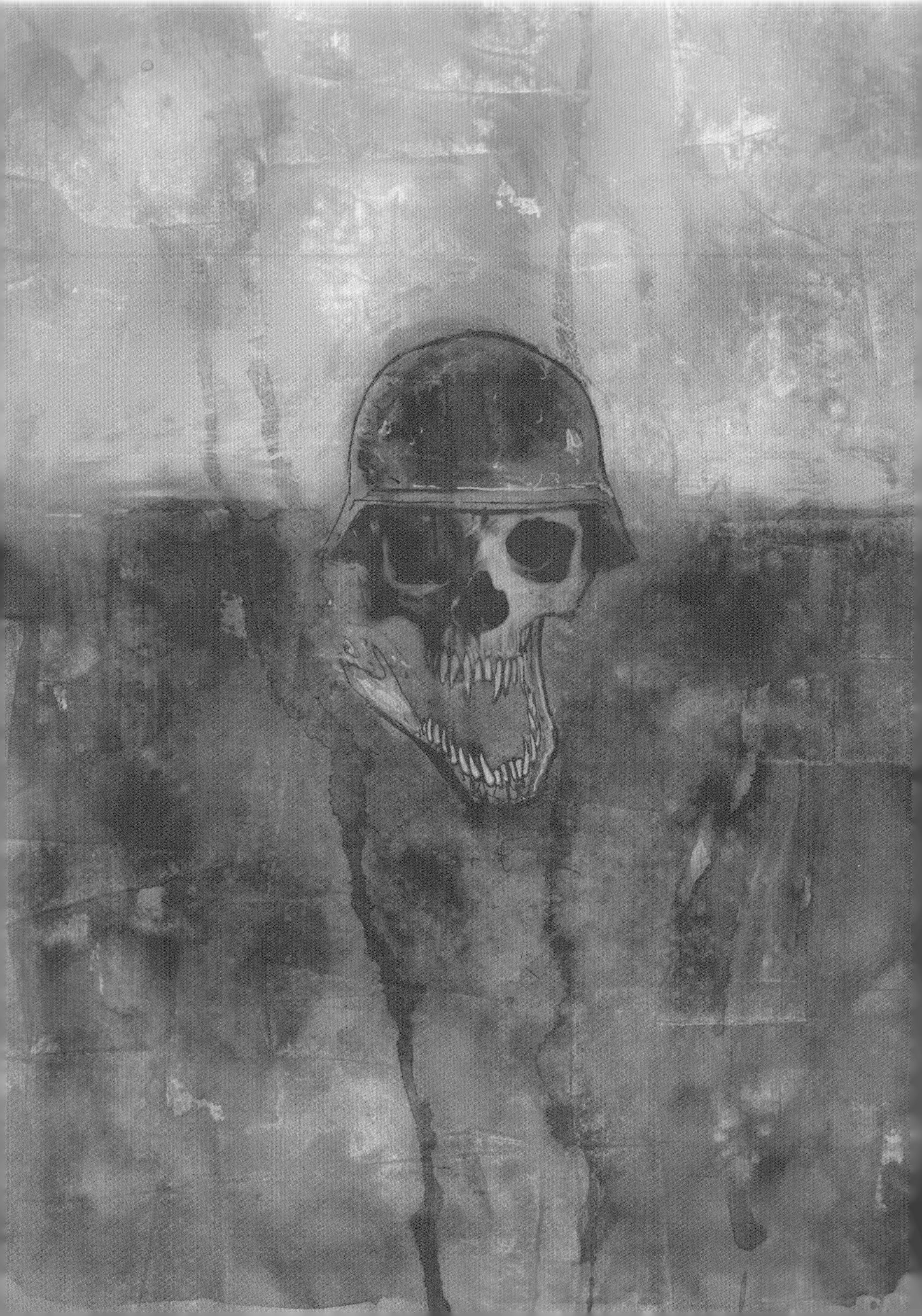

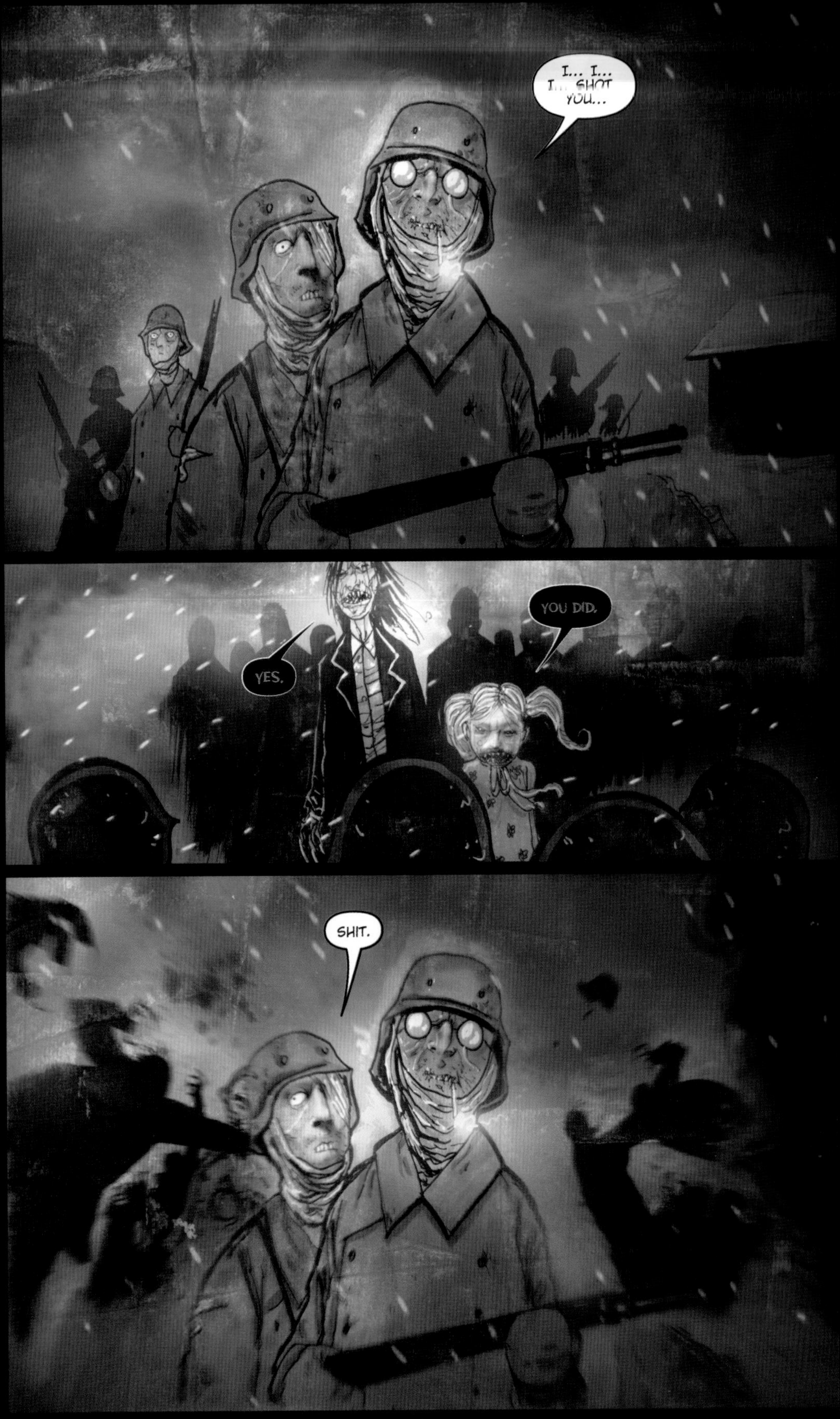
I... I... I... SHOT YOU...
YES.
YOU DID.
SHIT.

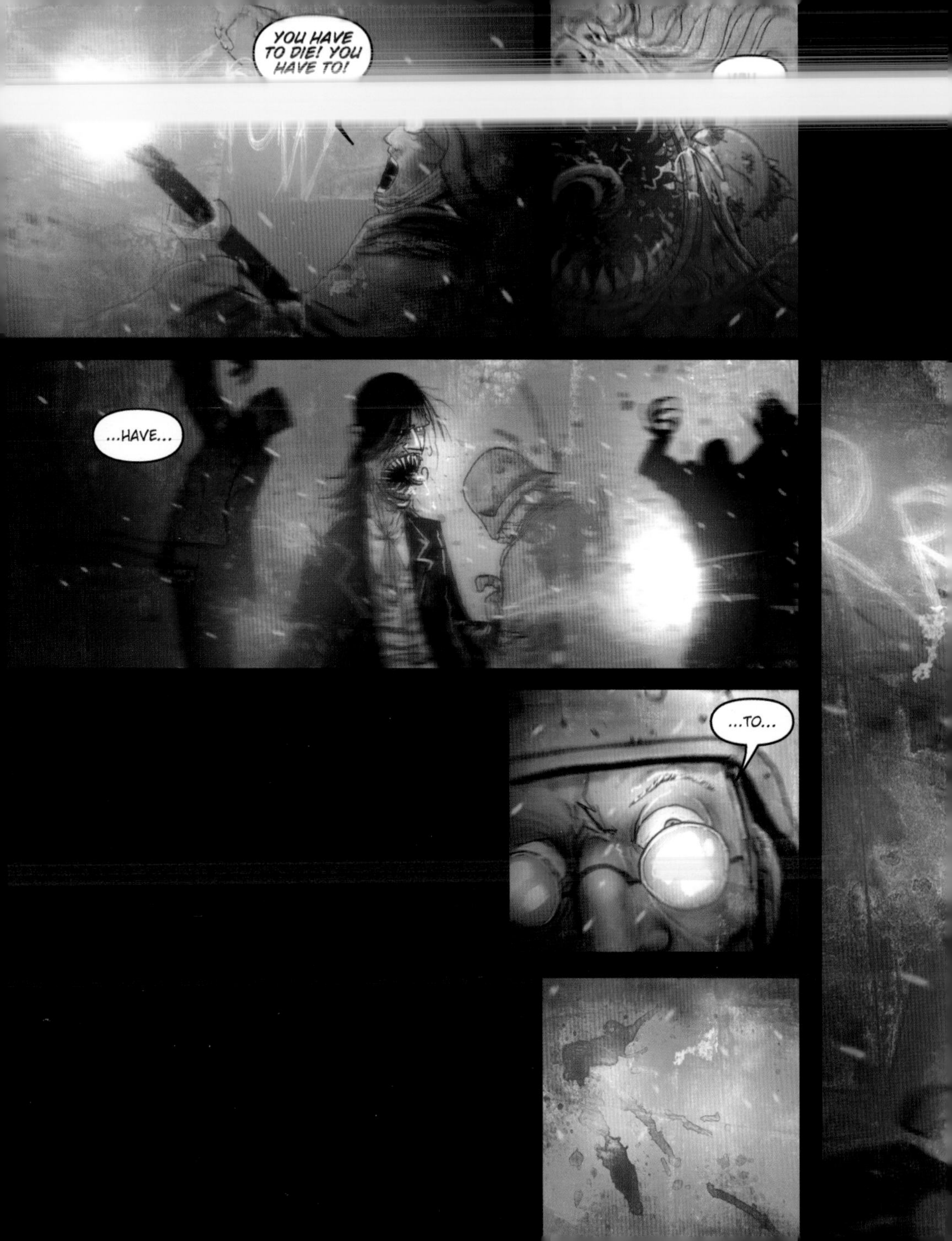
YOU HAVE TO DIE! YOU HAVE TO!
...HAVE...
...TO...

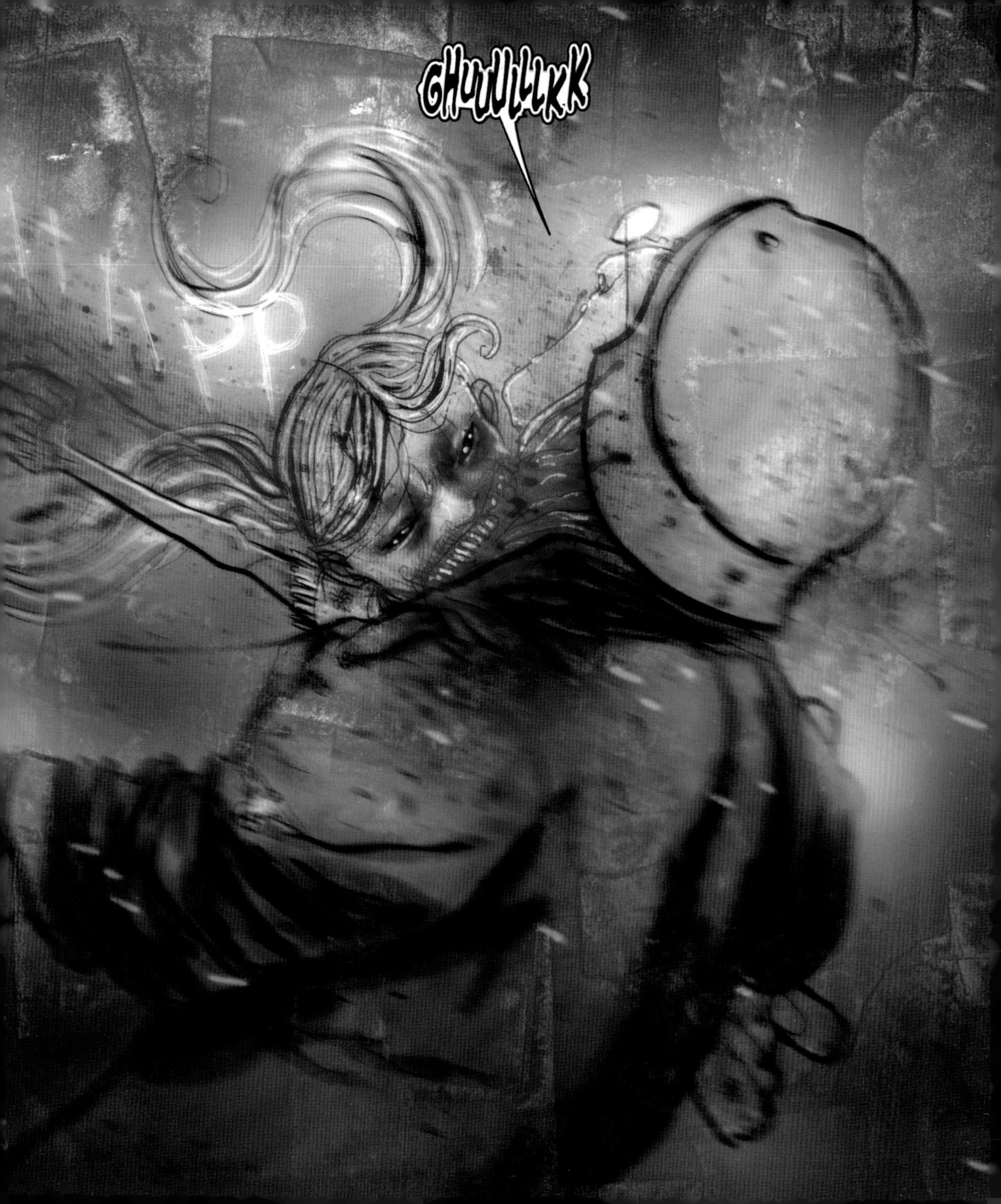
GHUUULLLKK

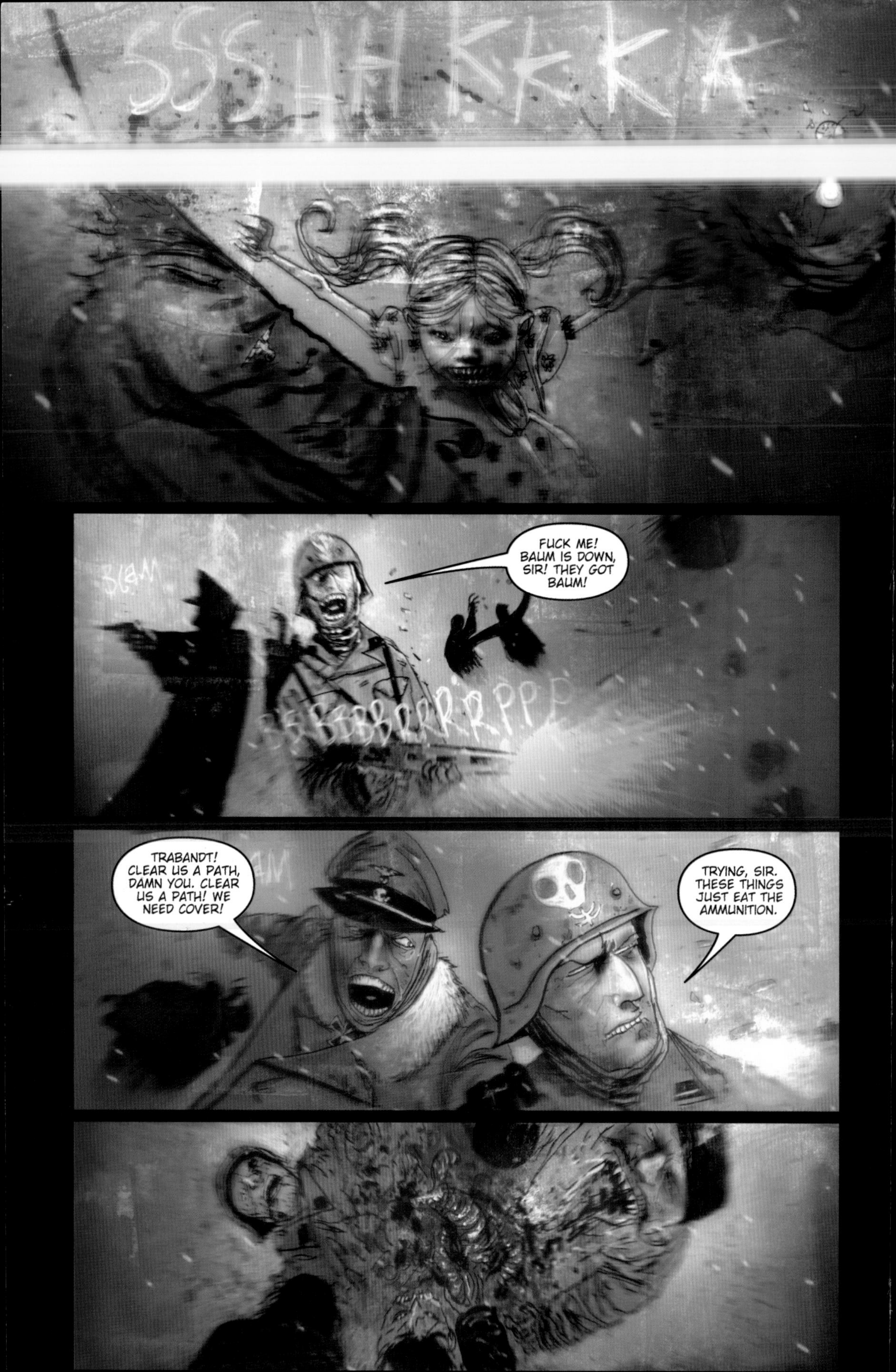
FUCK ME! BAUM IS DOWN, SIR! THEY GOT BAUM!
TRABANDT! CLEAR US A PATH, DAMN YOU. CLEAR US A PATH! WE NEED COVER!
TRYING, SIR. THESE THINGS JUST EAT THE AMMUNITION.

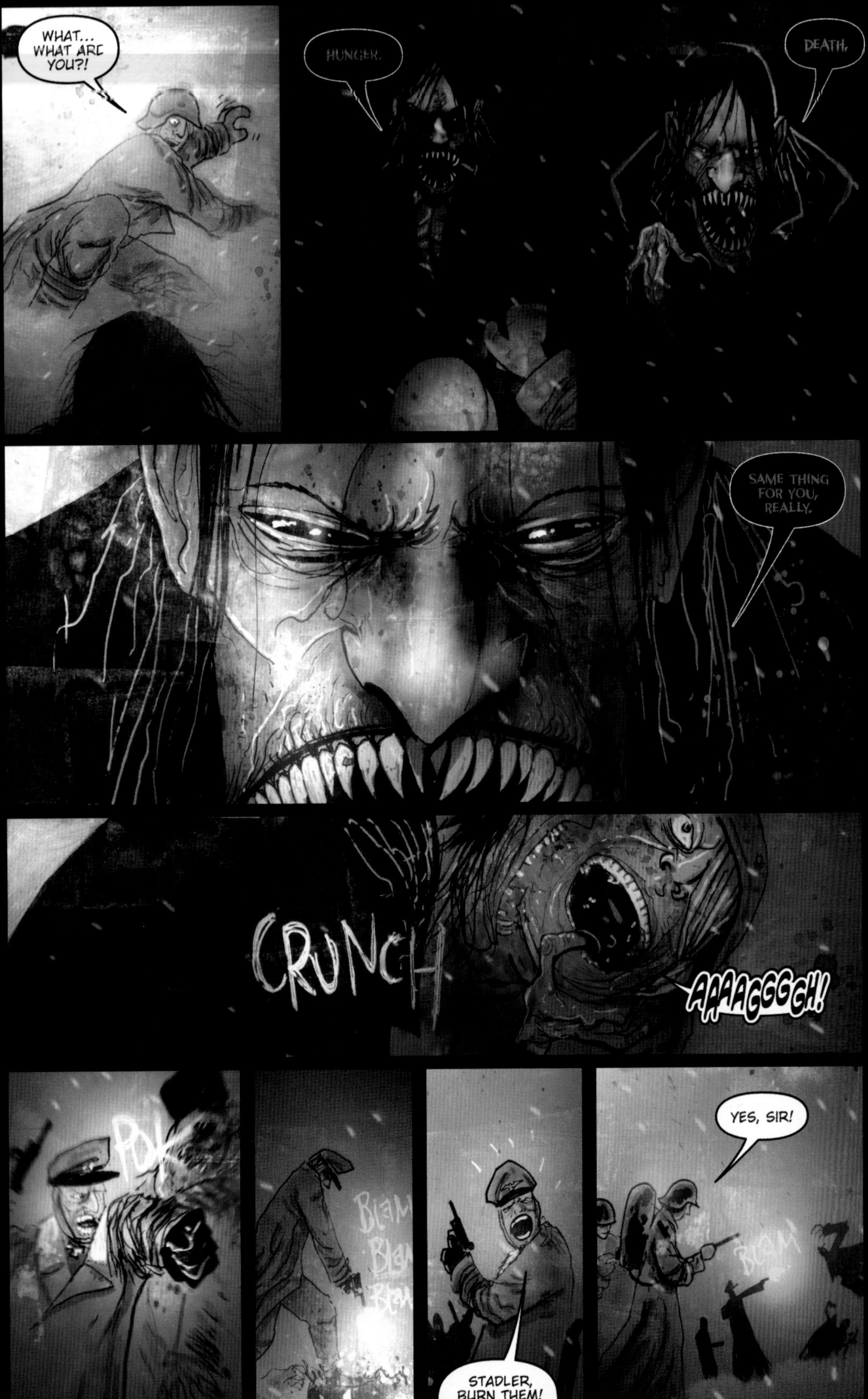
WHAT... WHAT ARE YOU?!
HUNGER.
DEATH.
SAME THING FOR YOU, REALLY.
CRUNCH
AAAAGGGGH!
STADLER, BURN THEM! BURN THEM!
YES, SIR!
BLAM

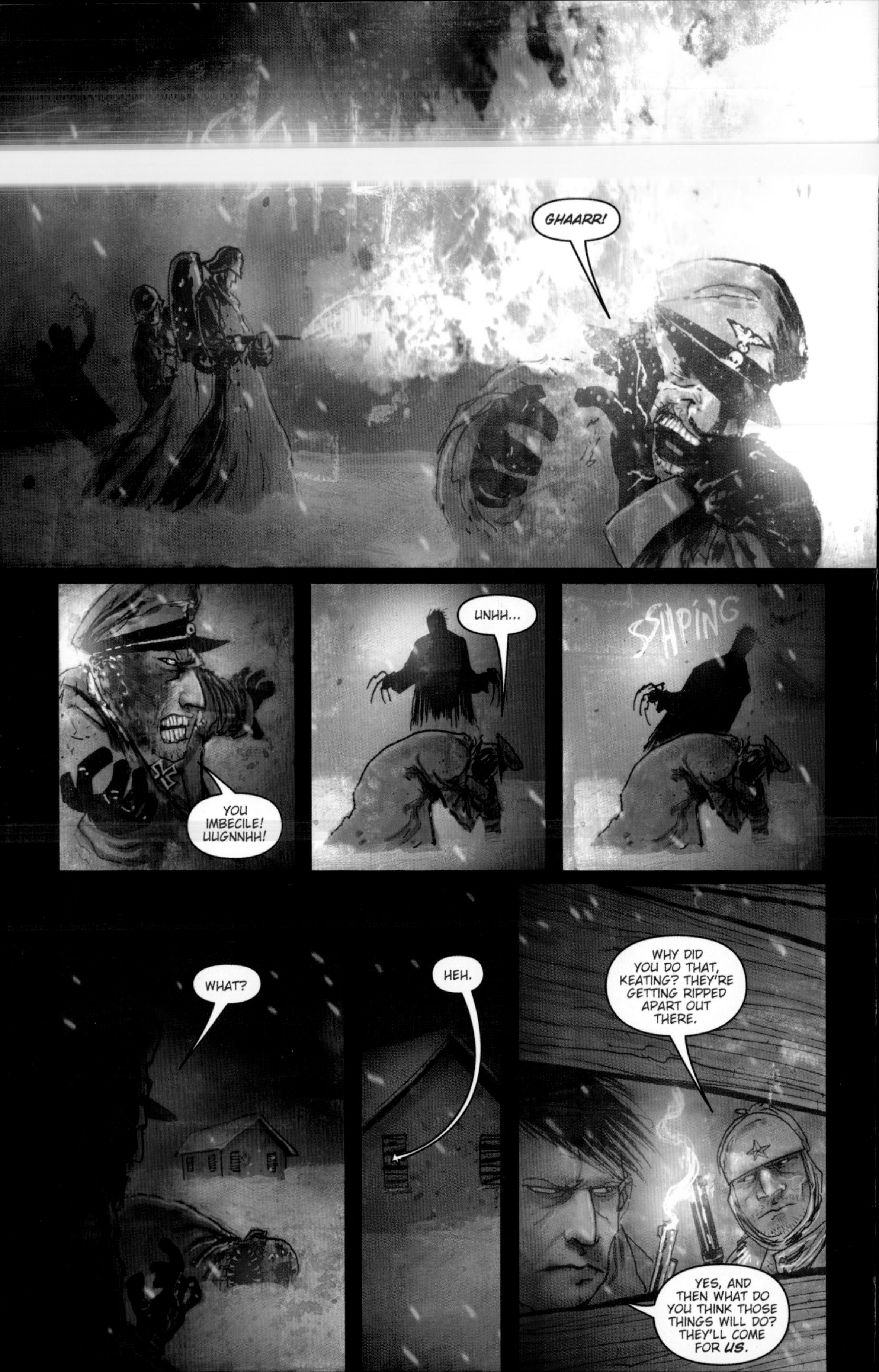
GHAARR!
YOU IMBECILE! UUGNNHH!
UNHH...
SSHPING
WHAT?
HEH.
WHY DID YOU DO THAT, KEATING? THEY'RE GETTING RIPPED APART OUT THERE.
YES, AND THEN WHAT DO YOU THINK THOSE THINGS WILL DO? THEY'LL COME FOR US.

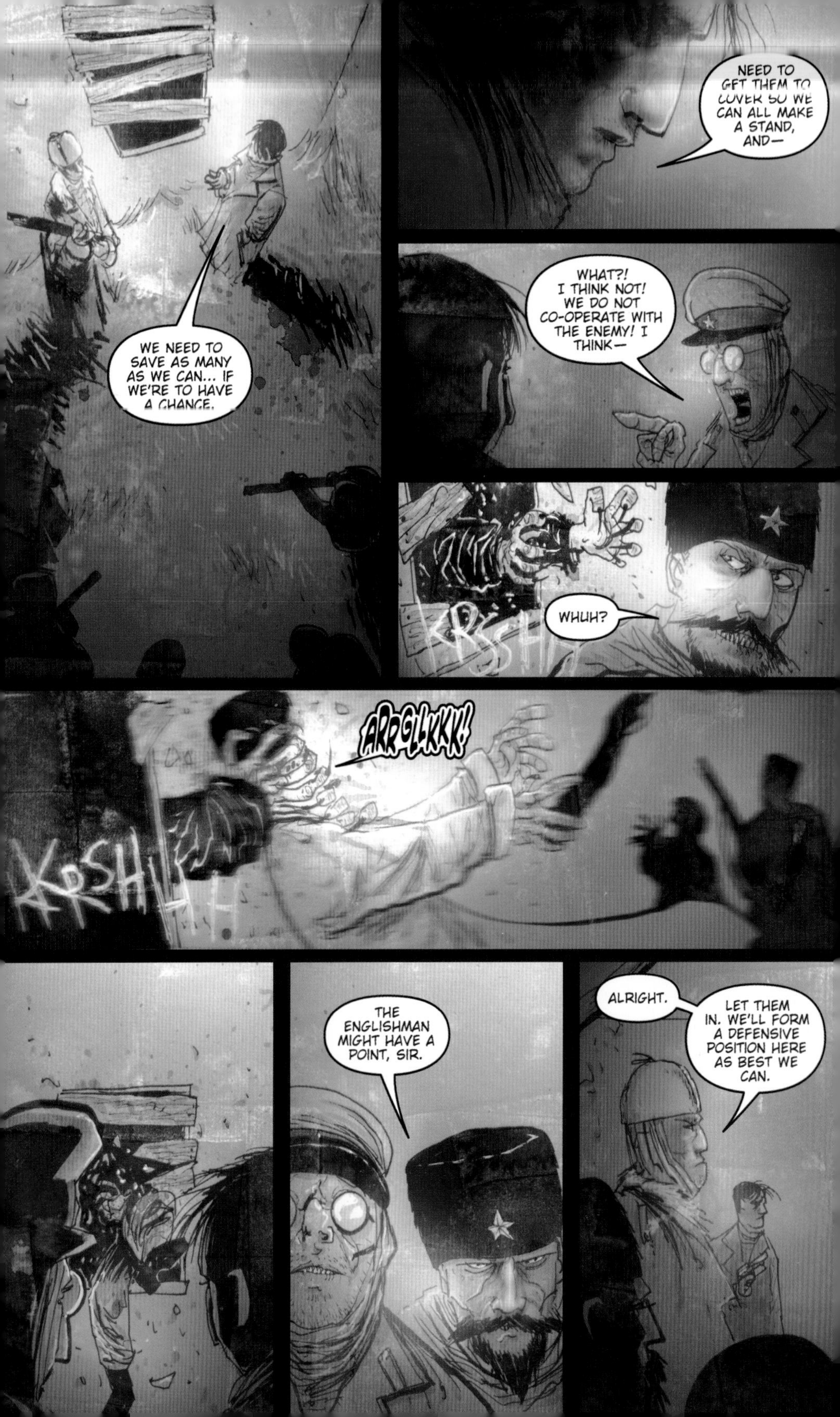
WE NEED TO SAVE AS MANY AS WE CAN... IF WE'RE TO HAVE A CHANCE.
NEED TO GET THEM TO COVER SO WE CAN ALL MAKE A STAND, AND—
WHAT?! I THINK NOT! WE DO NOT CO-OPERATE WITH THE ENEMY! I THINK—
WHUH?
KRSHH
ARRGLLKKK!
KRSHHHH
THE ENGLISHMAN MIGHT HAVE A POINT, SIR.
ALRIGHT.
LET THEM IN. WE'LL FORM A DEFENSIVE POSITION HERE AS BEST WE CAN.

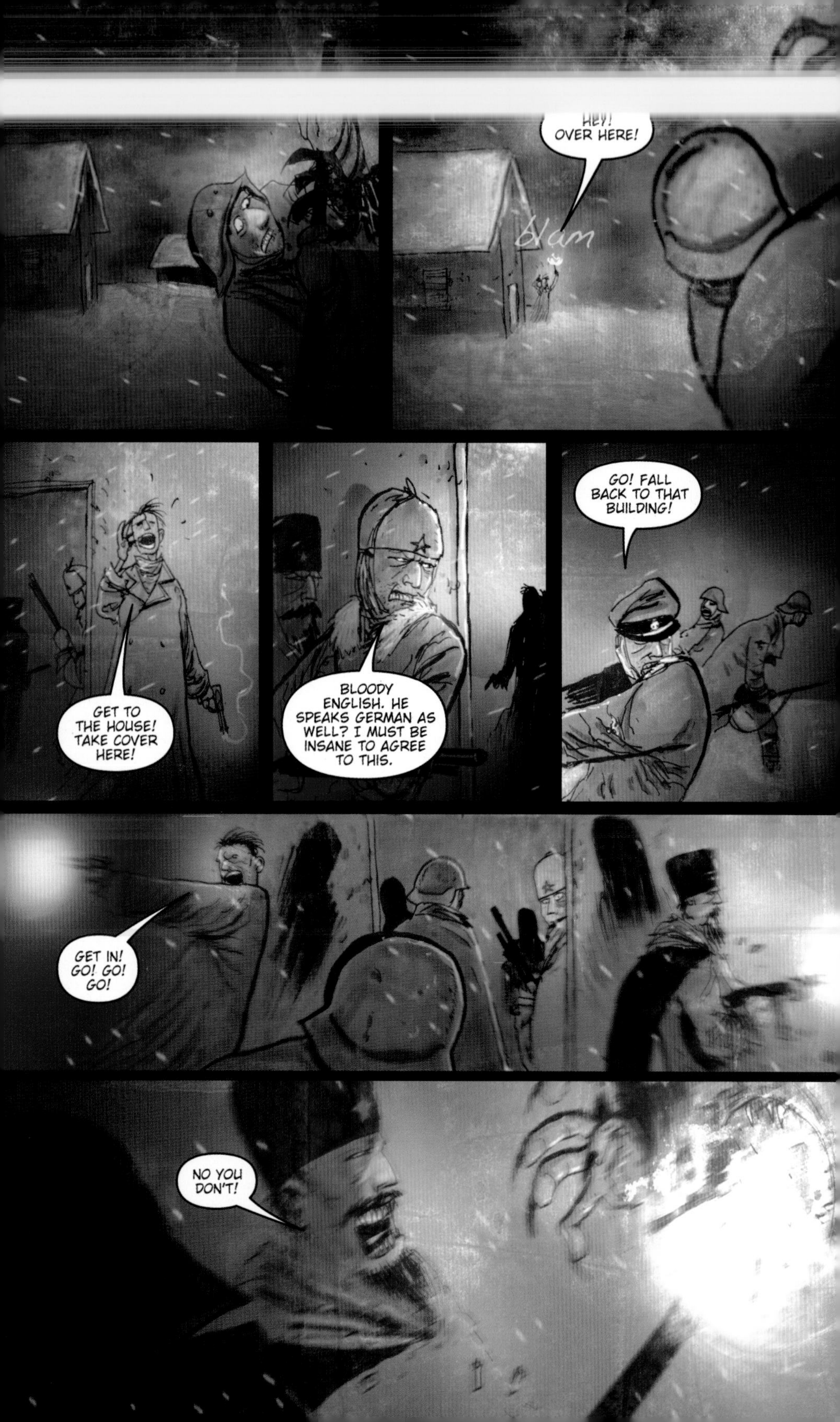
HEY! OVER HERE!
BLAM
GET TO THE HOUSE! TAKE COVER HERE!
BLOODY ENGLISH. HE SPEAKS GERMAN AS WELL? I MUST BE INSANE TO AGREE TO THIS.
GO! FALL BACK TO THAT BUILDING!
GET IN! GO! GO! GO!
NO YOU DON'T!

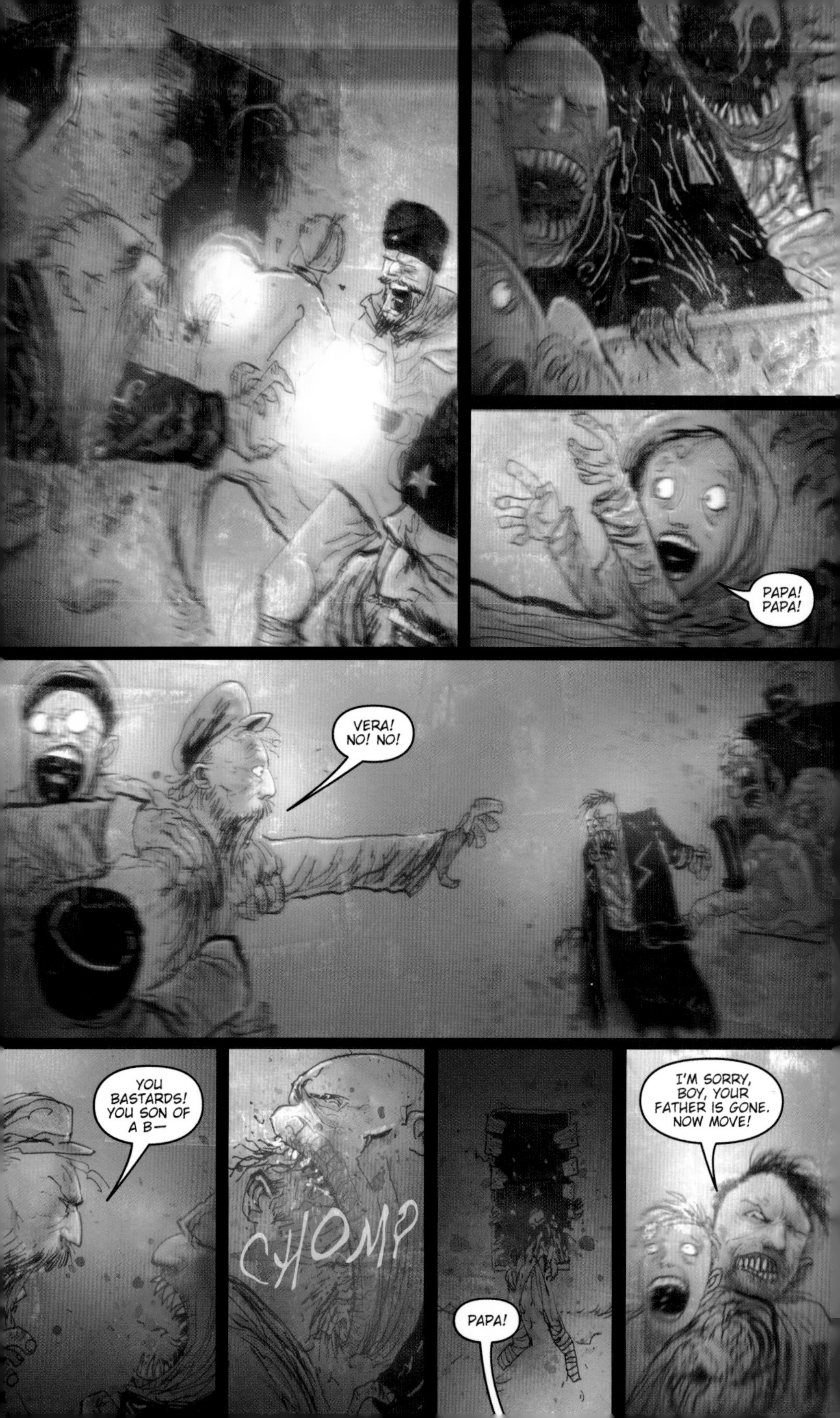
PAPA! PAPA!
VERA! NO! NO!
YOU BASTARDS! YOU SON OF A B—
CHOMP
PAPA!
I'M SORRY, BOY, YOUR FATHER IS GONE. NOW MOVE!

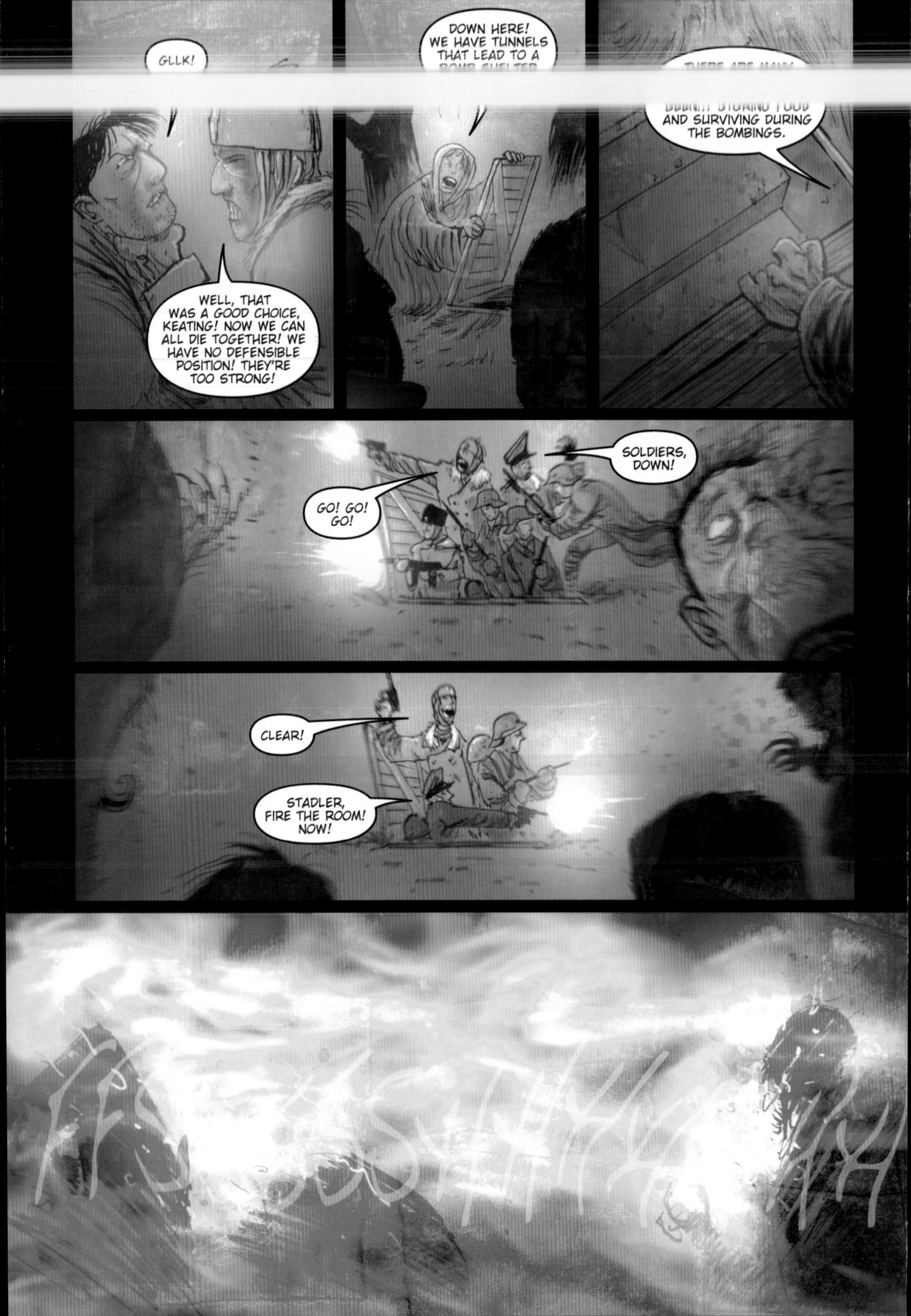
GLLK!
WELL, THAT WAS A GOOD CHOICE, KEATING! NOW WE CAN ALL DIE TOGETHER! WE HAVE NO DEFENSIBLE POSITION! THEY'RE TOO STRONG!
DOWN HERE! WE HAVE TUNNELS THAT LEAD TO A
AND SURVIVING DURING THE BOMBINGS.
GO! GO! GO!
SOLDIERS, DOWN!
CLEAR!
STADLER, FIRE THE ROOM! NOW!

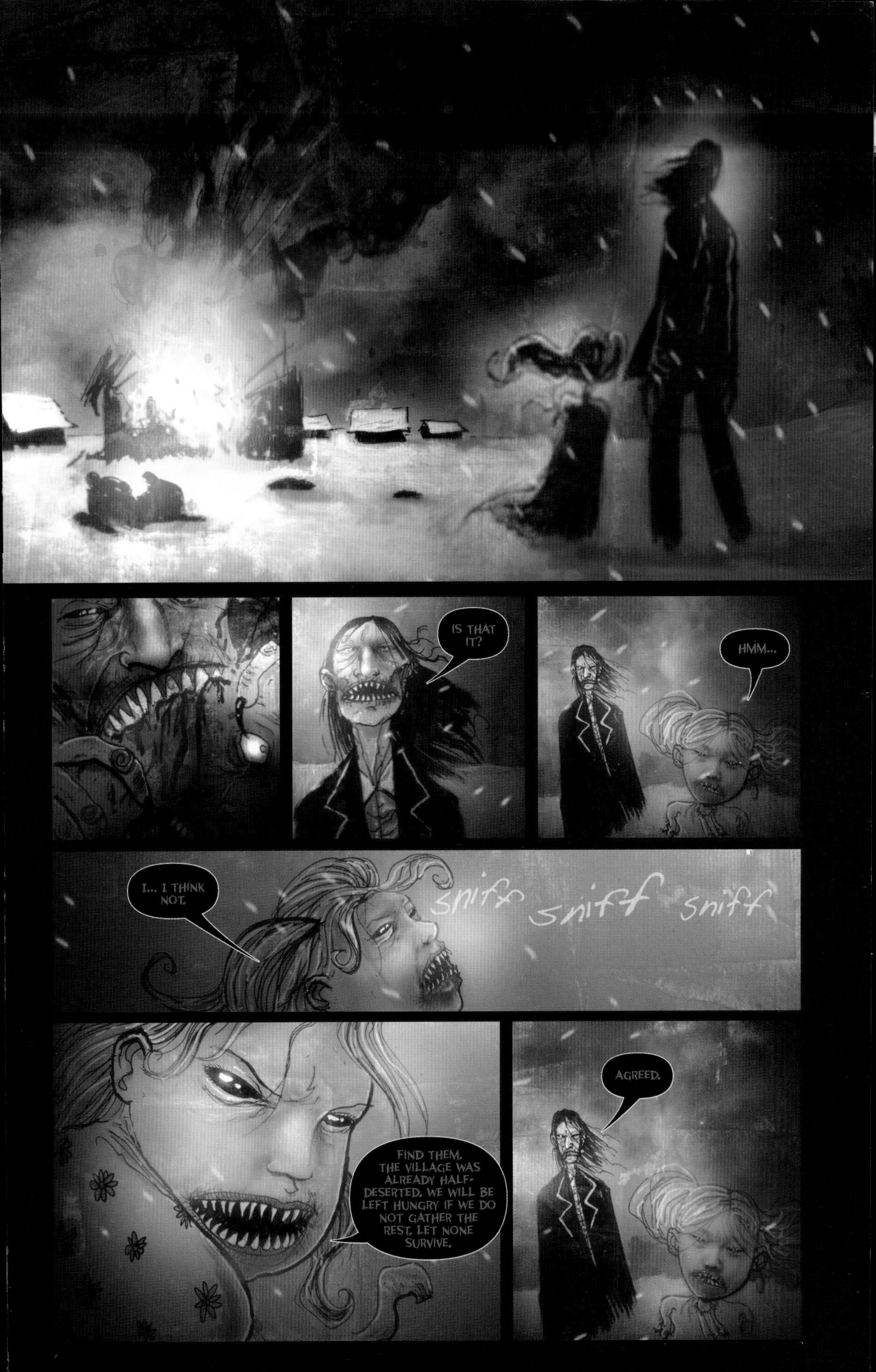
IS THAT IT?
HMM...
I... I THINK NOT.
sniff sniff sniff
FIND THEM. THE VILLAGE WAS ALREADY HALF-DESERTED. WE WILL BE LEFT HUNGRY IF WE DO NOT GATHER THE REST. LET NONE SURVIVE.
AGREED.

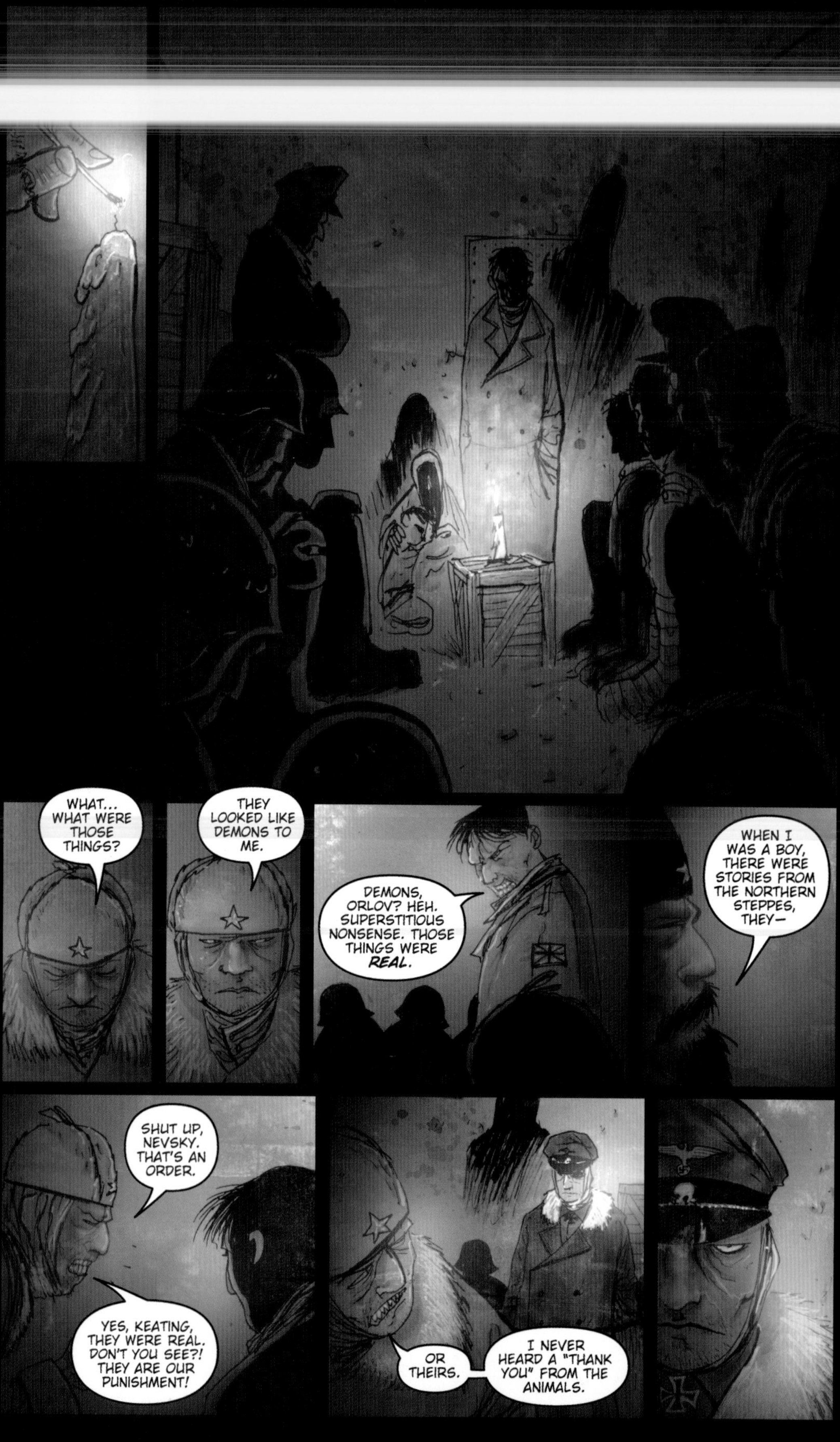
WHAT... WHAT WERE THOSE THINGS?
THEY LOOKED LIKE DEMONS TO ME.
DEMONS, ORLOV? HEH. SUPERSTITIOUS NONSENSE. THOSE THINGS WERE *REAL*.
WHEN I WAS A BOY, THERE WERE STORIES FROM THE NORTHERN STEPPES, THEY—
SHUT UP, NEVSKY. THAT'S AN ORDER.
YES, KEATING, THEY WERE REAL. DON'T YOU SEE?! THEY ARE OUR PUNISHMENT!
OR THEIRS.
I NEVER HEARD A "THANK YOU" FROM THE ANIMALS.

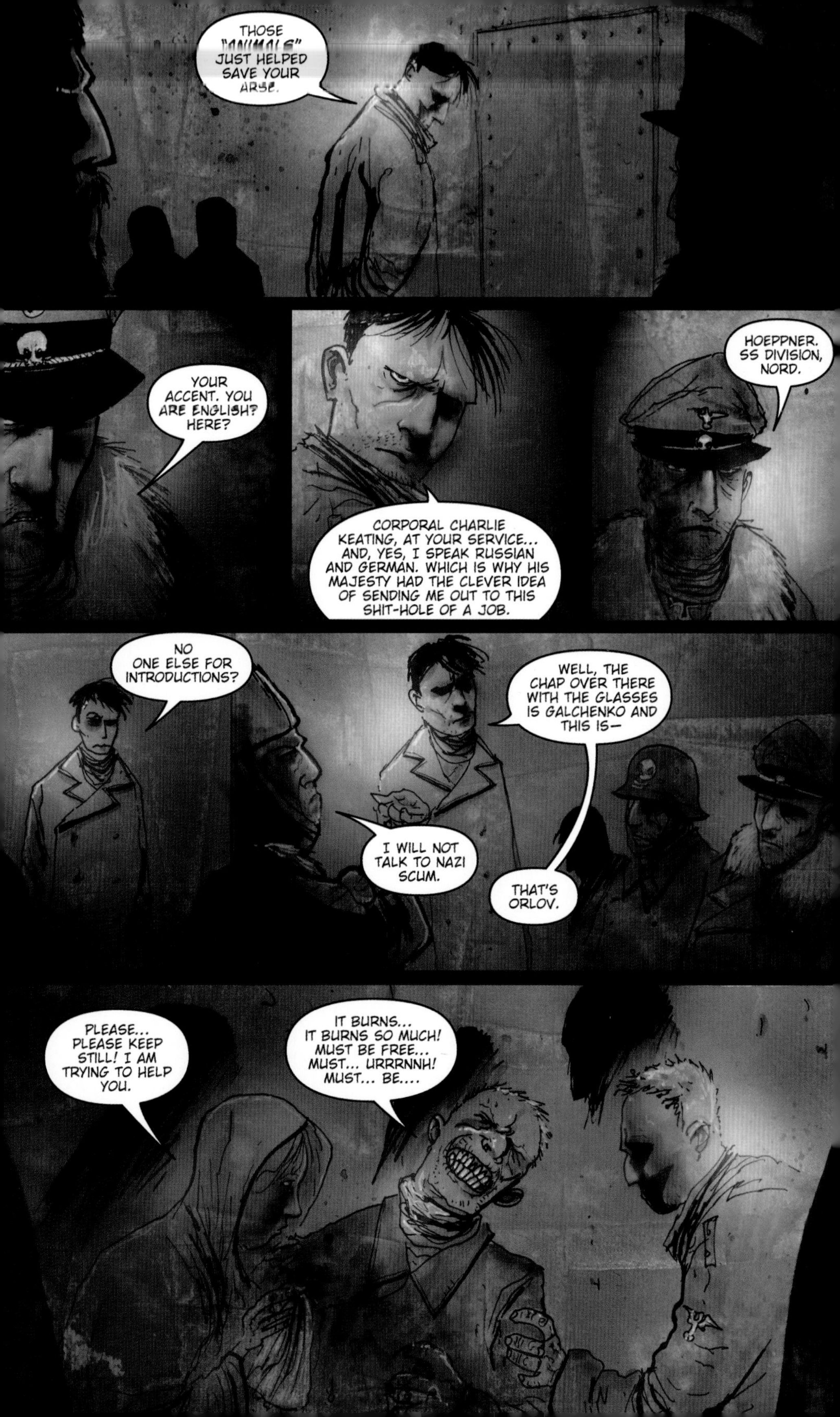
THOSE "ANIMALS" JUST HELPED SAVE YOUR ARSE.
YOUR ACCENT. YOU ARE ENGLISH? HERE?
CORPORAL CHARLIE KEATING, AT YOUR SERVICE... AND, YES, I SPEAK RUSSIAN AND GERMAN. WHICH IS WHY HIS MAJESTY HAD THE CLEVER IDEA OF SENDING ME OUT TO THIS SHIT-HOLE OF A JOB.
HOEPPNER. SS DIVISION, NORD.
NO ONE ELSE FOR INTRODUCTIONS?
WELL, THE CHAP OVER THERE WITH THE GLASSES IS GALCHENKO AND THIS IS—
I WILL NOT TALK TO NAZI SCUM.
THAT'S ORLOV.
PLEASE... PLEASE KEEP STILL! I AM TRYING TO HELP YOU.
IT BURNS... IT BURNS SO MUCH! MUST BE FREE... MUST... URRRNNH! MUST... BE....

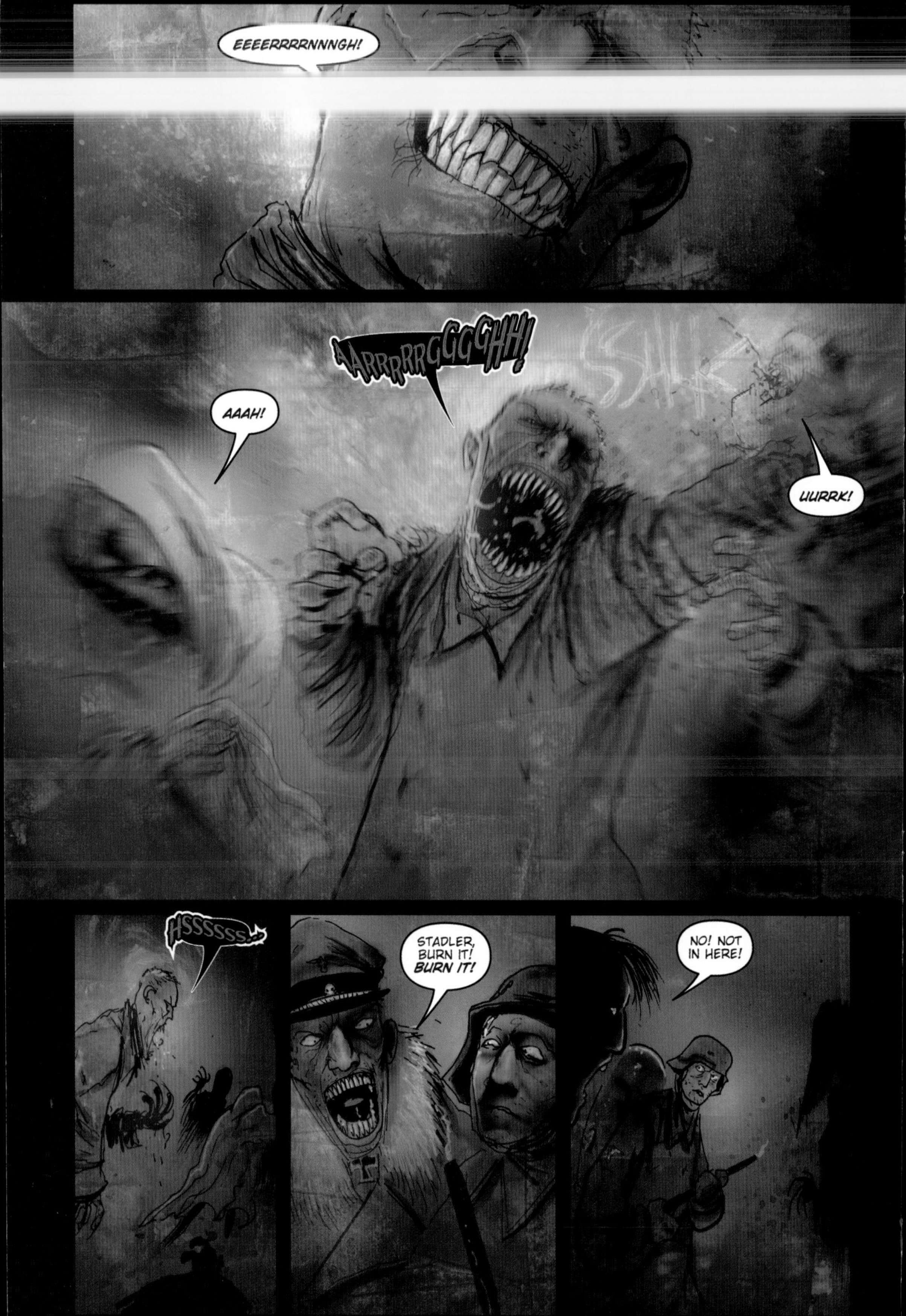
EEEERRRRNNNGH!
AARRRRRGGGGHH!
AAAH!
SHK
UURRK!
HSSSSSS
STADLER, BURN IT! BURN IT!
NO! NOT IN HERE!

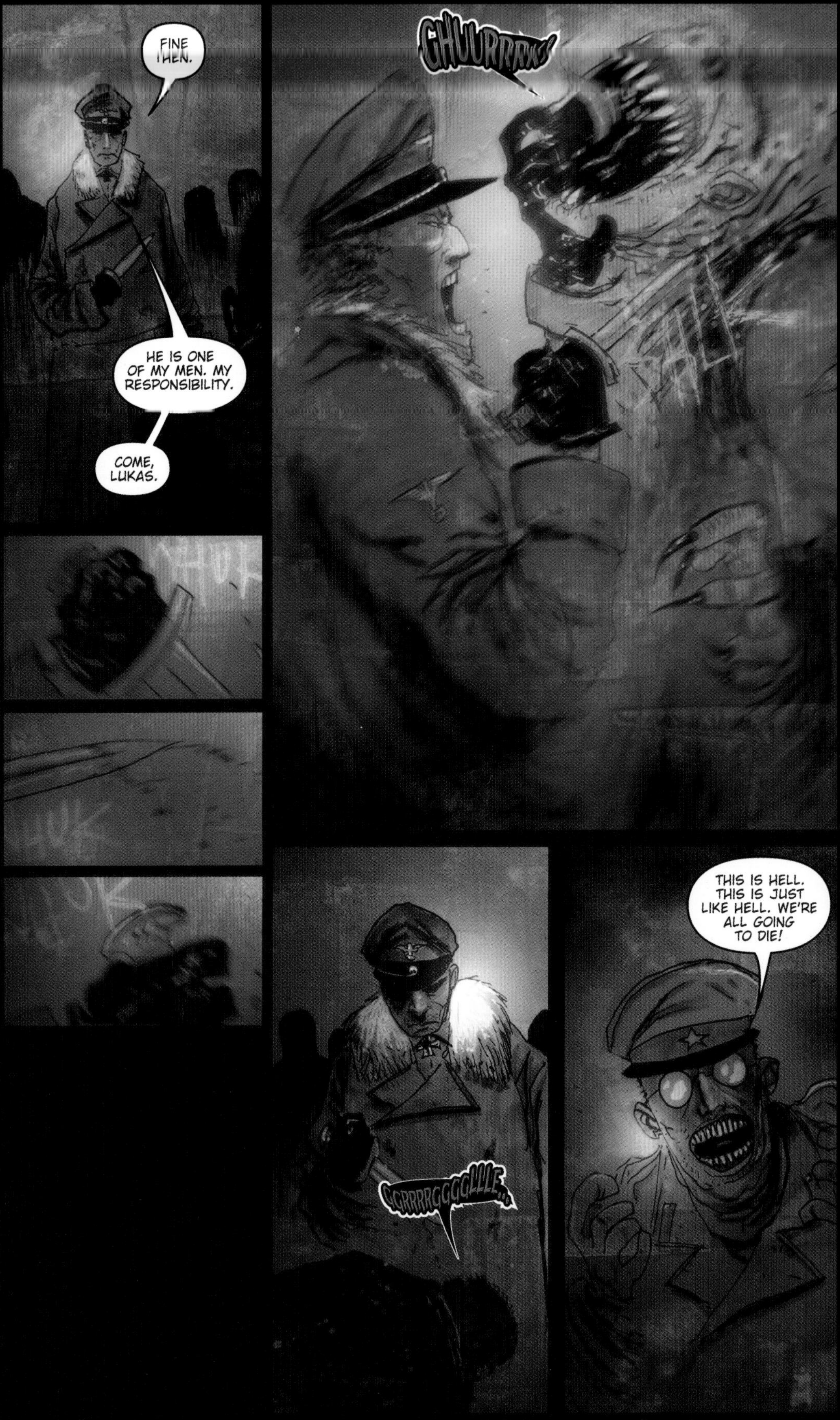
FINE THEN.
HE IS ONE OF MY MEN. MY RESPONSIBILITY.
COME, LUKAS.
GHUURRRK!
GGRRRRGGGLLLE...
THIS IS HELL. THIS IS JUST LIKE HELL. WE'RE ALL GOING TO DIE!

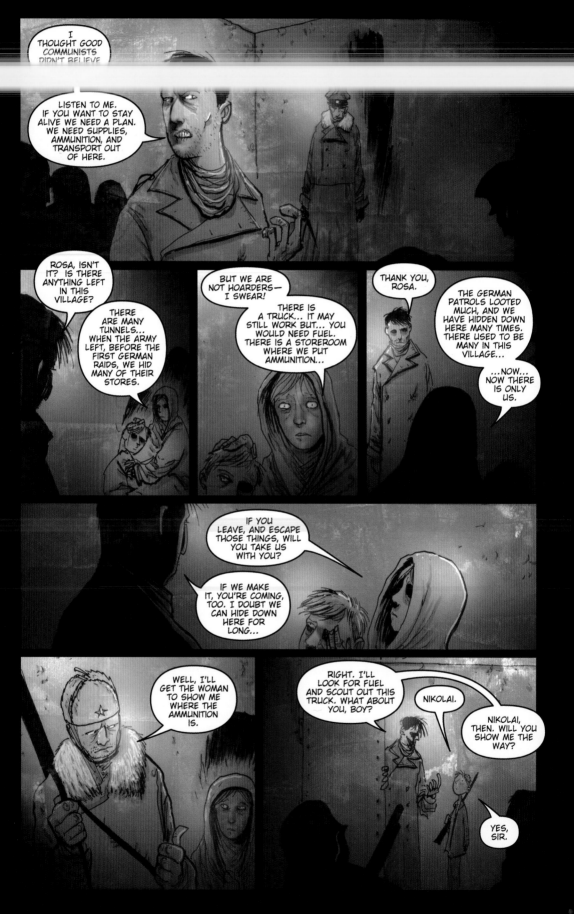

I THOUGHT GOOD COMMUNISTS DIDN'T BELIEVE

LISTEN TO ME. IF YOU WANT TO STAY ALIVE WE NEED A PLAN. WE NEED SUPPLIES, AMMUNITION, AND TRANSPORT OUT OF HERE.

ROSA, ISN'T IT? IS THERE ANYTHING LEFT IN THIS VILLAGE?

THERE ARE MANY TUNNELS... WHEN THE ARMY LEFT, BEFORE THE FIRST GERMAN RAIDS, WE HID MANY OF THEIR STORES.

BUT WE ARE NOT HOARDERS— I SWEAR!

THERE IS A TRUCK... IT MAY STILL WORK BUT... YOU WOULD NEED FUEL. THERE IS A STOREROOM WHERE WE PUT AMMUNITION...

THANK YOU, ROSA.

THE GERMAN PATROLS LOOTED MUCH, AND WE HAVE HIDDEN DOWN HERE MANY TIMES. THERE USED TO BE MANY IN THIS VILLAGE...

...NOW... NOW THERE IS ONLY US.

IF YOU LEAVE, AND ESCAPE THOSE THINGS, WILL YOU TAKE US WITH YOU?

IF WE MAKE IT, YOU'RE COMING, TOO. I DOUBT WE CAN HIDE DOWN HERE FOR LONG...

WELL, I'LL GET THE WOMAN TO SHOW ME WHERE THE AMMUNITION IS.

RIGHT. I'LL LOOK FOR FUEL AND SCOUT OUT THIS TRUCK. WHAT ABOUT YOU, BOY?

NIKOLAI.

NIKOLAI, THEN. WILL YOU SHOW ME THE WAY?

YES, SIR.

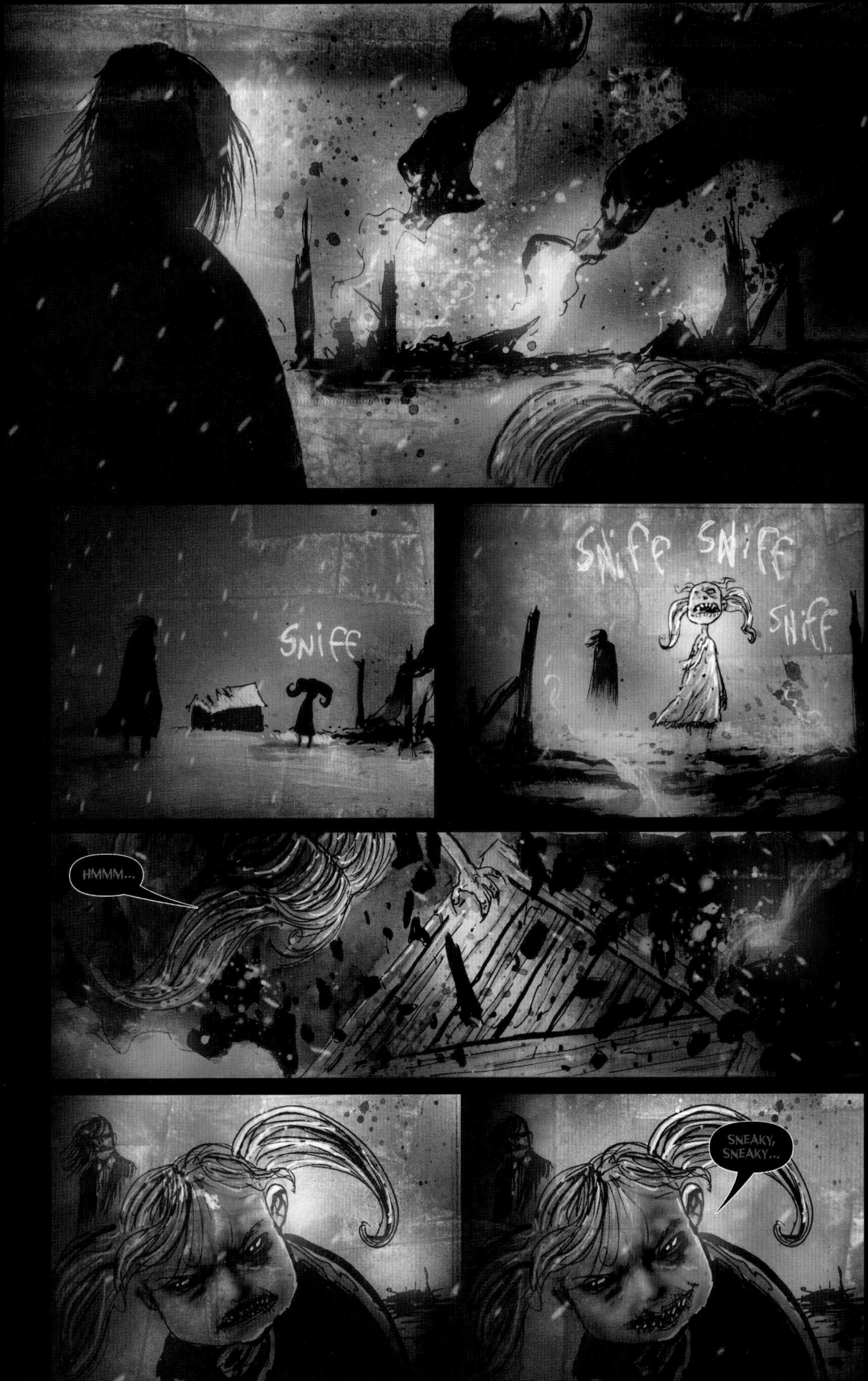
SNIFF
SNIFF SNIFF
SNIFF
HMMM...
SNEAKY, SNEAKY...

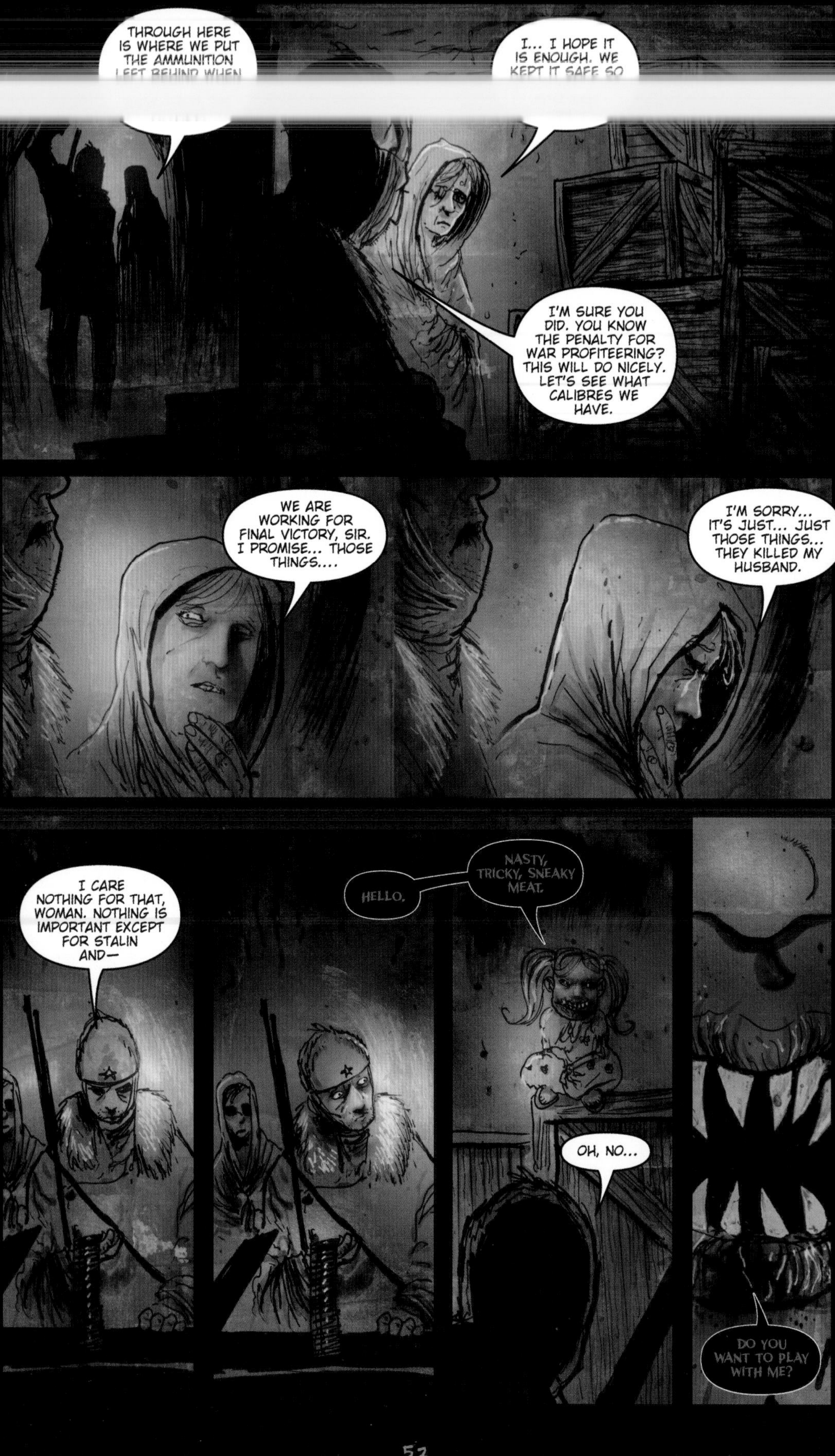
THROUGH HERE IS WHERE WE PUT THE AMMUNITION
I... I HOPE IT IS ENOUGH. WE
I'M SURE YOU DID. YOU KNOW THE PENALTY FOR WAR PROFITEERING? THIS WILL DO NICELY. LET'S SEE WHAT CALIBRES WE HAVE.
WE ARE WORKING FOR FINAL VICTORY, SIR. I PROMISE... THOSE THINGS....
I'M SORRY... IT'S JUST... JUST THOSE THINGS... THEY KILLED MY HUSBAND.
I CARE NOTHING FOR THAT, WOMAN. NOTHING IS IMPORTANT EXCEPT FOR STALIN AND—
HELLO.
NASTY, TRICKY, SNEAKY MEAT.
OH, NO...
DO YOU WANT TO PLAY WITH ME?

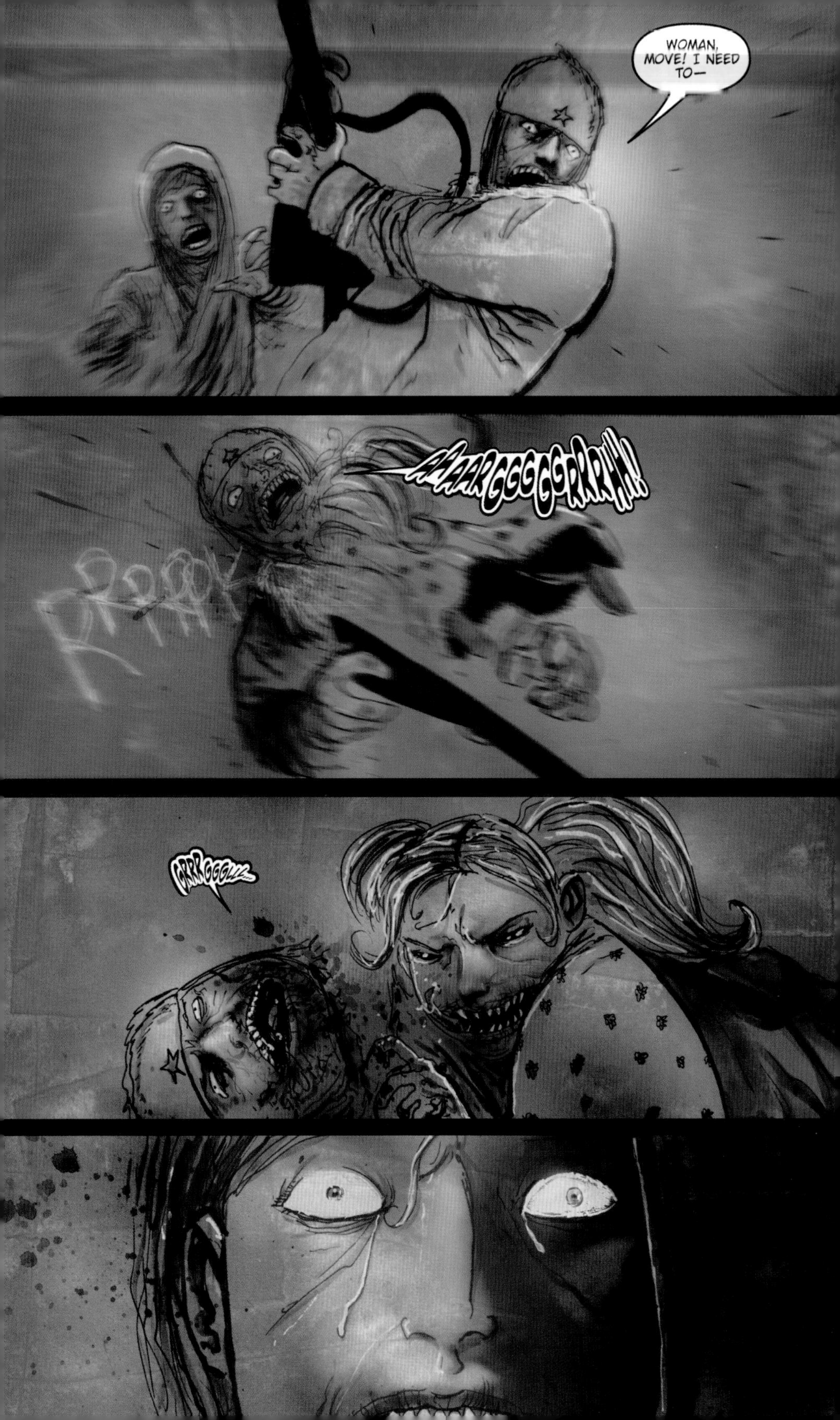
WOMAN, MOVE! I NEED TO—
AAAARGGGGGRRRAH!
GRRROGGLL...

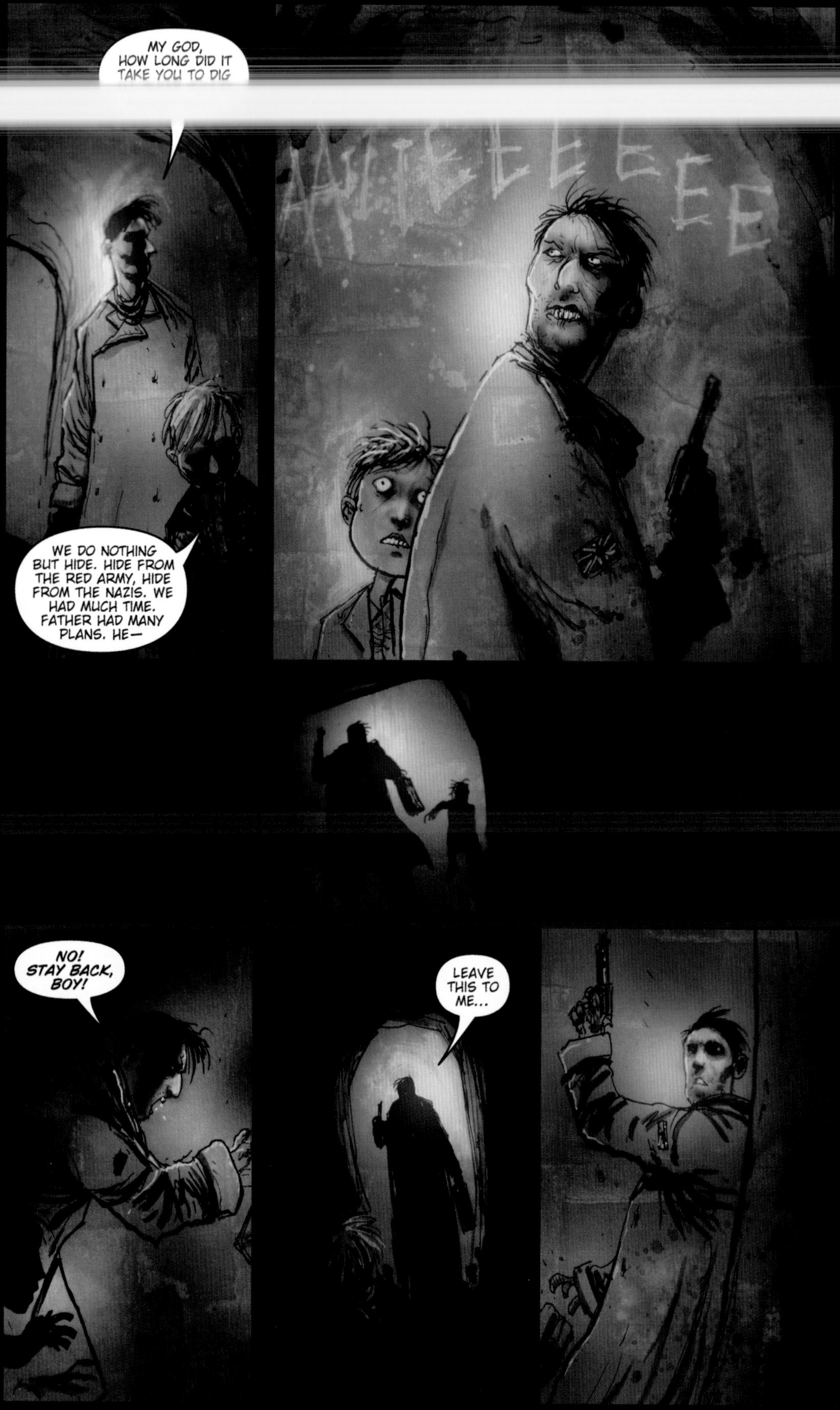

MY GOD, HOW LONG DID IT TAKE YOU TO DIG
WE DO NOTHING BUT HIDE. HIDE FROM THE RED ARMY, HIDE FROM THE NAZIS. WE HAD MUCH TIME. FATHER HAD MANY PLANS. HE—
NO! STAY BACK, BOY!
LEAVE THIS TO ME...

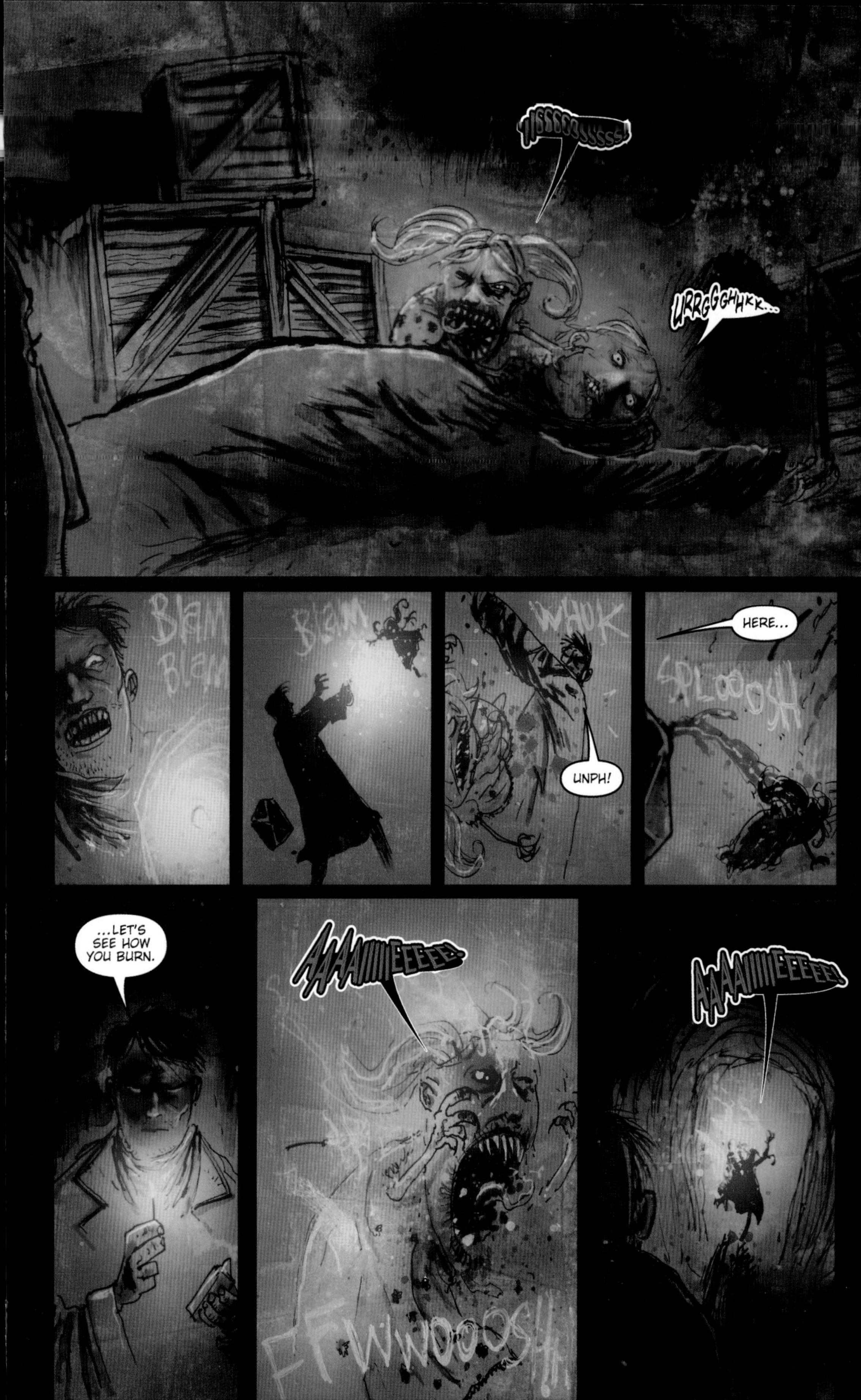
HISSSSSSSSSSS!
URRGGGHHKK...
BLAM
BLAM
BLAM
WHUK
UNPH!
HERE...
SPLOOOSH
...LET'S SEE HOW YOU BURN.
AAAAIIIIIEEEEE!
AAAAIIIIIEEEEE!
FFWWOOOSH

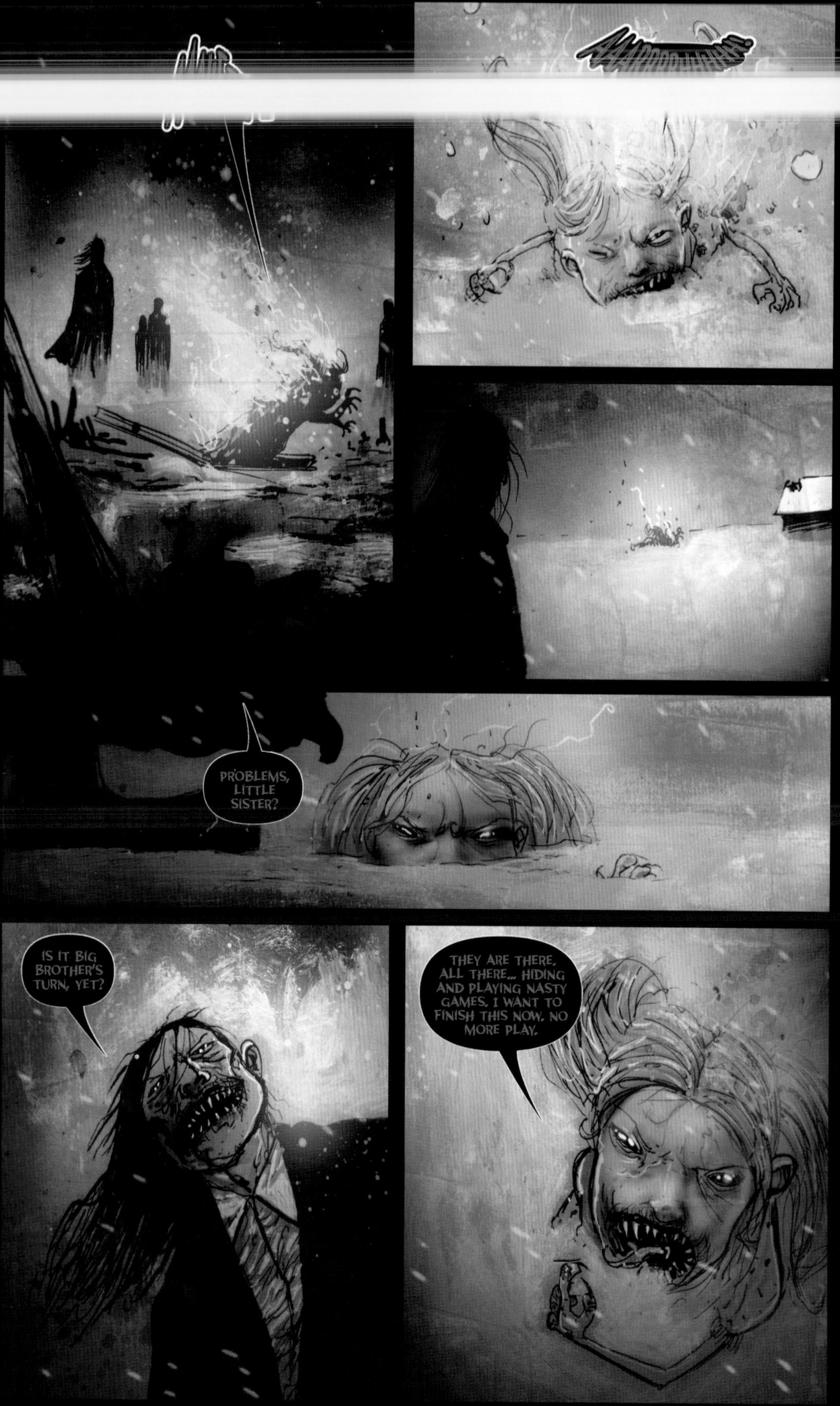
PROBLEMS, LITTLE SISTER?
IS IT BIG BROTHER'S TURN, YET?
THEY ARE THERE, ALL THERE... HIDING AND PLAYING NASTY GAMES. I WANT TO FINISH THIS NOW. NO MORE PLAY.

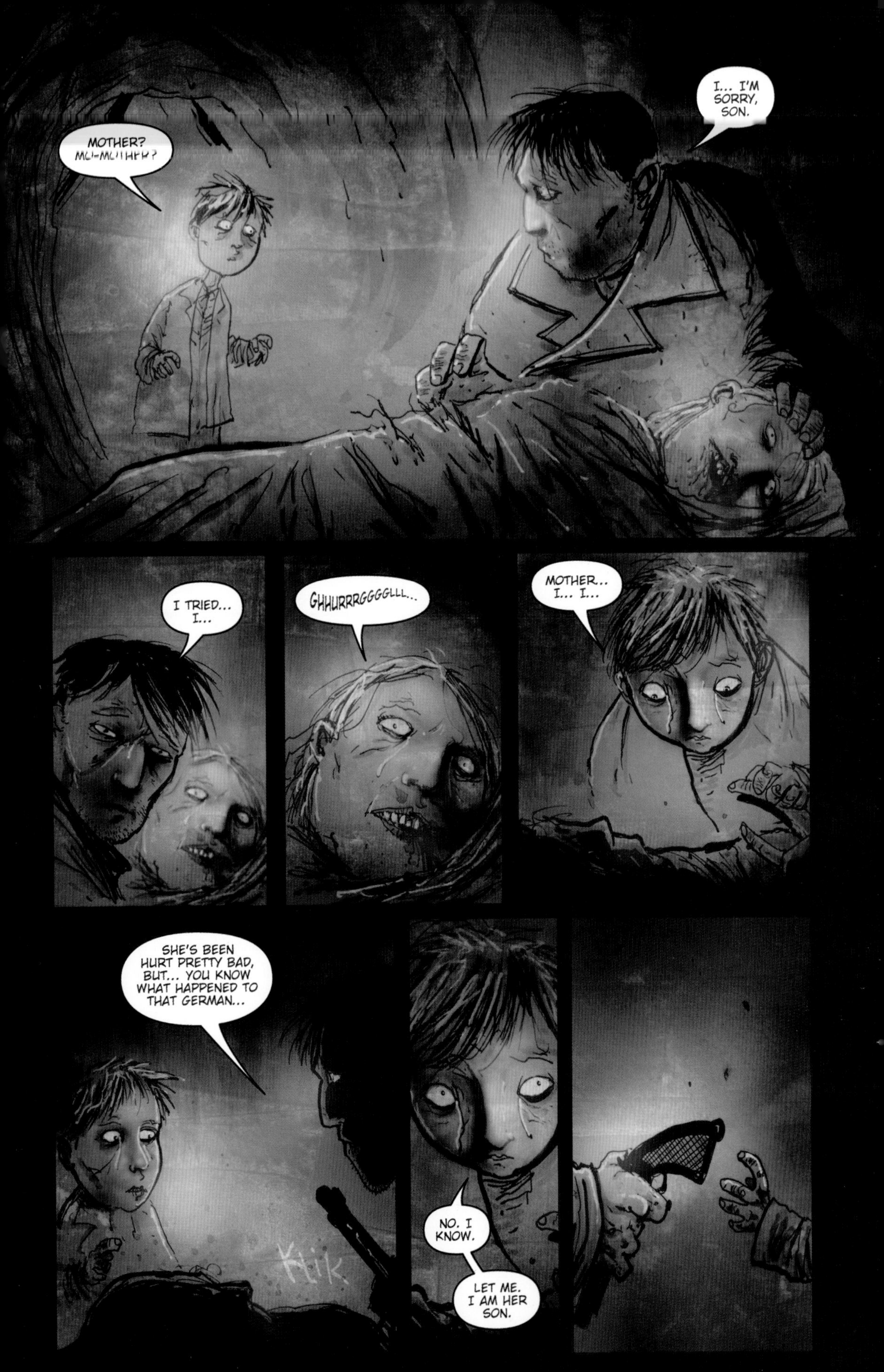
MOTHER?
MO-MOTHER?
I... I'M
SORRY,
SON.
I TRIED...
I...
GHHURRRGGGGLLL...
MOTHER...
I... I...
SHE'S BEEN
HURT PRETTY BAD,
BUT... YOU KNOW
WHAT HAPPENED TO
THAT GERMAN...
KLIK
NO. I
KNOW.
LET ME.
I AM HER
SON.

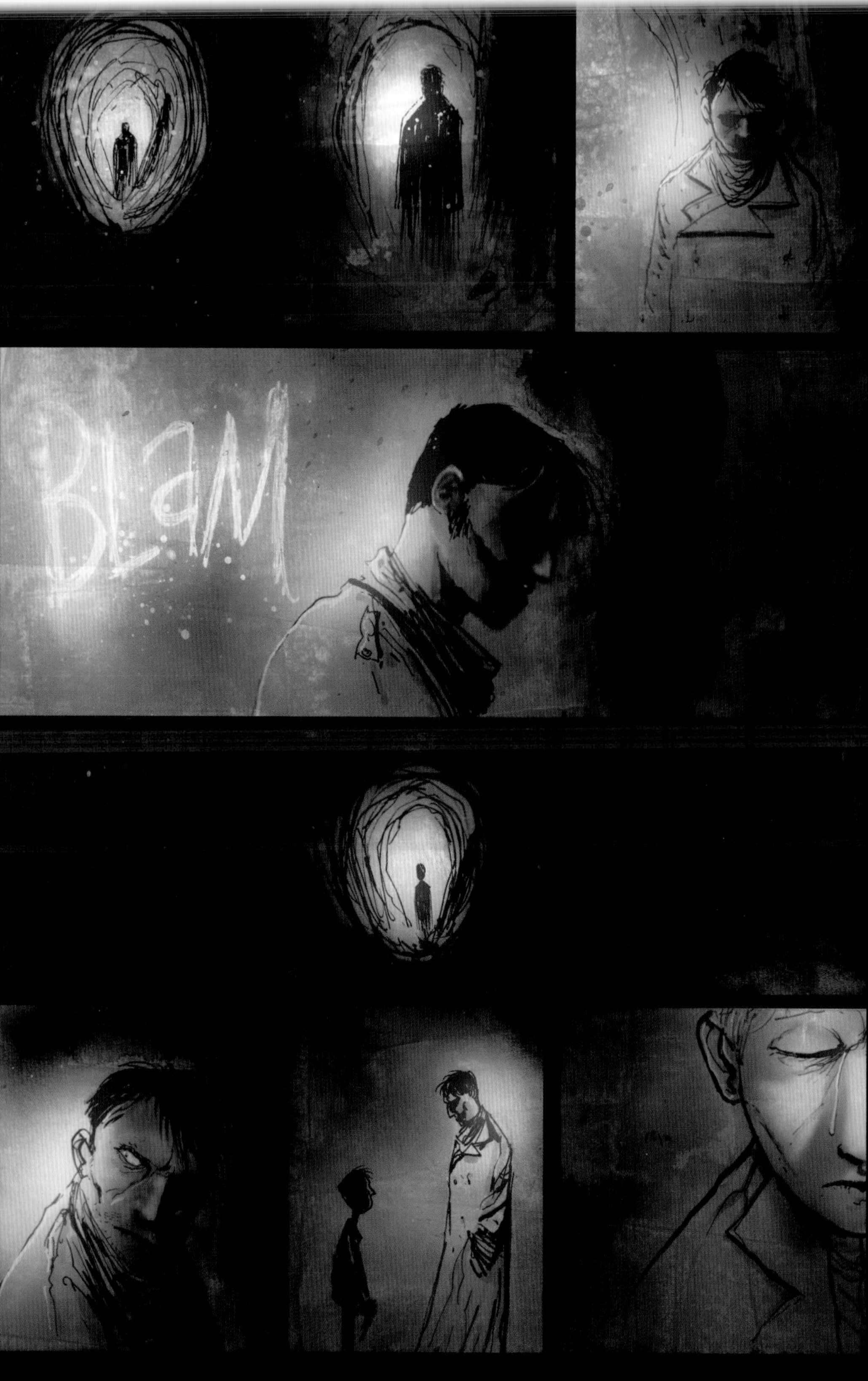
BLAM

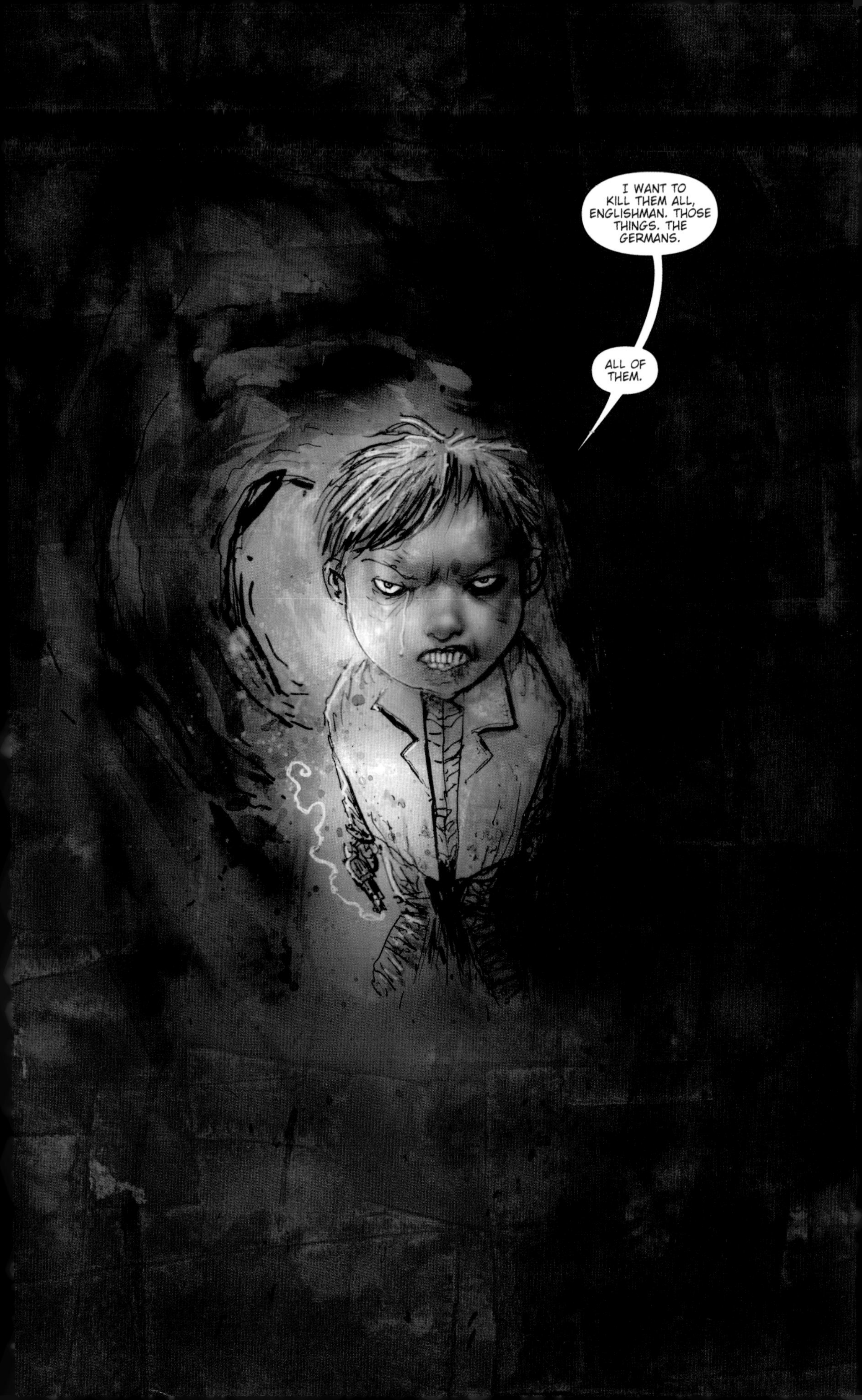
I WANT TO KILL THEM ALL, ENGLISHMAN. THOSE THINGS. THE GERMANS.
ALL OF THEM.

Chapter Three

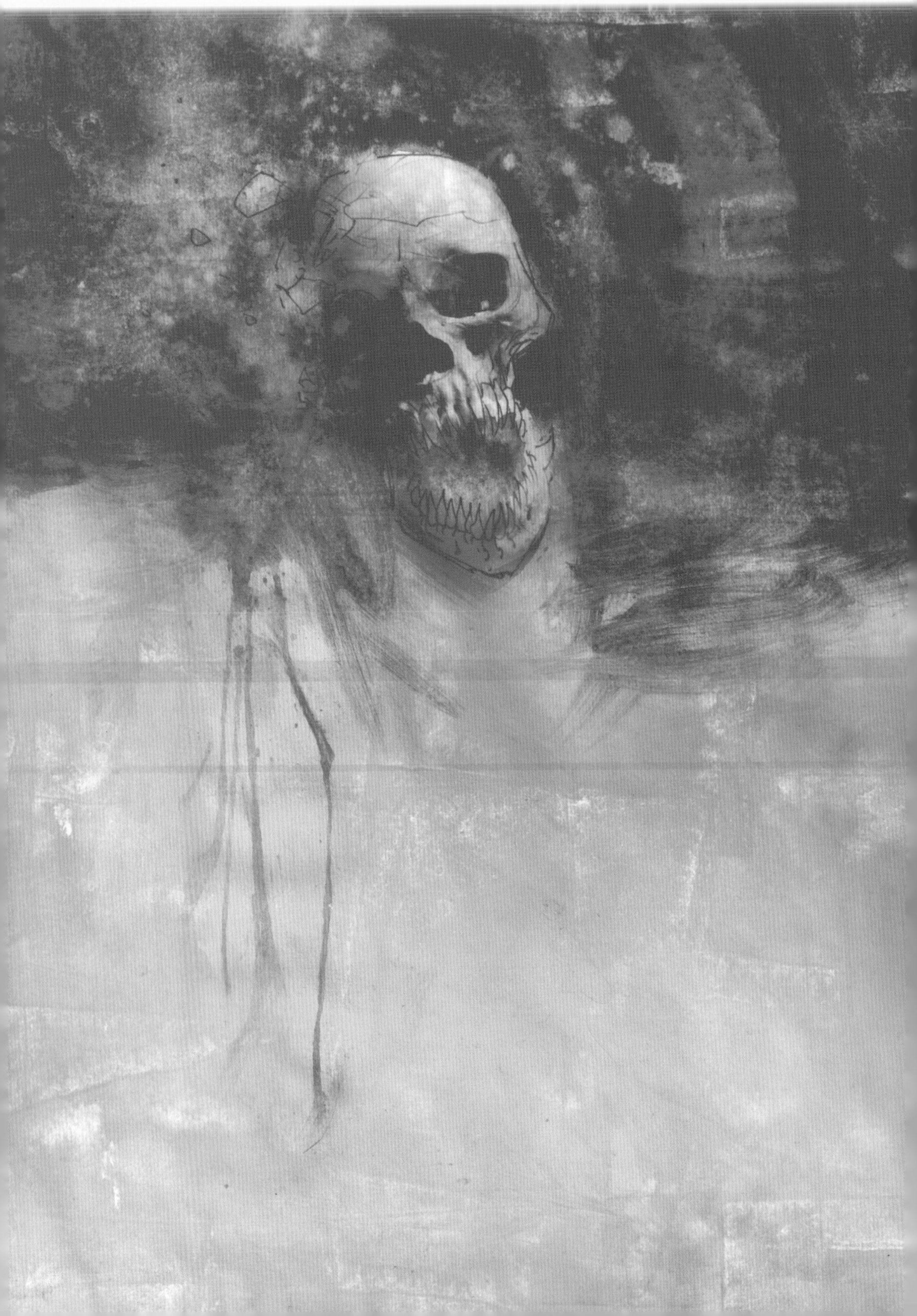

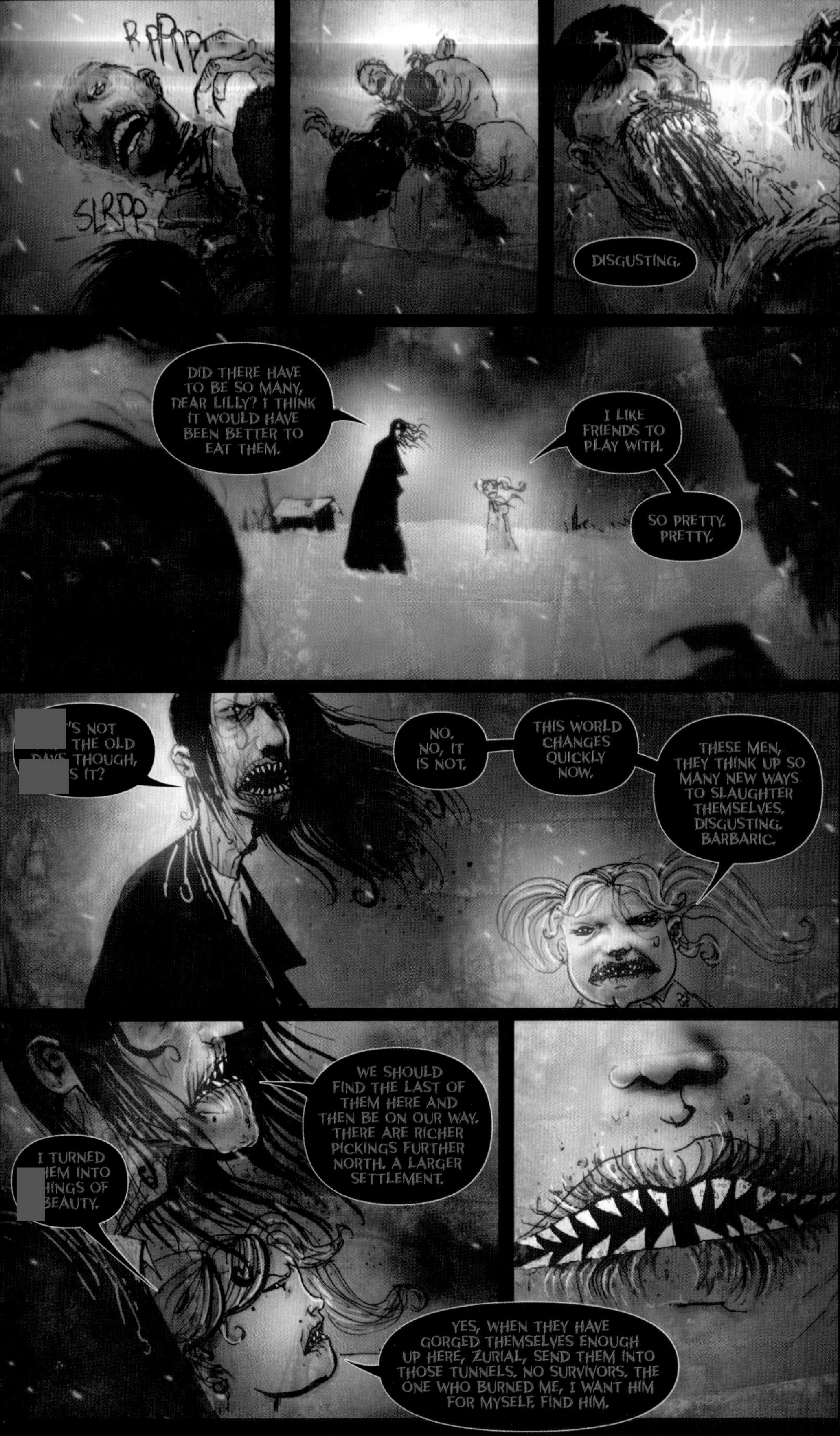
RPPPP
SLRPP
DISGUSTING.
DID THERE HAVE TO BE SO MANY, DEAR LILLY? I THINK IT WOULD HAVE BEEN BETTER TO EAT THEM.
I LIKE FRIENDS TO PLAY WITH.
SO PRETTY. PRETTY.
[redacted]'S NOT THE OLD [redacted] THOUGH, [redacted]S IT?
NO. NO, IT IS NOT.
THIS WORLD CHANGES QUICKLY NOW.
THESE MEN, THEY THINK UP SO MANY NEW WAYS TO SLAUGHTER THEMSELVES. DISGUSTING. BARBARIC.
WE SHOULD FIND THE LAST OF THEM HERE AND THEN BE ON OUR WAY. THERE ARE RICHER PICKINGS FURTHER NORTH. A LARGER SETTLEMENT.
I TURNED [redacted]HEM INTO [redacted]HINGS OF [redacted]EAUTY.
YES, WHEN THEY HAVE GORGED THEMSELVES ENOUGH UP HERE, ZURIAL, SEND THEM INTO THOSE TUNNELS. NO SURVIVORS. THE ONE WHO BURNED ME, I WANT HIM FOR MYSELF. FIND HIM.

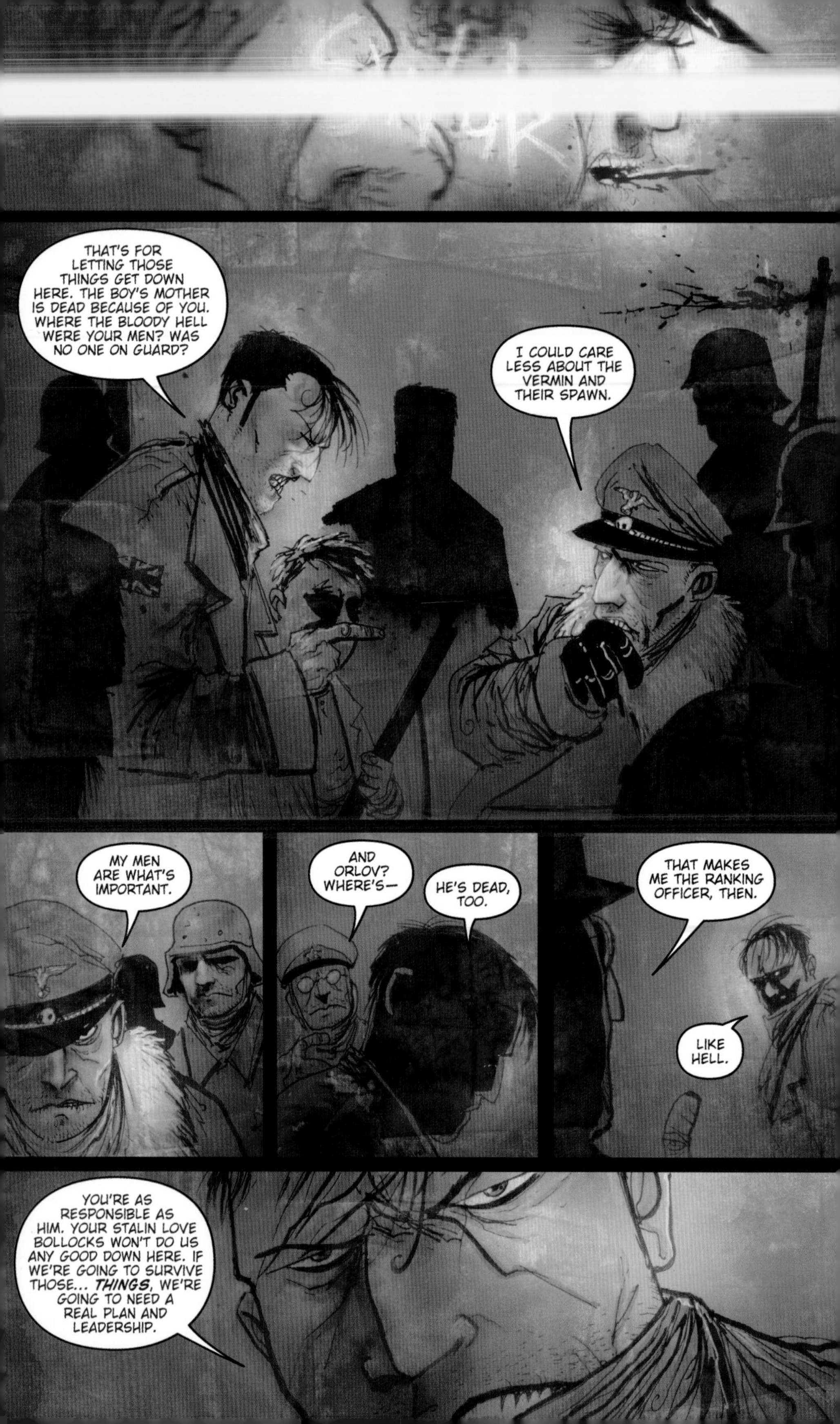
THAT'S FOR LETTING THOSE THINGS GET DOWN HERE. THE BOY'S MOTHER IS DEAD BECAUSE OF YOU. WHERE THE BLOODY HELL WERE YOUR MEN? WAS NO ONE ON GUARD?
I COULD CARE LESS ABOUT THE VERMIN AND THEIR SPAWN.
MY MEN ARE WHAT'S IMPORTANT.
AND ORLOV? WHERE'S—
HE'S DEAD, TOO.
THAT MAKES ME THE RANKING OFFICER, THEN.
LIKE HELL.
YOU'RE AS RESPONSIBLE AS HIM. YOUR STALIN LOVE BOLLOCKS WON'T DO US ANY GOOD DOWN HERE. IF WE'RE GOING TO SURVIVE THOSE... *THINGS*, WE'RE GOING TO NEED A REAL PLAN AND LEADERSHIP.

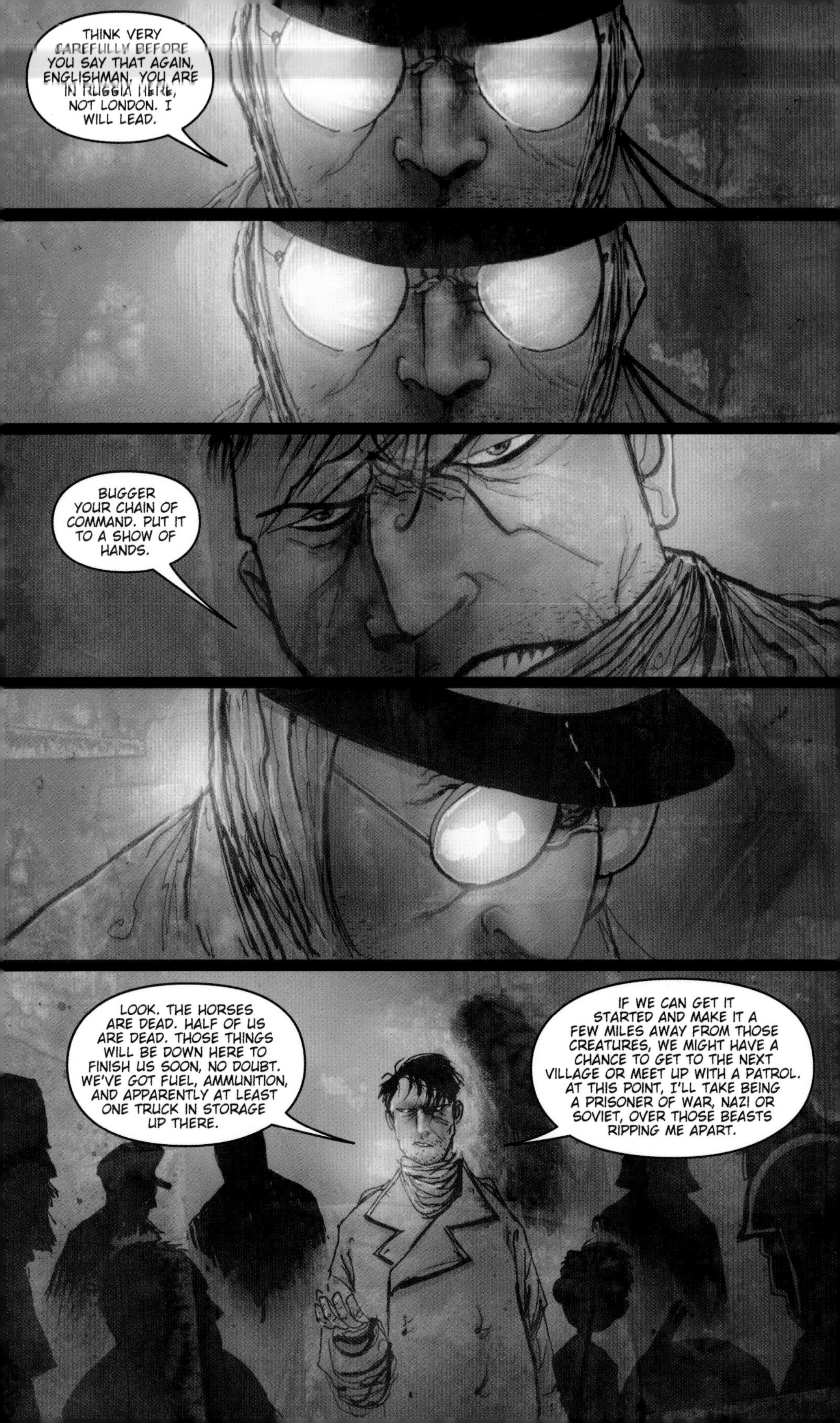
THINK VERY CAREFULLY BEFORE YOU SAY THAT AGAIN, ENGLISHMAN. YOU ARE IN RUSSIA HERE, NOT LONDON. I WILL LEAD.
BUGGER YOUR CHAIN OF COMMAND. PUT IT TO A SHOW OF HANDS.
LOOK. THE HORSES ARE DEAD. HALF OF US ARE DEAD. THOSE THINGS WILL BE DOWN HERE TO FINISH US SOON, NO DOUBT. WE'VE GOT FUEL, AMMUNITION, AND APPARENTLY AT LEAST ONE TRUCK IN STORAGE UP THERE.
IF WE CAN GET IT STARTED AND MAKE IT A FEW MILES AWAY FROM THOSE CREATURES, WE MIGHT HAVE A CHANCE TO GET TO THE NEXT VILLAGE OR MEET UP WITH A PATROL. AT THIS POINT, I'LL TAKE BEING A PRISONER OF WAR, NAZI OR SOVIET, OVER THOSE BEASTS RIPPING ME APART.

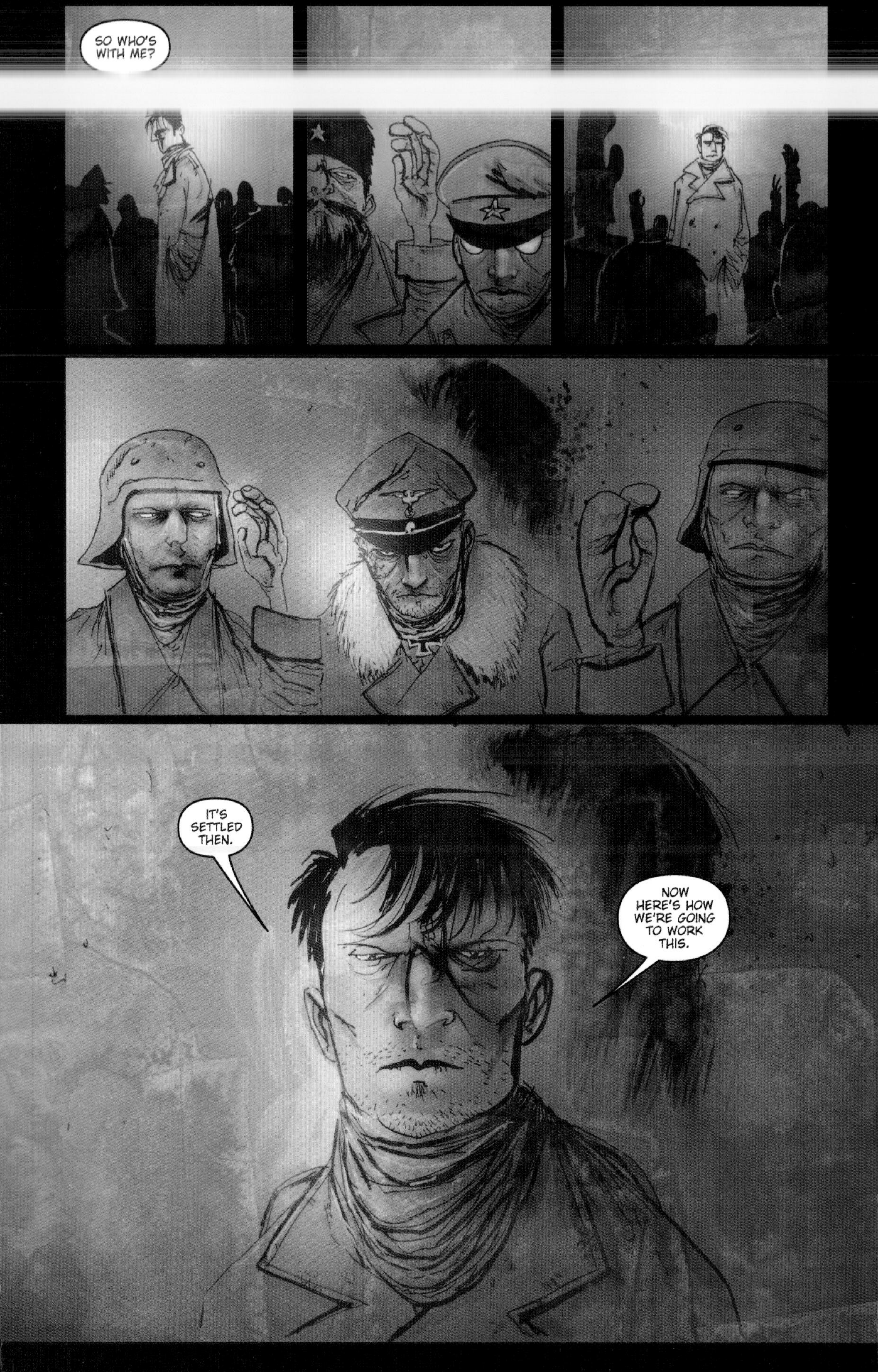
SO WHO'S WITH ME?
IT'S SETTLED THEN.
NOW HERE'S HOW WE'RE GOING TO WORK THIS.

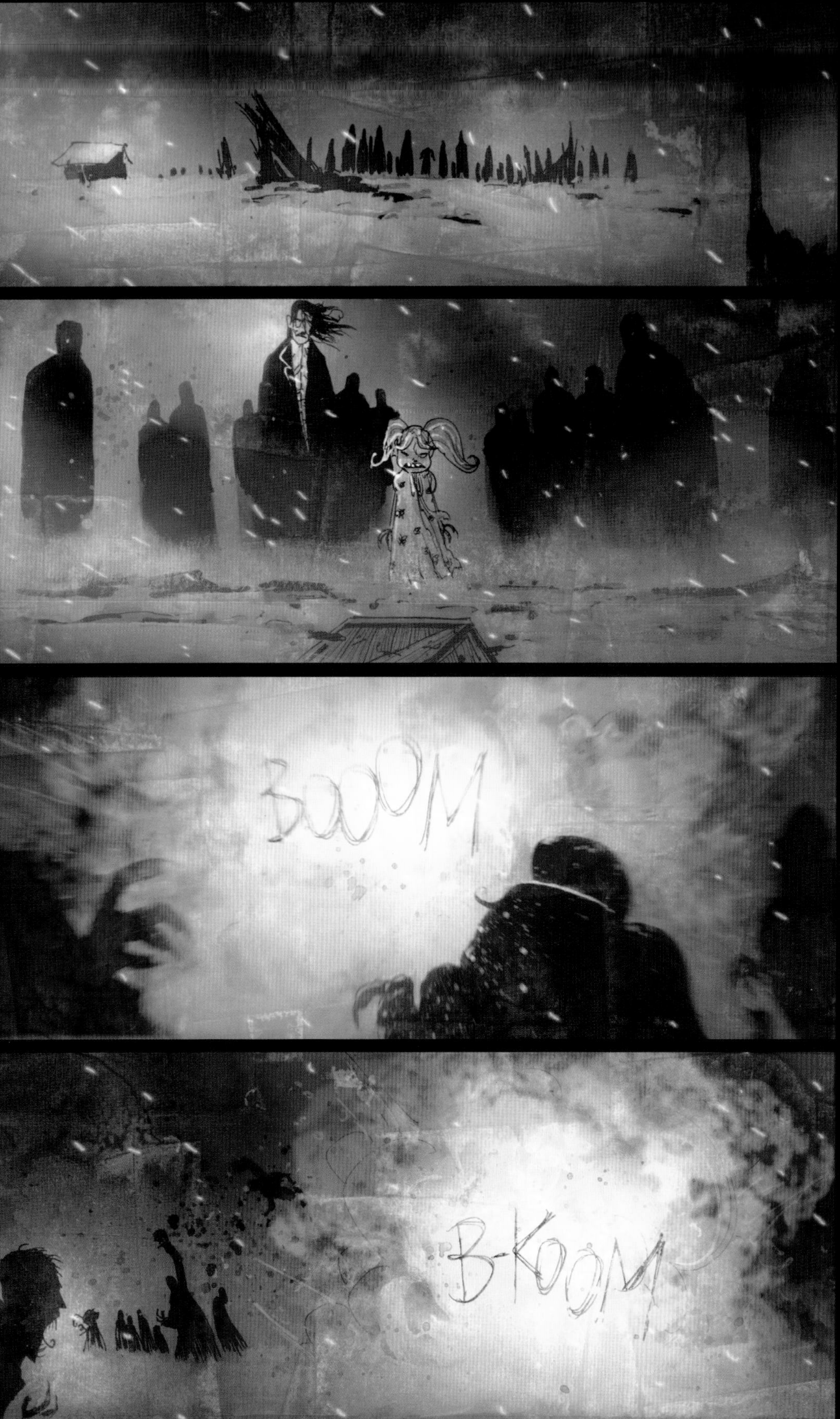
BOOOM
B-KOOM

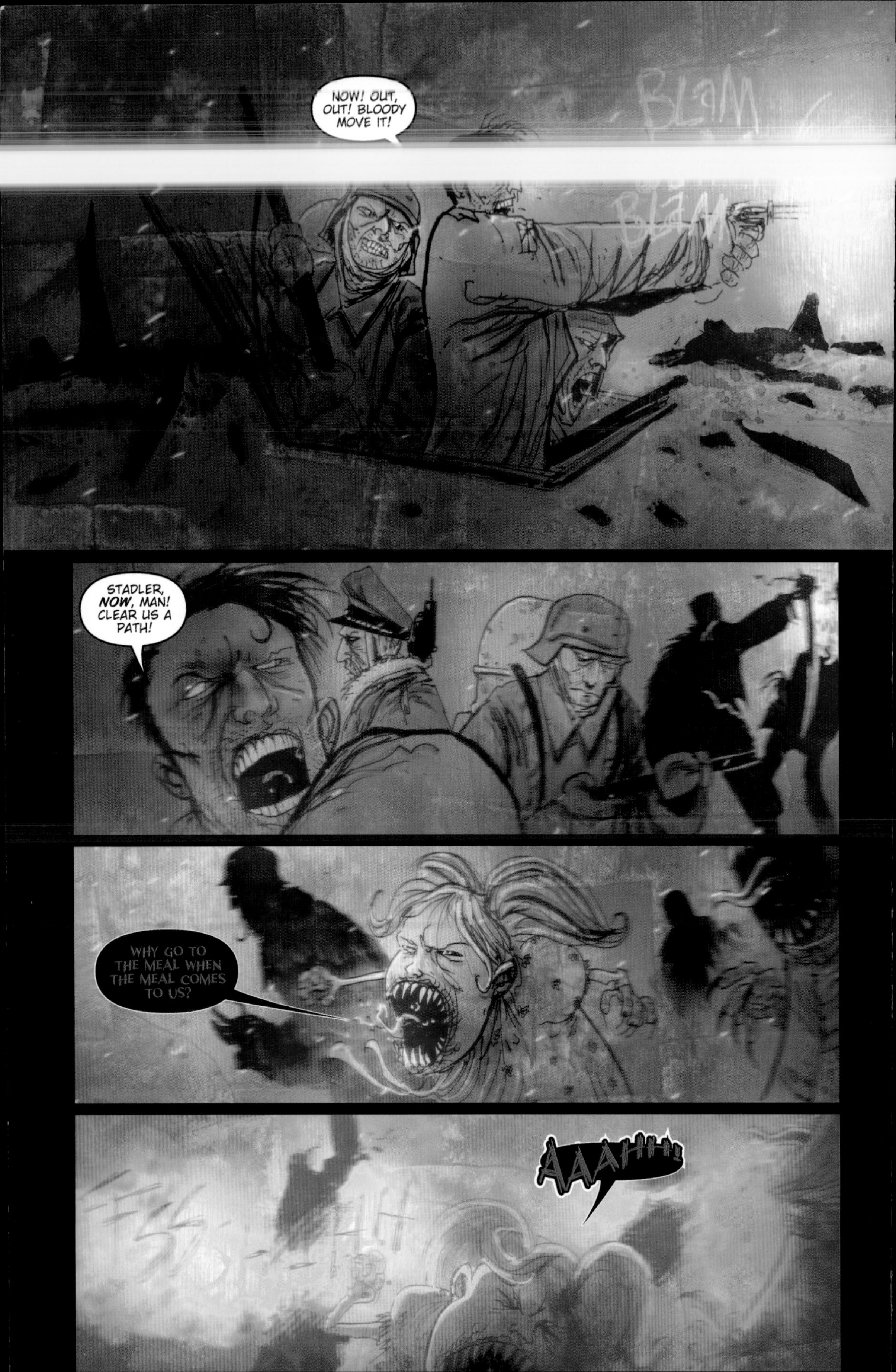
BLAM
NOW! OUT, OUT! BLOODY MOVE IT!
BLAM
STADLER, NOW, MAN! CLEAR US A PATH!
WHY GO TO THE MEAL WHEN THE MEAL COMES TO US?
AAAHHH

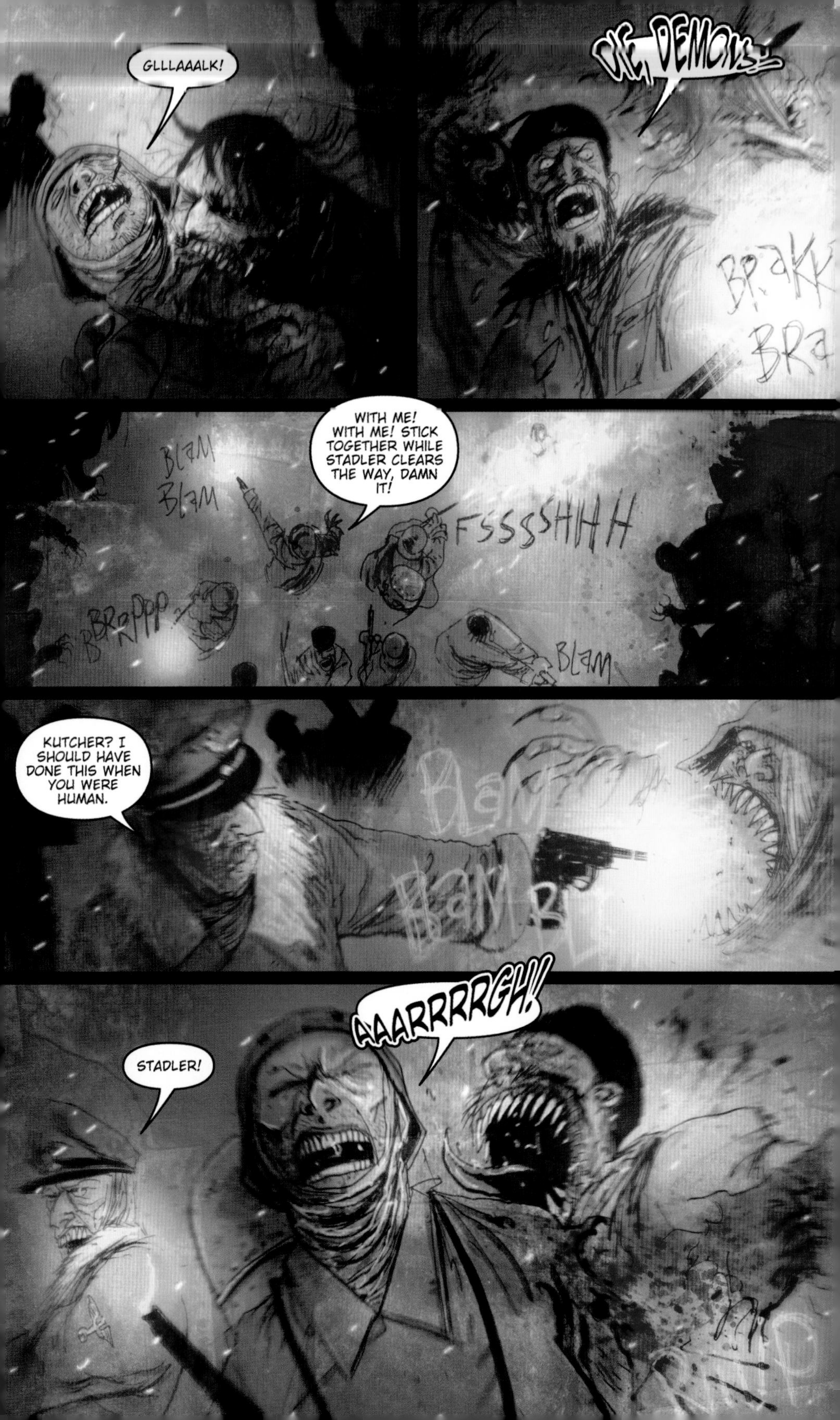
GLLLAAALK!
DIE, DEMONS!
BRAKK
BRA
BLAM
BLAM
WITH ME! WITH ME! STICK TOGETHER WHILE STADLER CLEARS THE WAY, DAMN IT!
FSSSSHHH
BRRPPP
BLAM
KUTCHER? I SHOULD HAVE DONE THIS WHEN YOU WERE HUMAN.
BLAM
BLAM
STADLER!
AAARRRRGH!

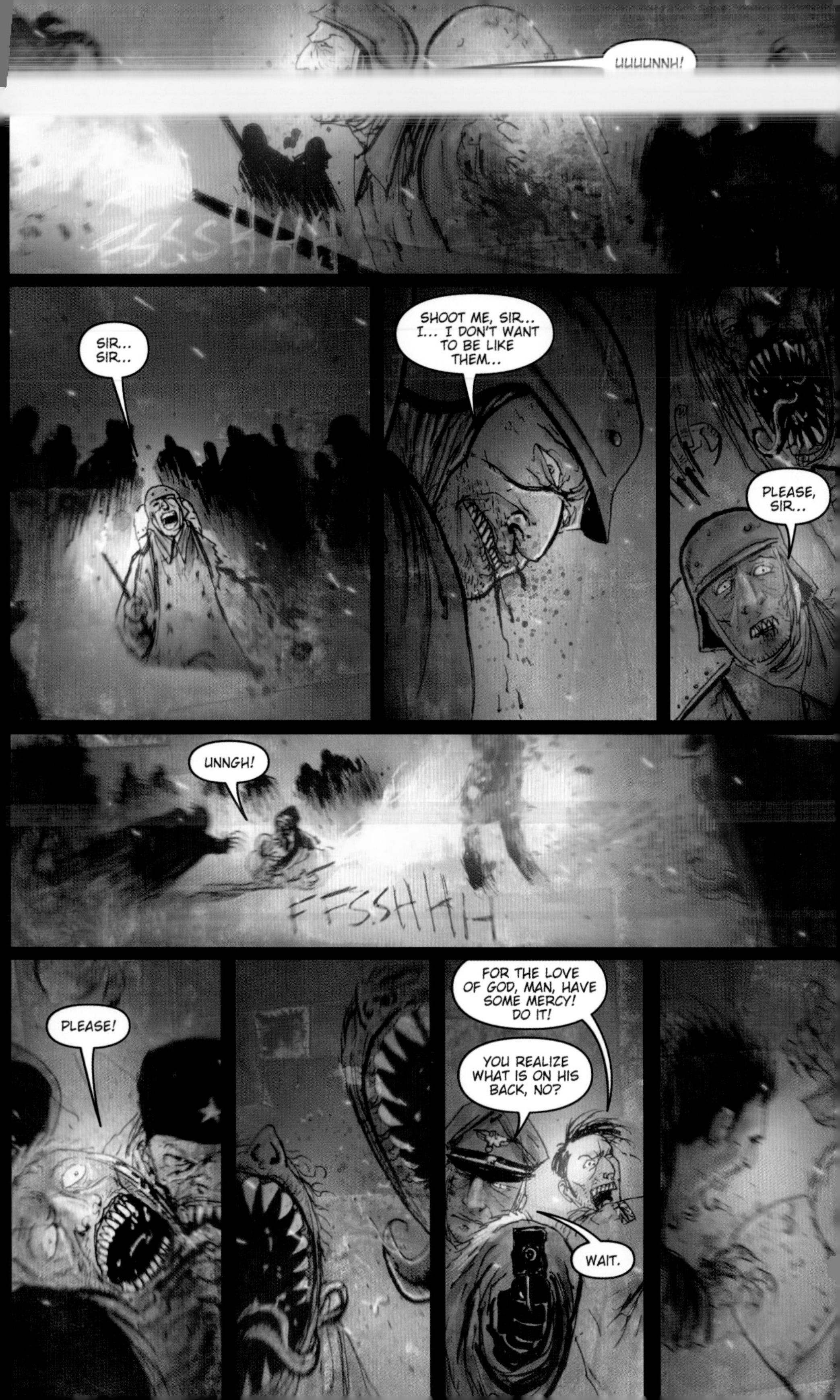
UUUUNNH!
FFSSHHH
SIR... SIR...
SHOOT ME, SIR... I... I DON'T WANT TO BE LIKE THEM...
PLEASE, SIR...
UNNGH!
FFSSHHH
PLEASE!
FOR THE LOVE OF GOD, MAN, HAVE SOME MERCY! DO IT!
YOU REALIZE WHAT IS ON HIS BACK, NO?
WAIT.

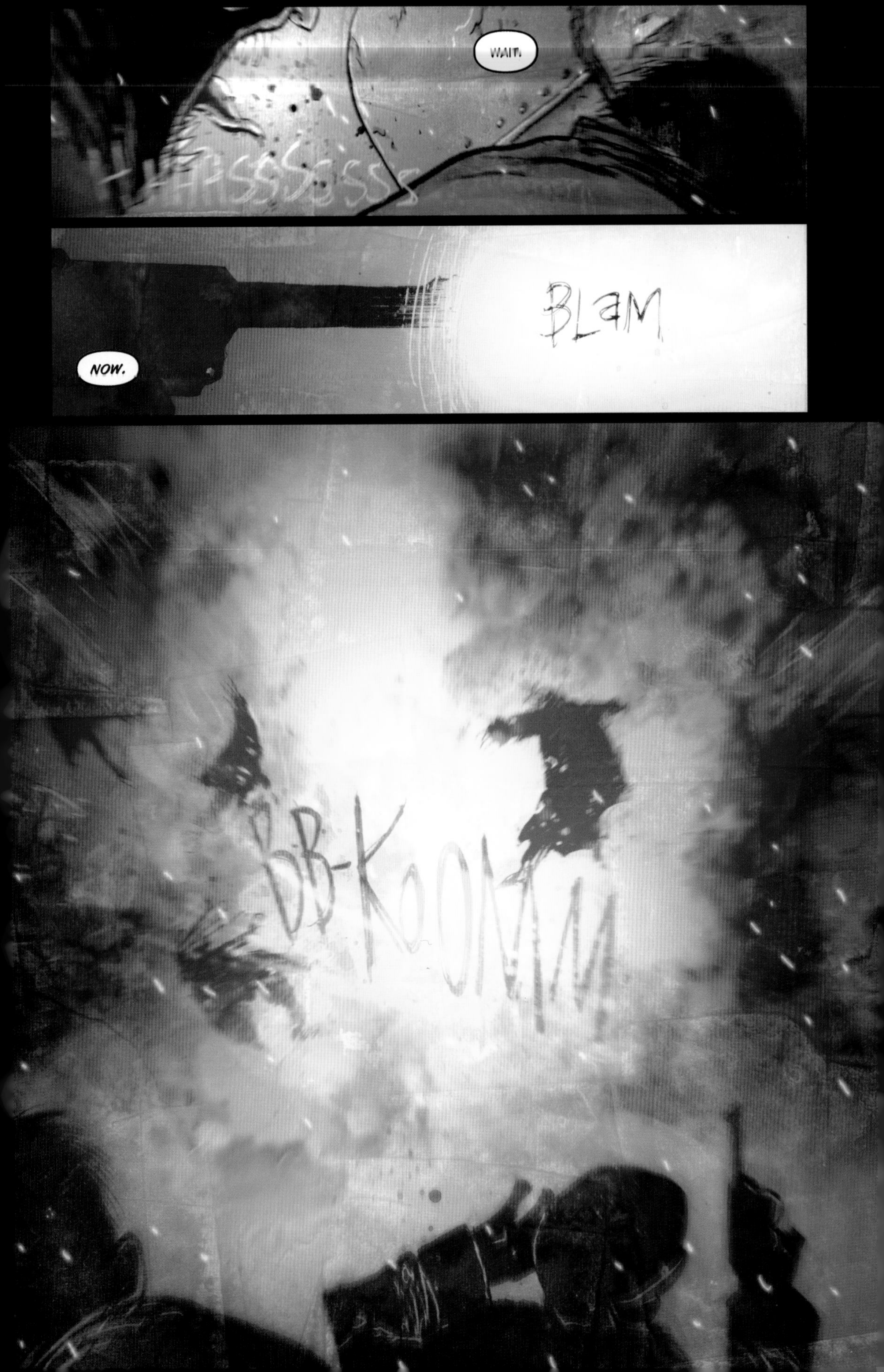
WAIT.
HFSSSSSSSS
BLAM
NOW.
BB-KOOMM

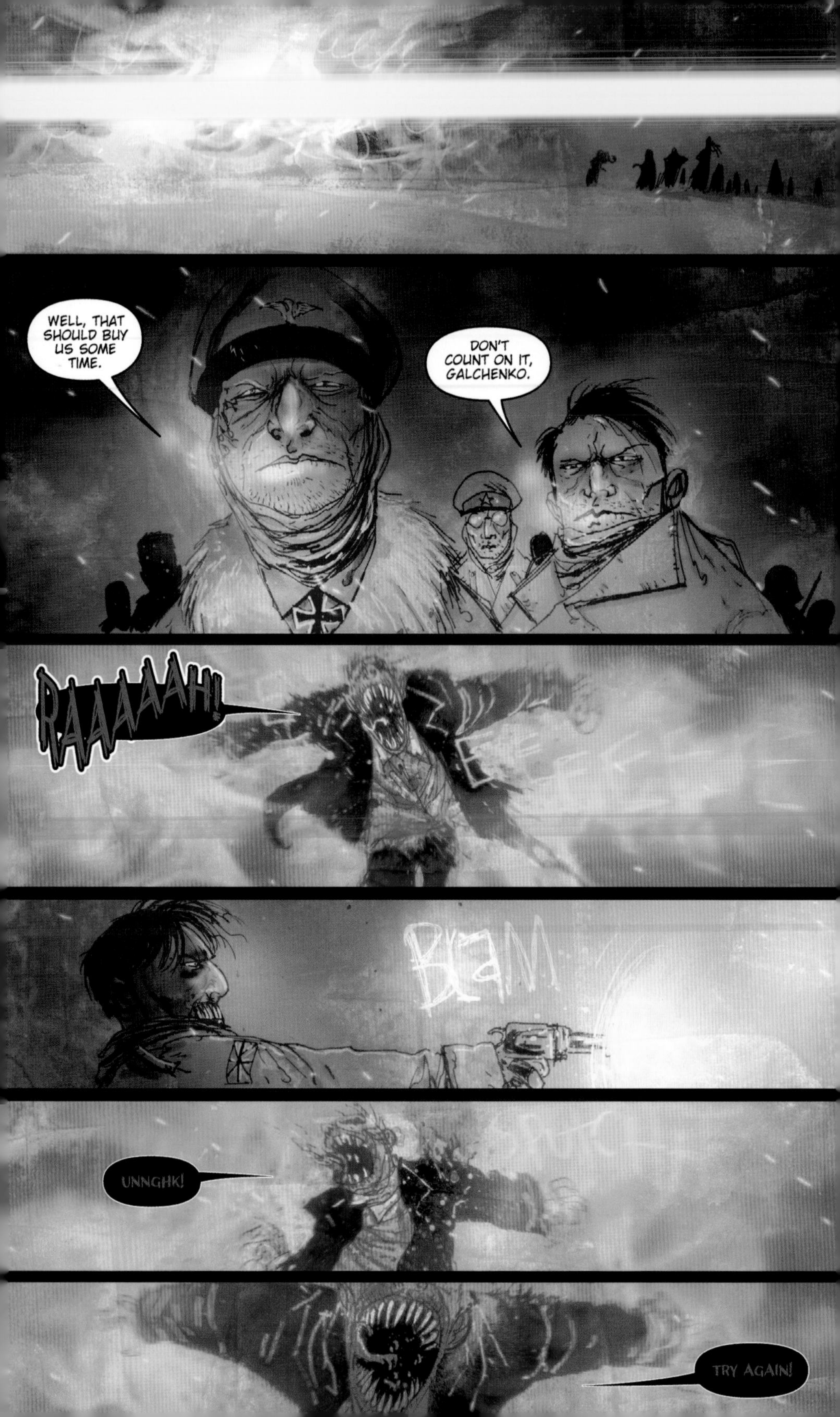
WELL, THAT SHOULD BUY US SOME TIME.
DON'T COUNT ON IT, GALCHENKO.
RAAAAAAH!
BLAM
UNNGHK!
TRY AGAIN!

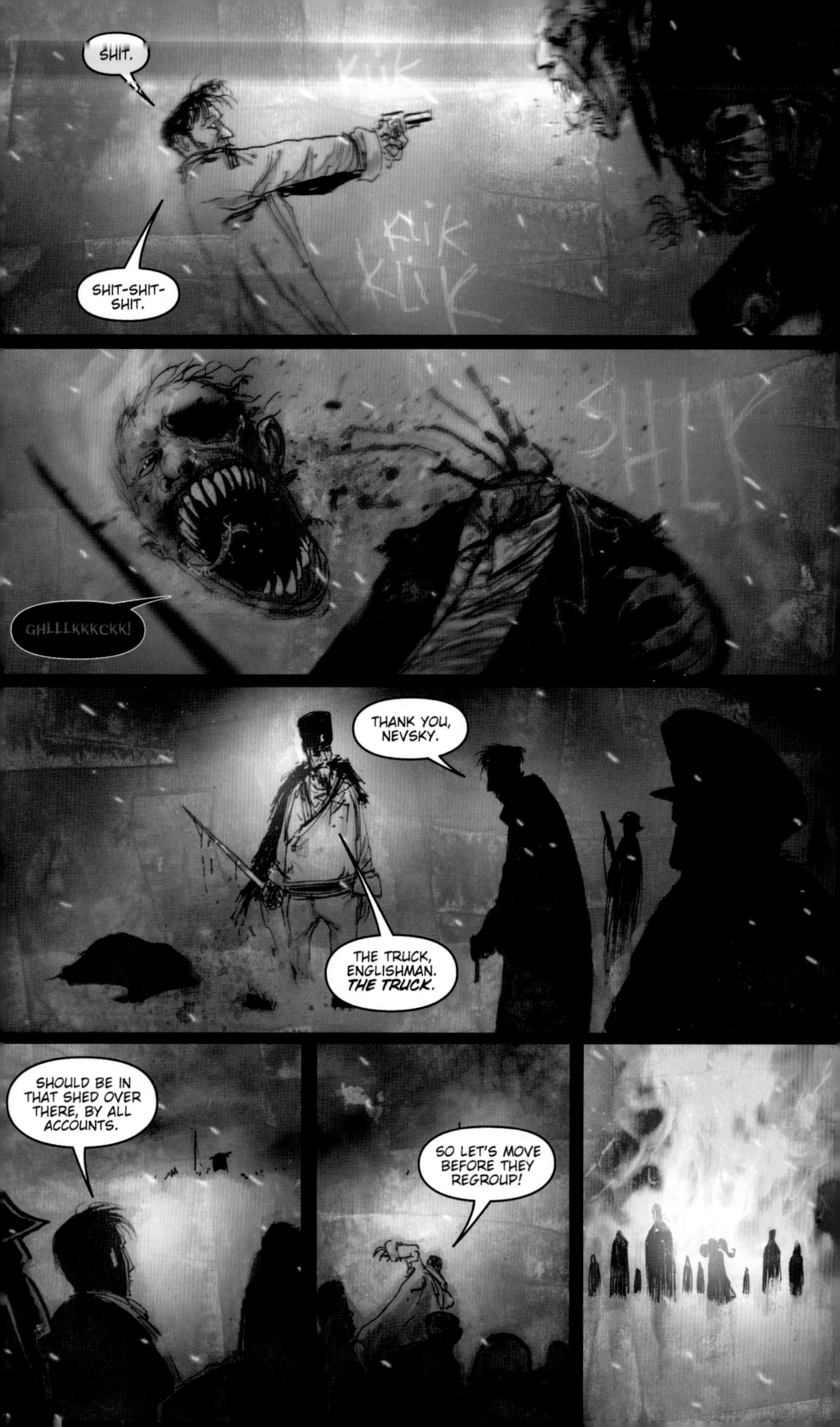
SHIT.
KLIK
SHIT-SHIT-SHIT.
KLIK KLIK
SHLK
GHLLLKKKCKK!
THANK YOU, NEVSKY.
THE TRUCK, ENGLISHMAN. *THE TRUCK.*
SHOULD BE IN THAT SHED OVER THERE, BY ALL ACCOUNTS.
SO LET'S MOVE BEFORE THEY REGROUP!

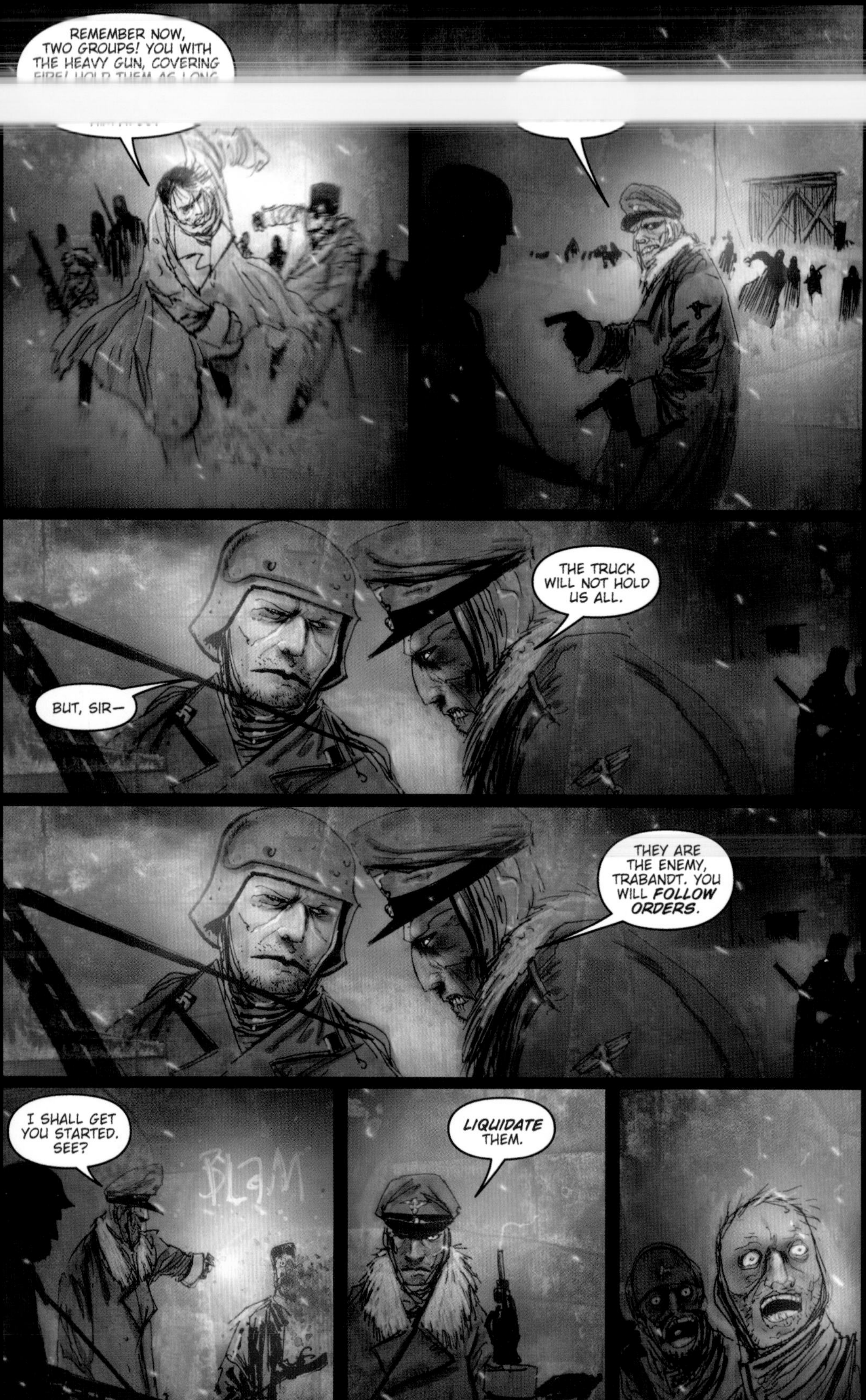
REMEMBER NOW, TWO GROUPS! YOU WITH THE HEAVY GUN, COVERING
THE TRUCK WILL NOT HOLD US ALL.
BUT, SIR—
THEY ARE THE ENEMY, TRABANDT. YOU WILL *FOLLOW ORDERS*.
I SHALL GET YOU STARTED. SEE?
BLAM
LIQUIDATE THEM.

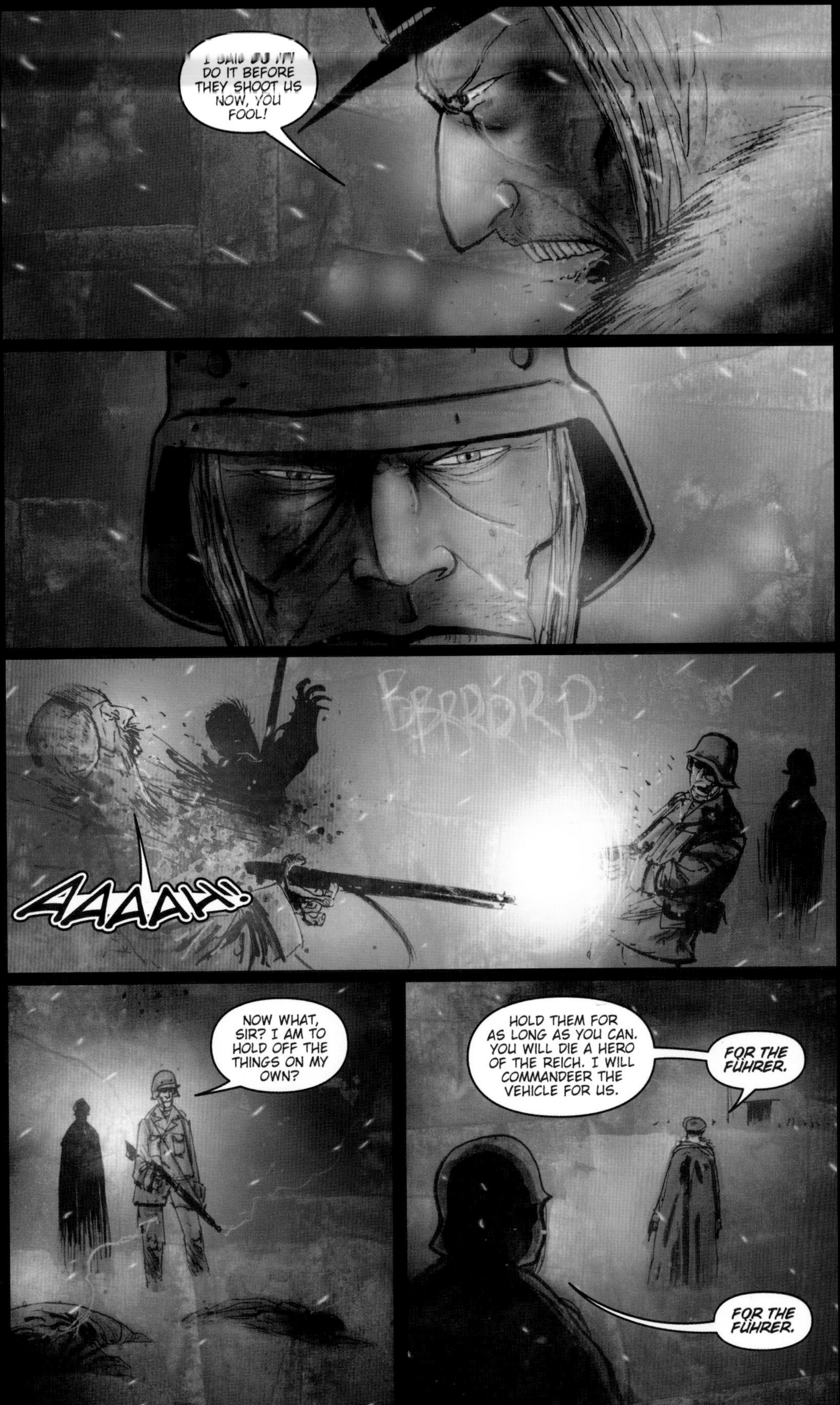
DO IT BEFORE THEY SHOOT US NOW, YOU FOOL!
AAAAH!
NOW WHAT, SIR? I AM TO HOLD OFF THE THINGS ON MY OWN?
HOLD THEM FOR AS LONG AS YOU CAN. YOU WILL DIE A HERO OF THE REICH. I WILL COMMANDEER THE VEHICLE FOR US.
FOR THE FÜHRER.
FOR THE FÜHRER.

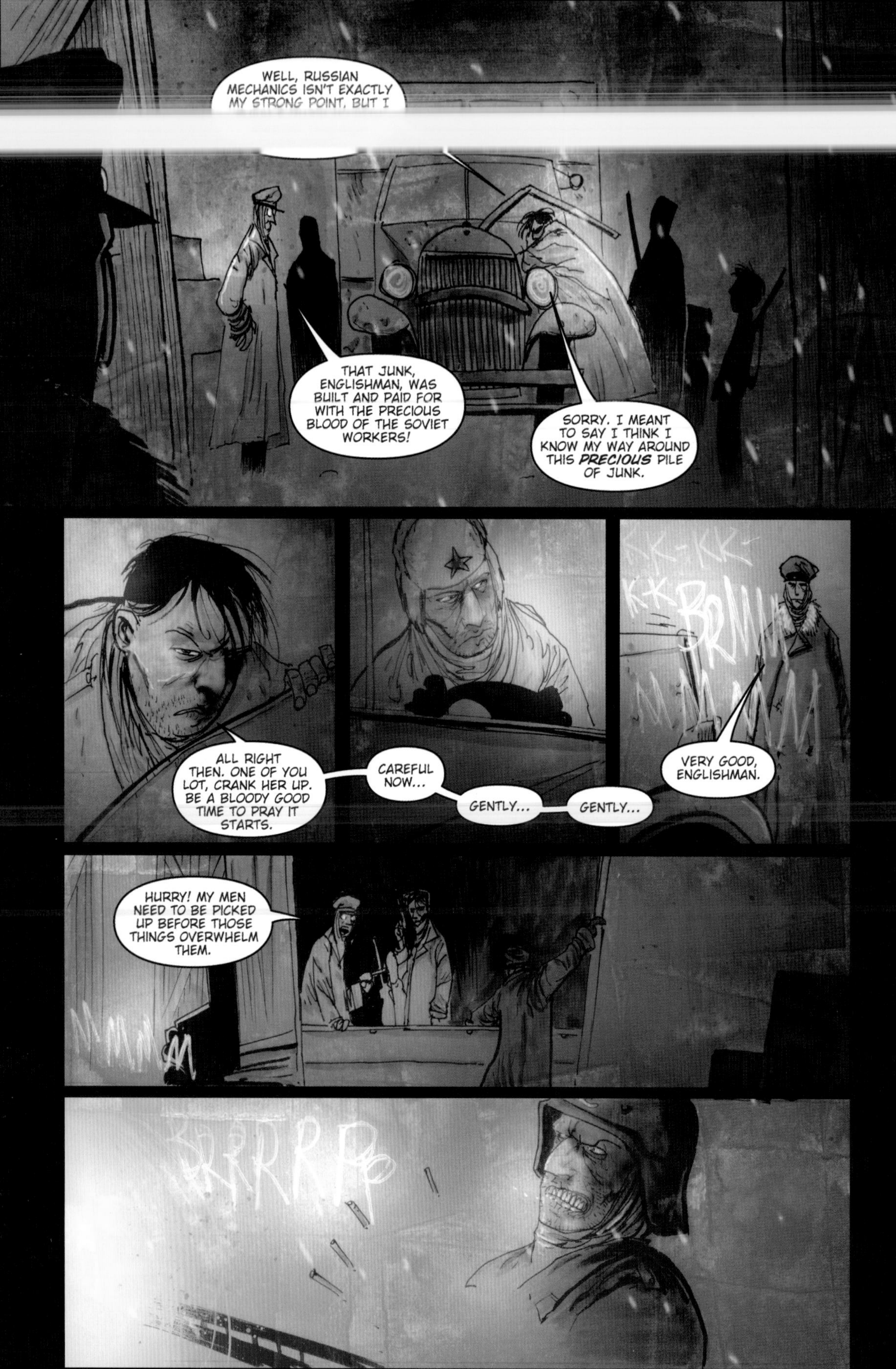
WELL, RUSSIAN MECHANICS ISN'T EXACTLY MY STRONG POINT, BUT I
THAT JUNK, ENGLISHMAN, WAS BUILT AND PAID FOR WITH THE PRECIOUS BLOOD OF THE SOVIET WORKERS!
SORRY. I MEANT TO SAY I THINK I KNOW MY WAY AROUND THIS ***PRECIOUS*** PILE OF JUNK.
ALL RIGHT THEN. ONE OF YOU LOT, CRANK HER UP. BE A BLOODY GOOD TIME TO PRAY IT STARTS.
CAREFUL NOW...
GENTLY...
GENTLY...
VERY GOOD, ENGLISHMAN.
HURRY! MY MEN NEED TO BE PICKED UP BEFORE THOSE THINGS OVERWHELM THEM.

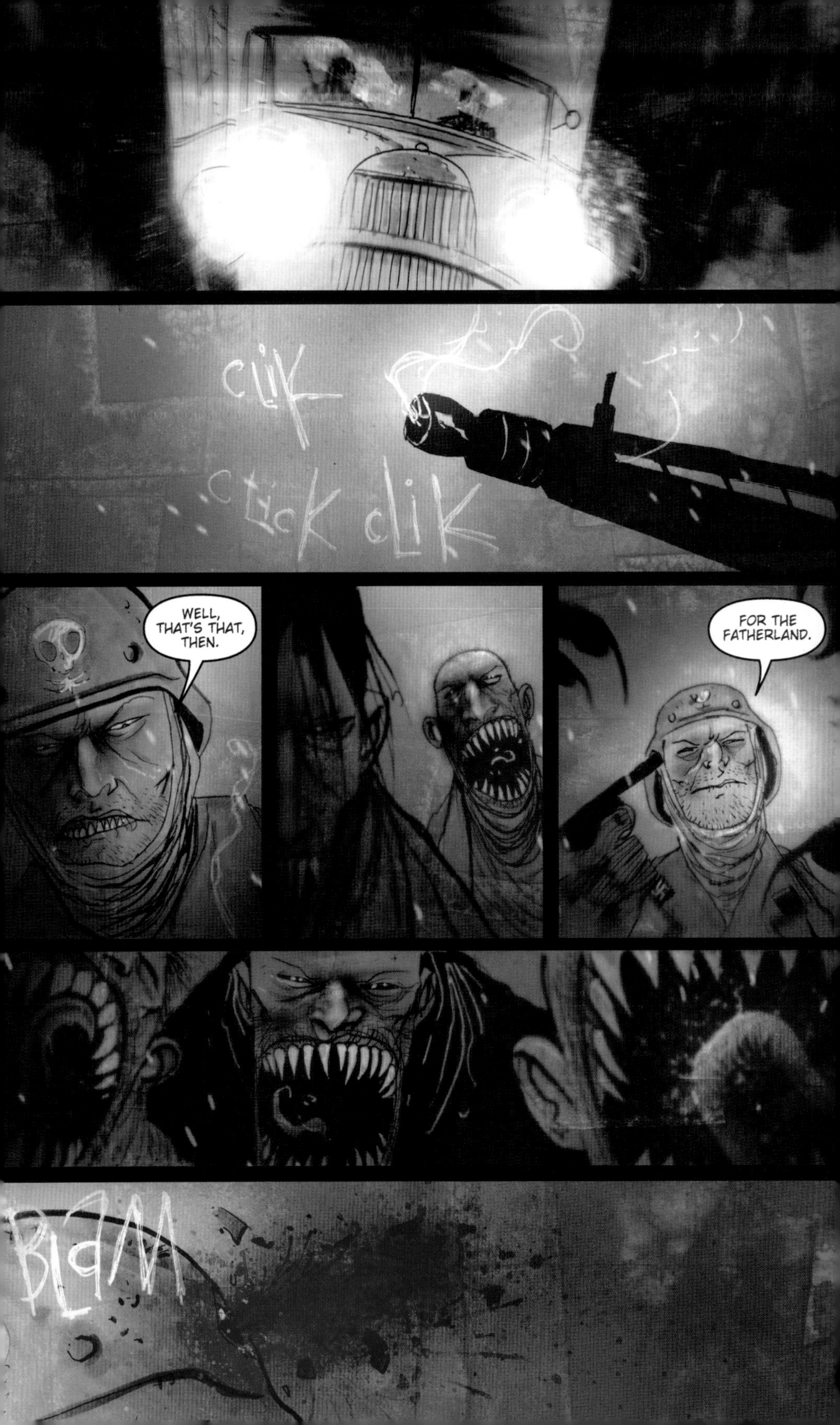
CLIK
CLICK CLIK
WELL, THAT'S THAT, THEN.
FOR THE FATHERLAND.
BLAM

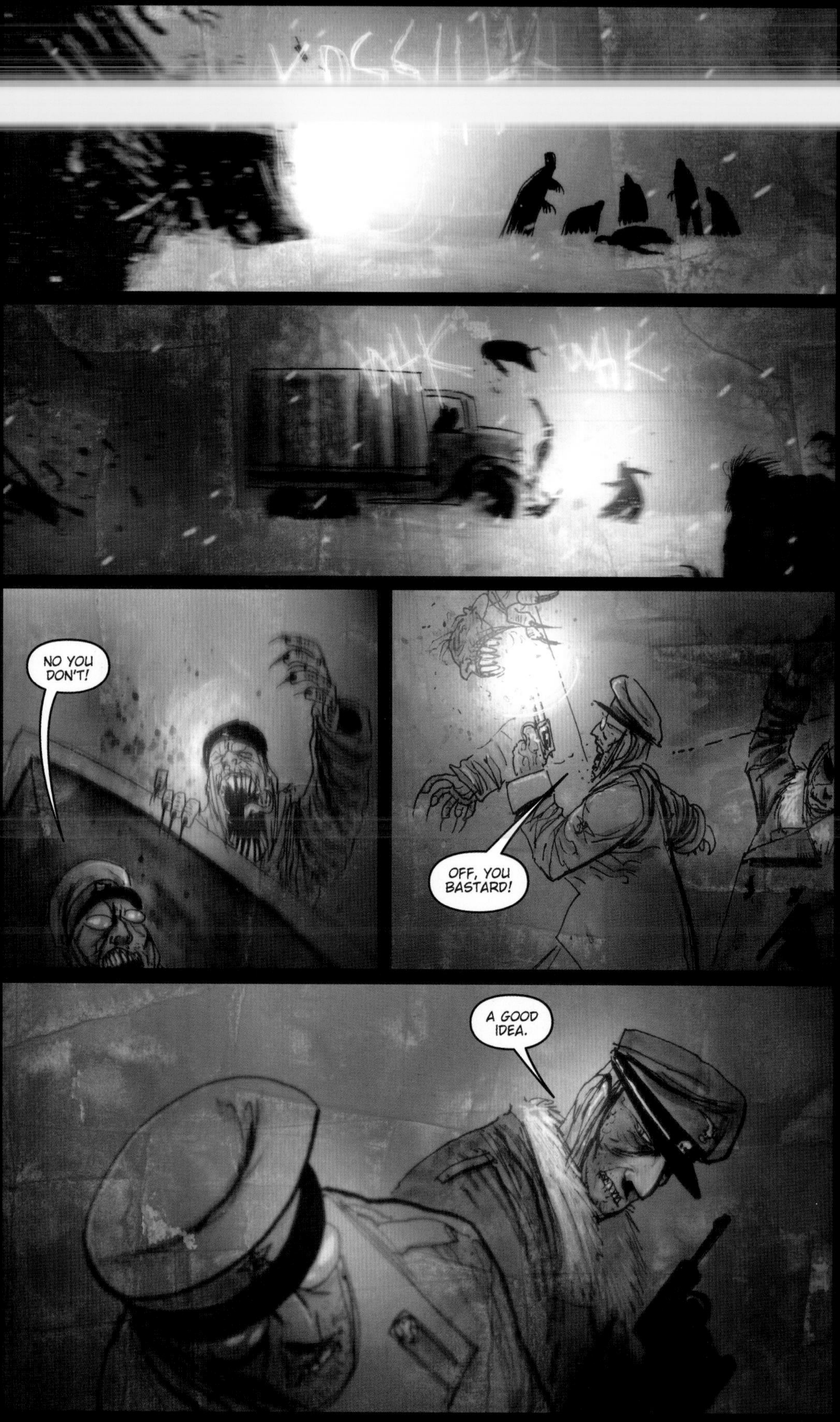
NO YOU DON'T!
OFF, YOU BASTARD!
A GOOD IDEA.

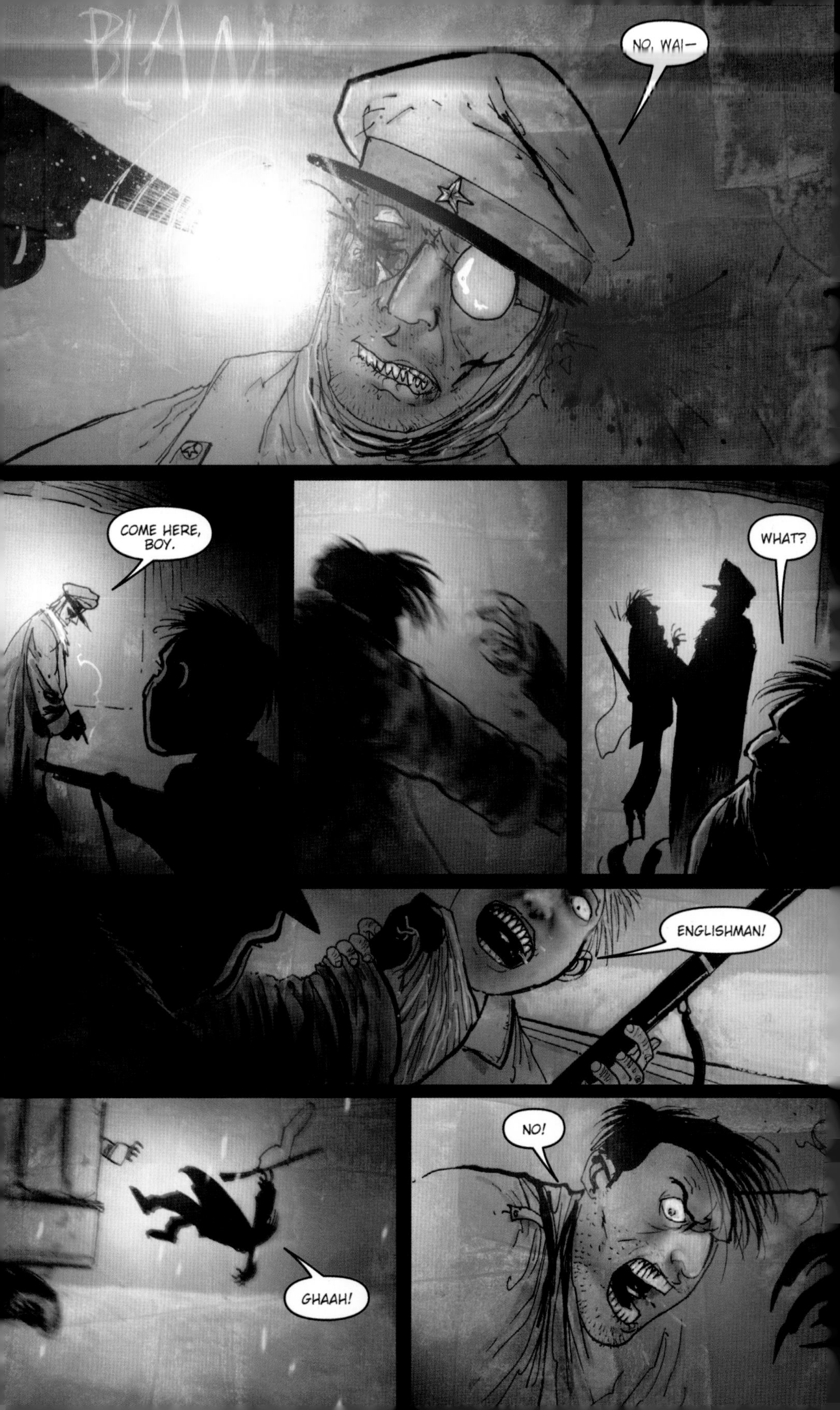
NO, WAI—
COME HERE, BOY.
WHAT?
ENGLISHMAN!
GHAAH!
NO!

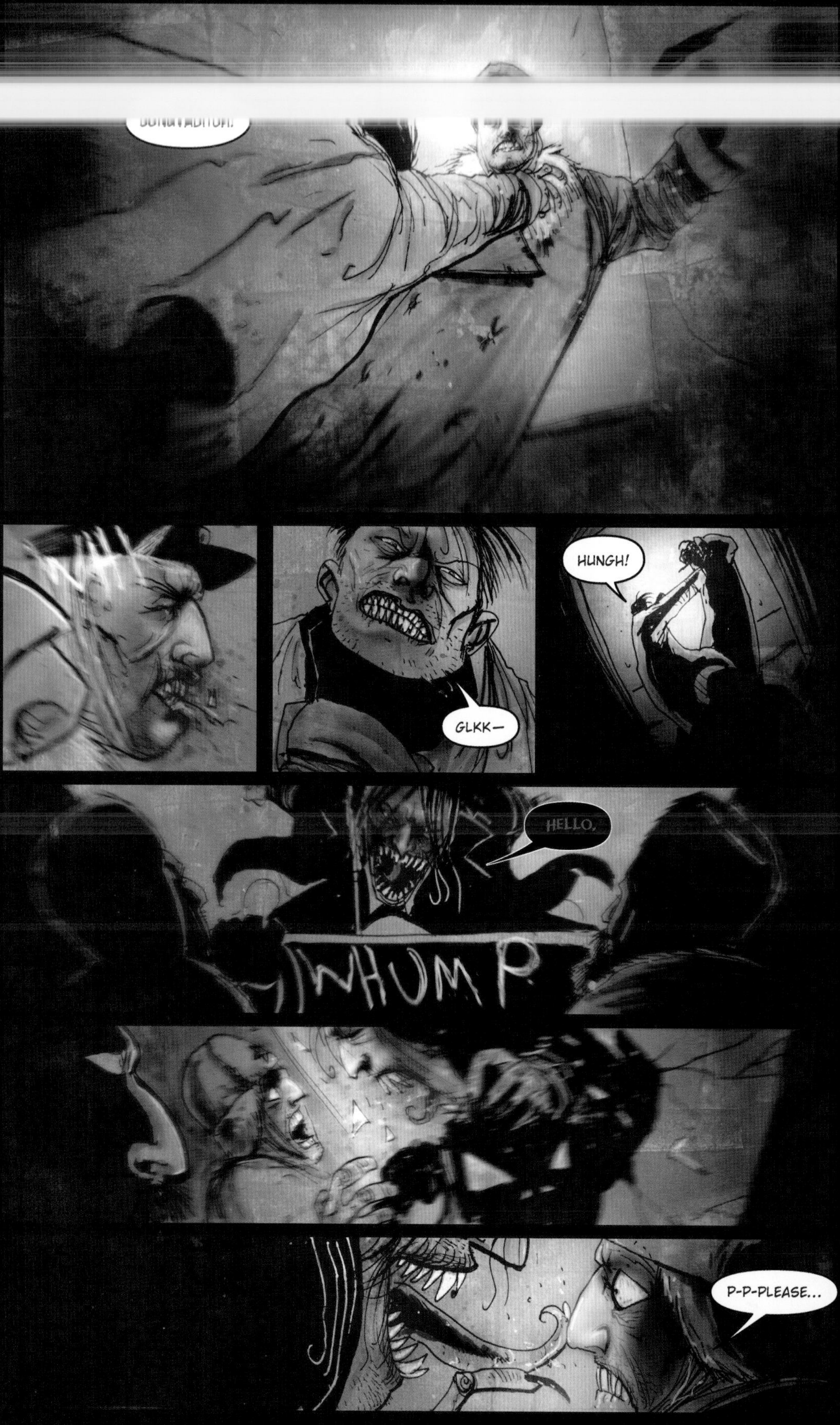
HUNGH!
GLKK—
HELLO.
WHUMP
P-P-PLEASE...

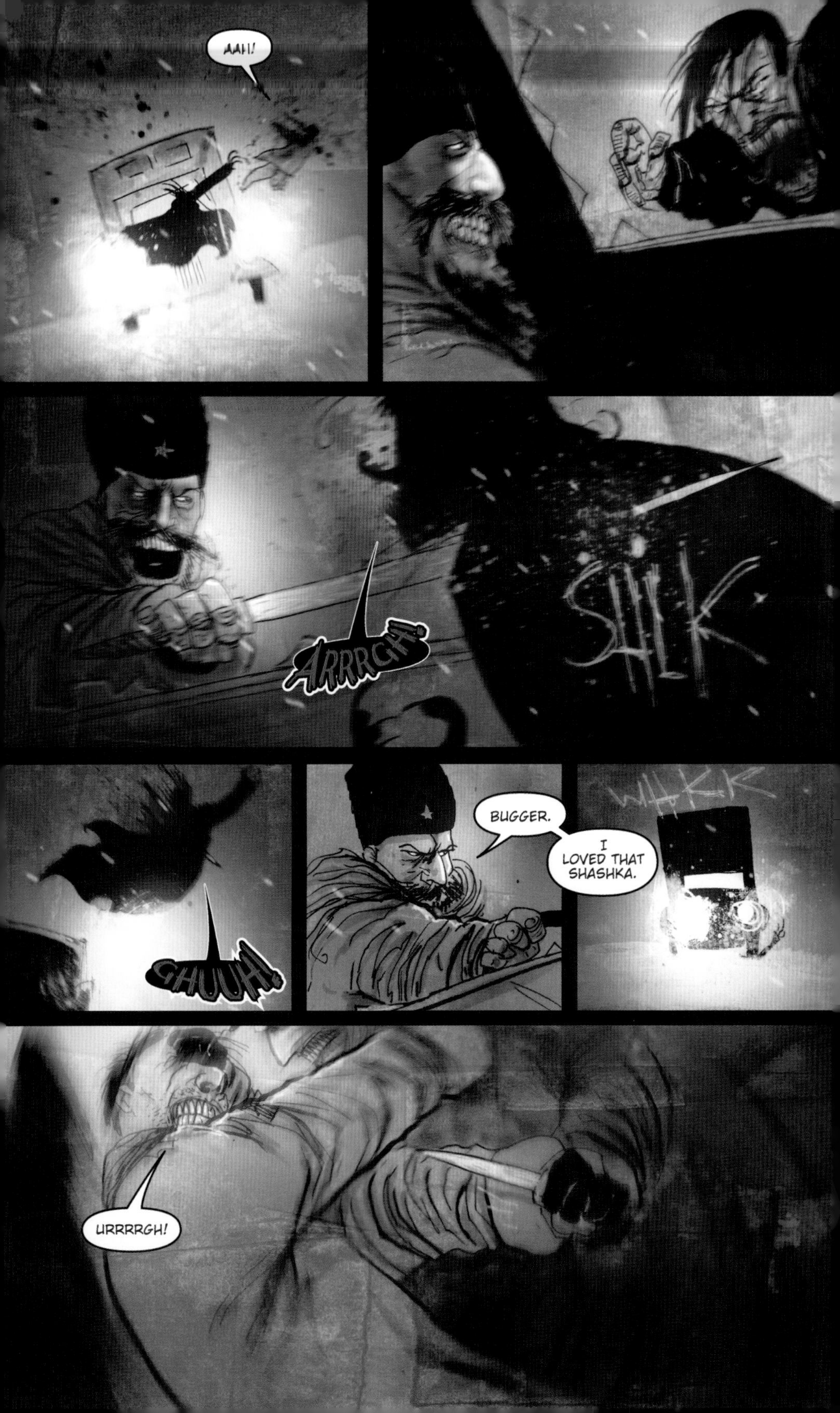
AAH!
ARRRGH!
SHLK
GHUUH!
BUGGER.
I LOVED THAT SHASHKA.
URRRRGH!

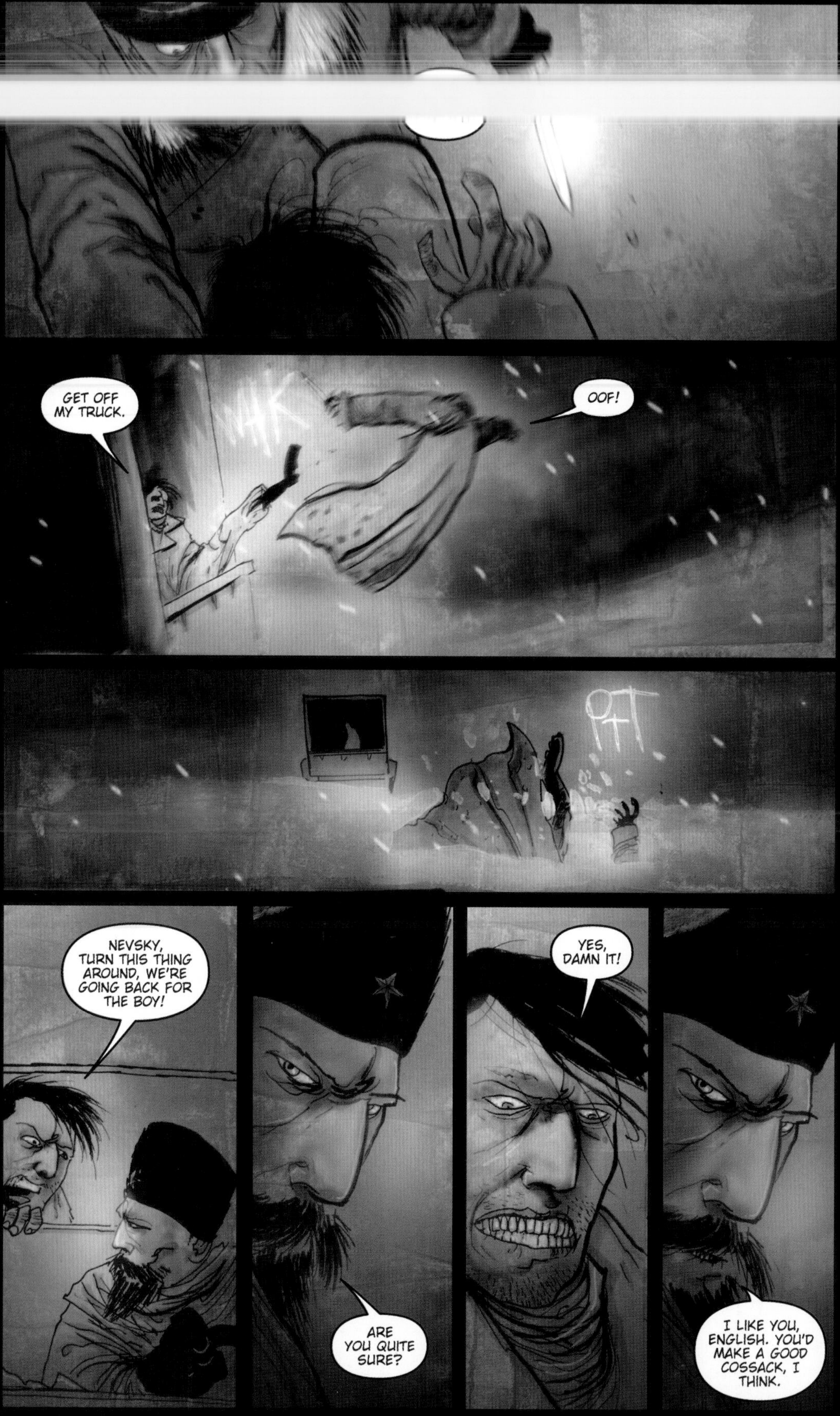
GET OFF MY TRUCK.
OOF!
NEVSKY, TURN THIS THING AROUND, WE'RE GOING BACK FOR THE BOY!
ARE YOU QUITE SURE?
YES, DAMN IT!
I LIKE YOU, ENGLISH. YOU'D MAKE A GOOD COSSACK, I THINK.

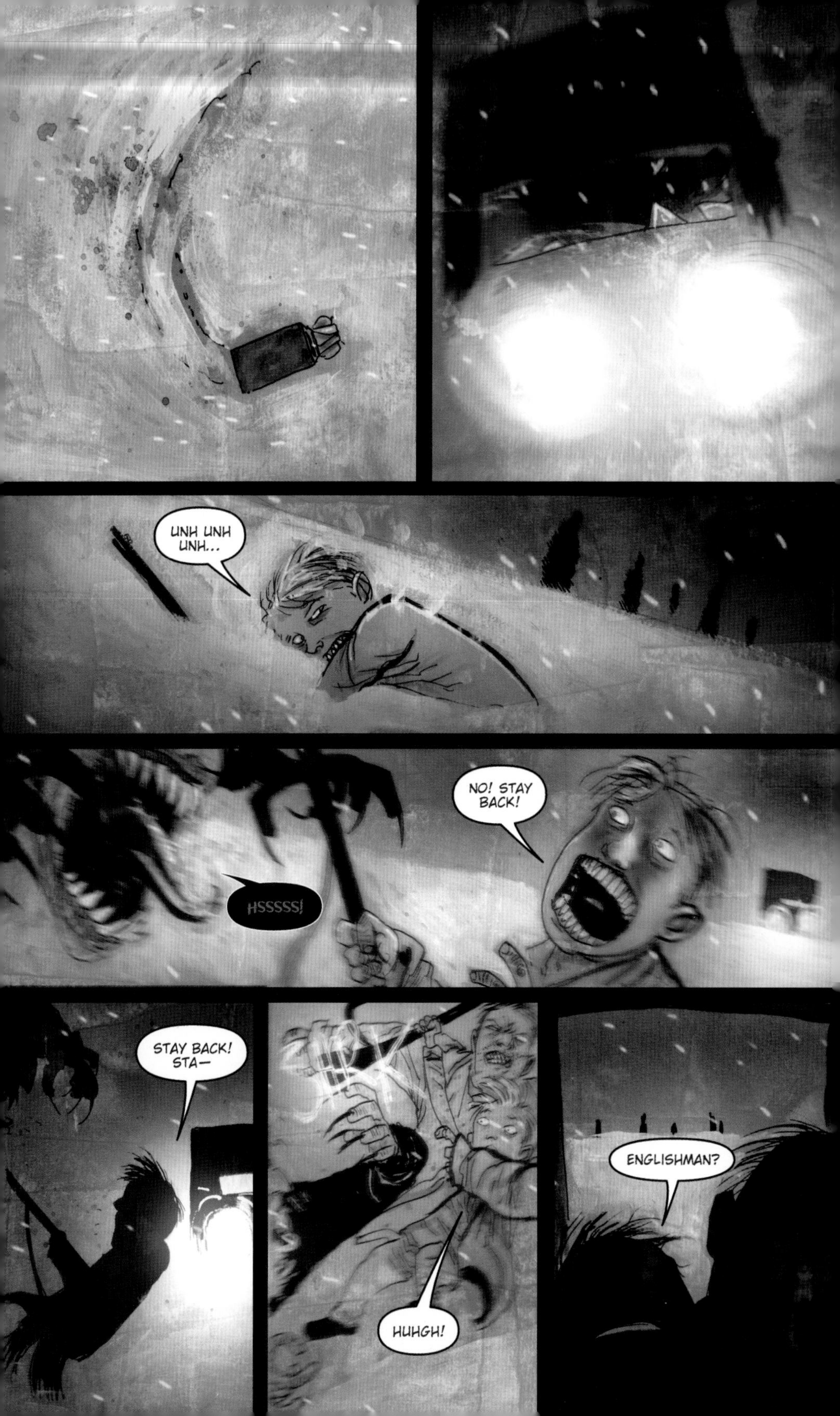
UNH UNH UNH...
NO! STAY BACK!
HSSSSS!
STAY BACK! STA—
HUHGH!
ENGLISHMAN?

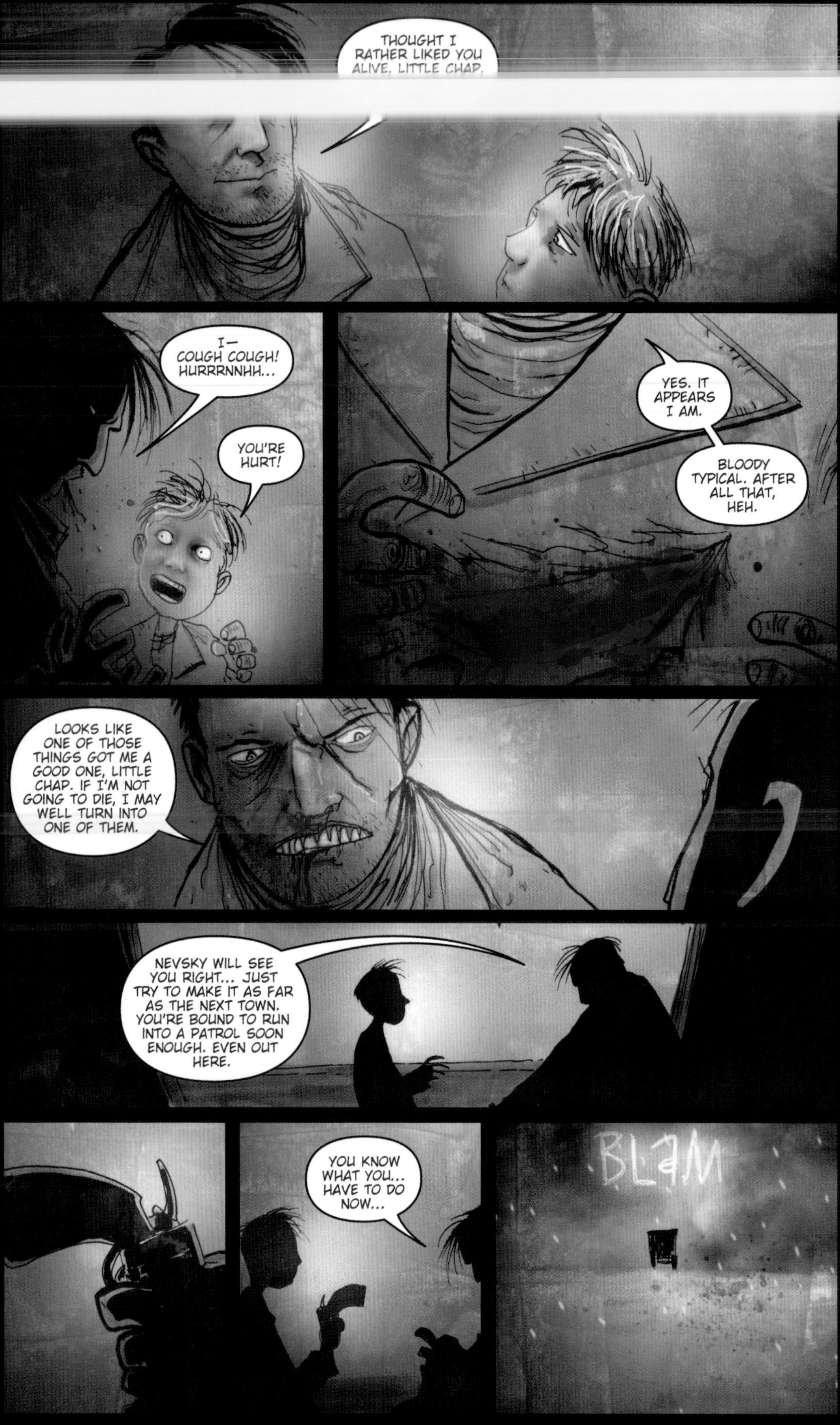
THOUGHT I RATHER LIKED YOU ALIVE, LITTLE CHAP.
I— COUGH COUGH! HURRRNNHH...
YOU'RE HURT!
YES. IT APPEARS I AM.
BLOODY TYPICAL. AFTER ALL THAT, HEH.
LOOKS LIKE ONE OF THOSE THINGS GOT ME A GOOD ONE, LITTLE CHAP. IF I'M NOT GOING TO DIE, I MAY WELL TURN INTO ONE OF THEM.
NEVSKY WILL SEE YOU RIGHT... JUST TRY TO MAKE IT AS FAR AS THE NEXT TOWN. YOU'RE BOUND TO RUN INTO A PATROL SOON ENOUGH. EVEN OUT HERE.
YOU KNOW WHAT YOU... HAVE TO DO NOW...
BLAM

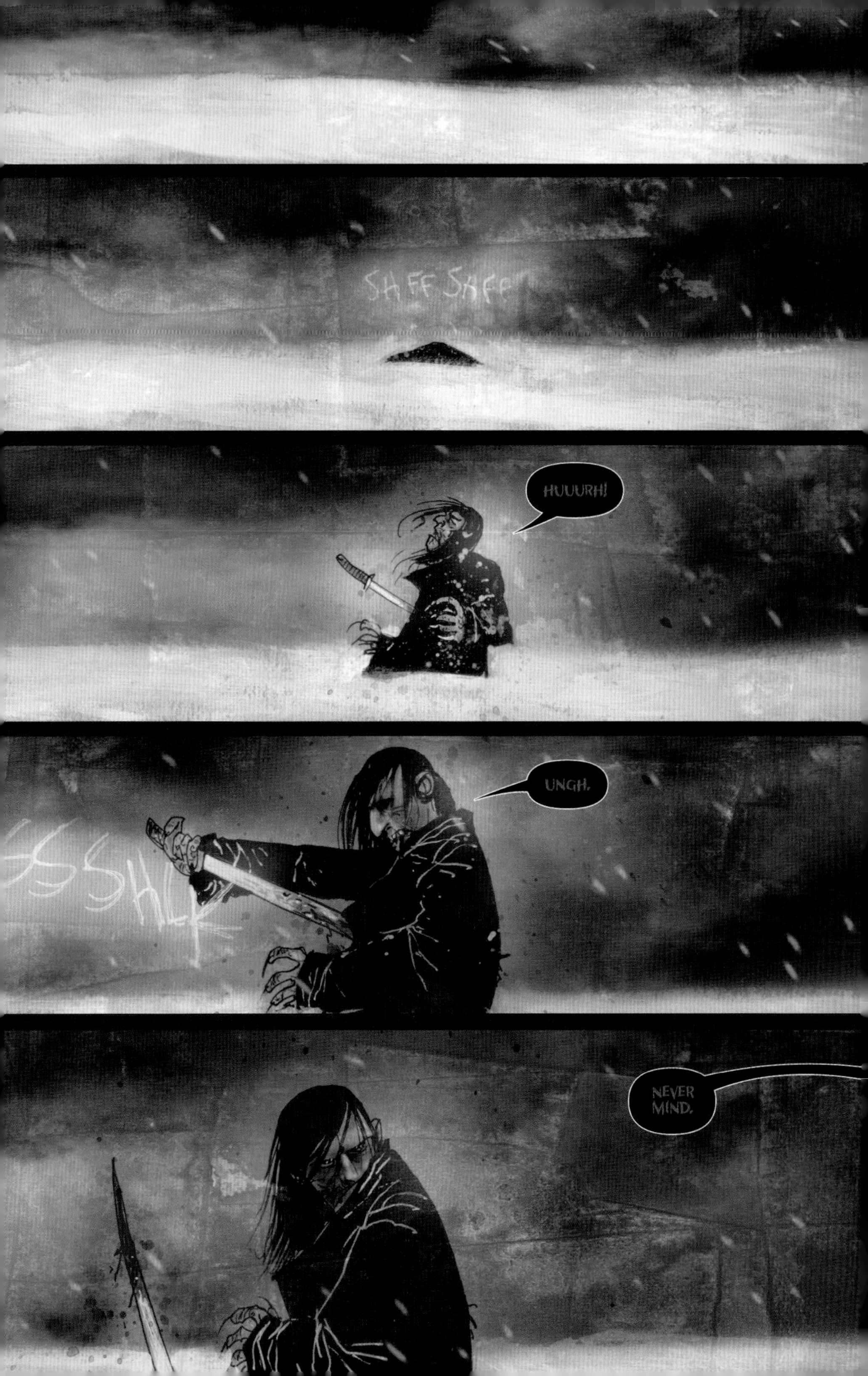
SHFF SHFF
HUUURH!
UNGH.
SSSHLK
NEVER MIND.

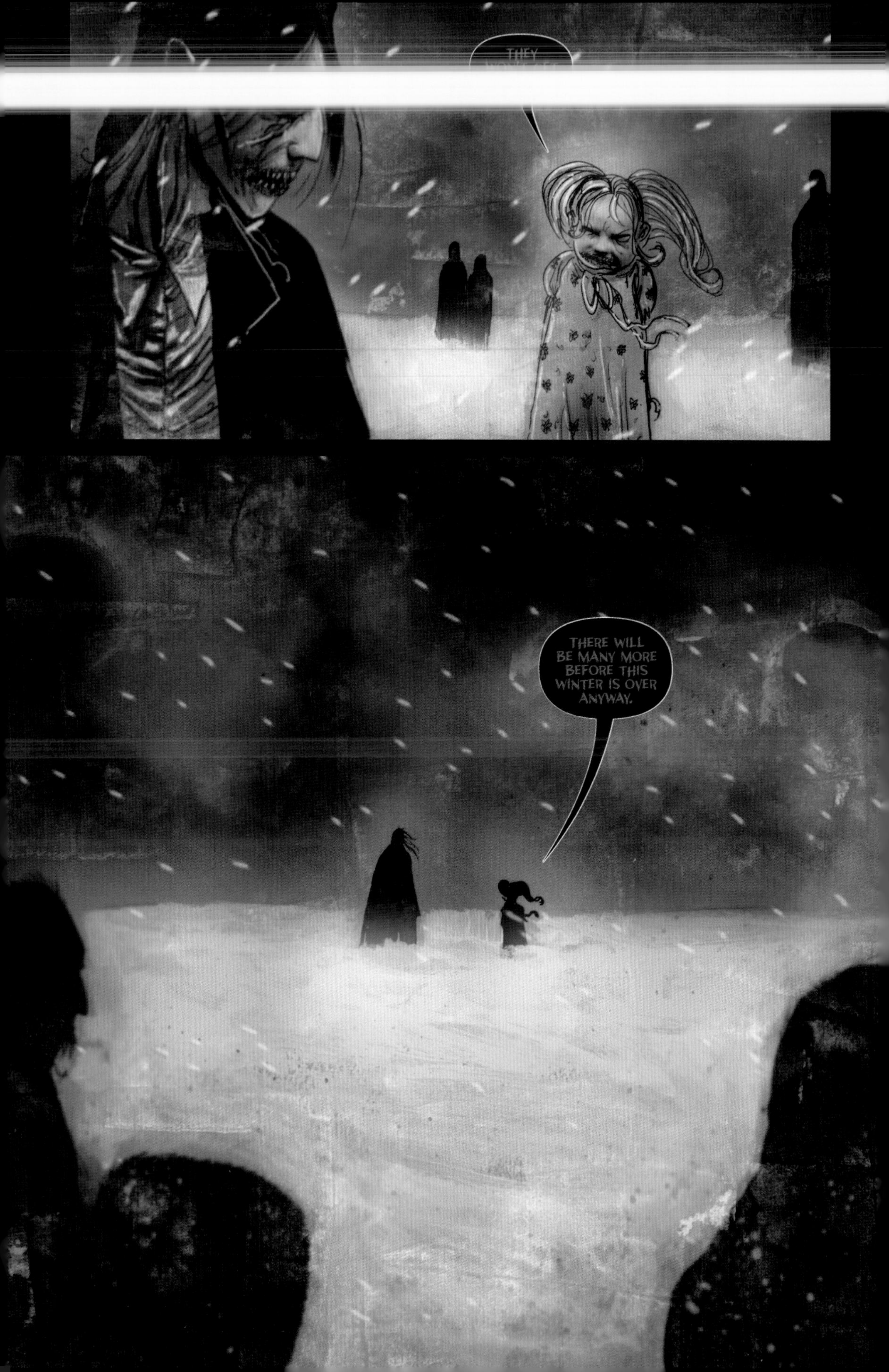
THEY
THERE WILL BE MANY MORE BEFORE THIS WINTER IS OVER ANYWAY.

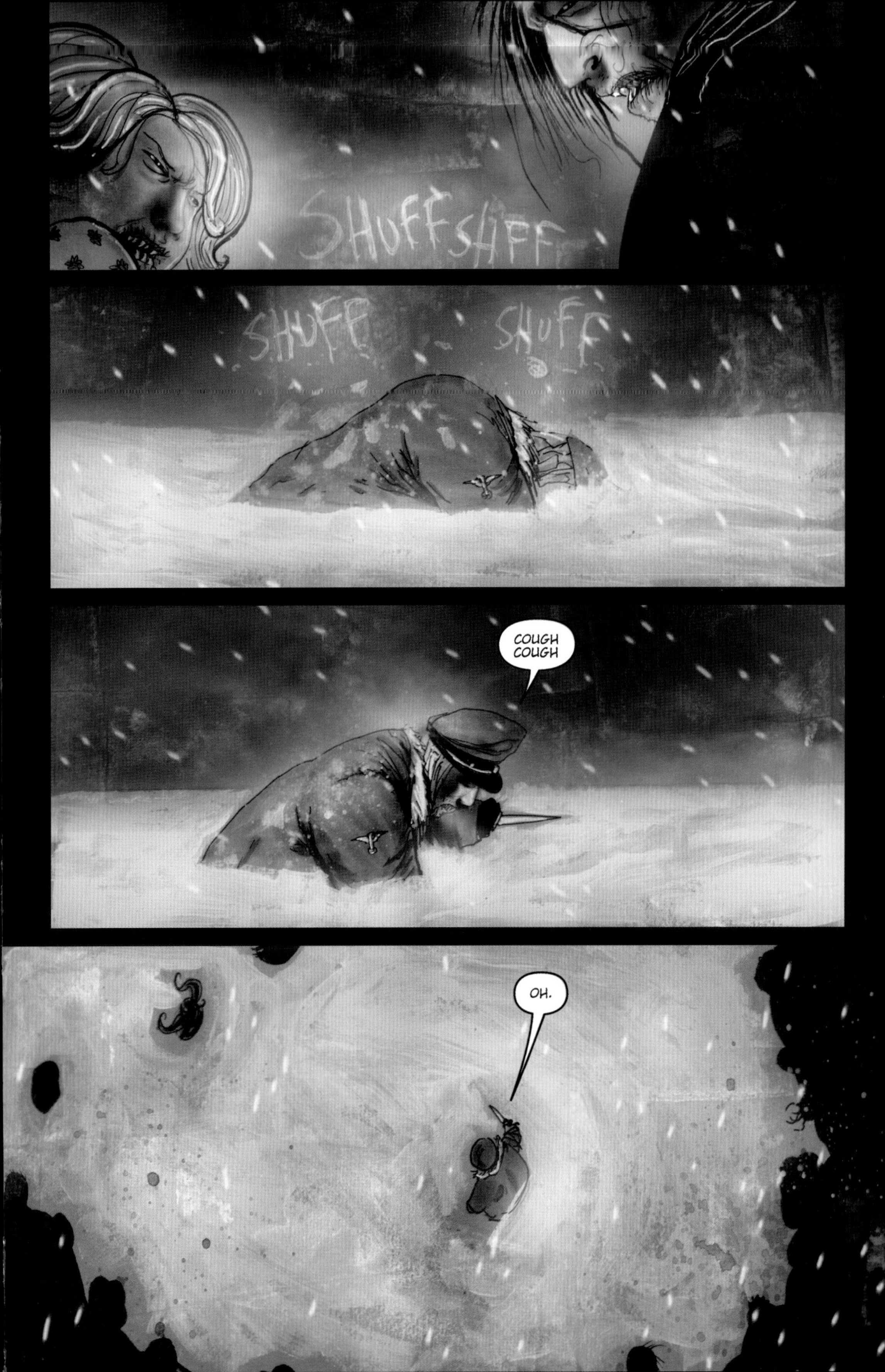
SHUFFSHUFF
SHUFF SHUFF
COUGH COUGH
OH.

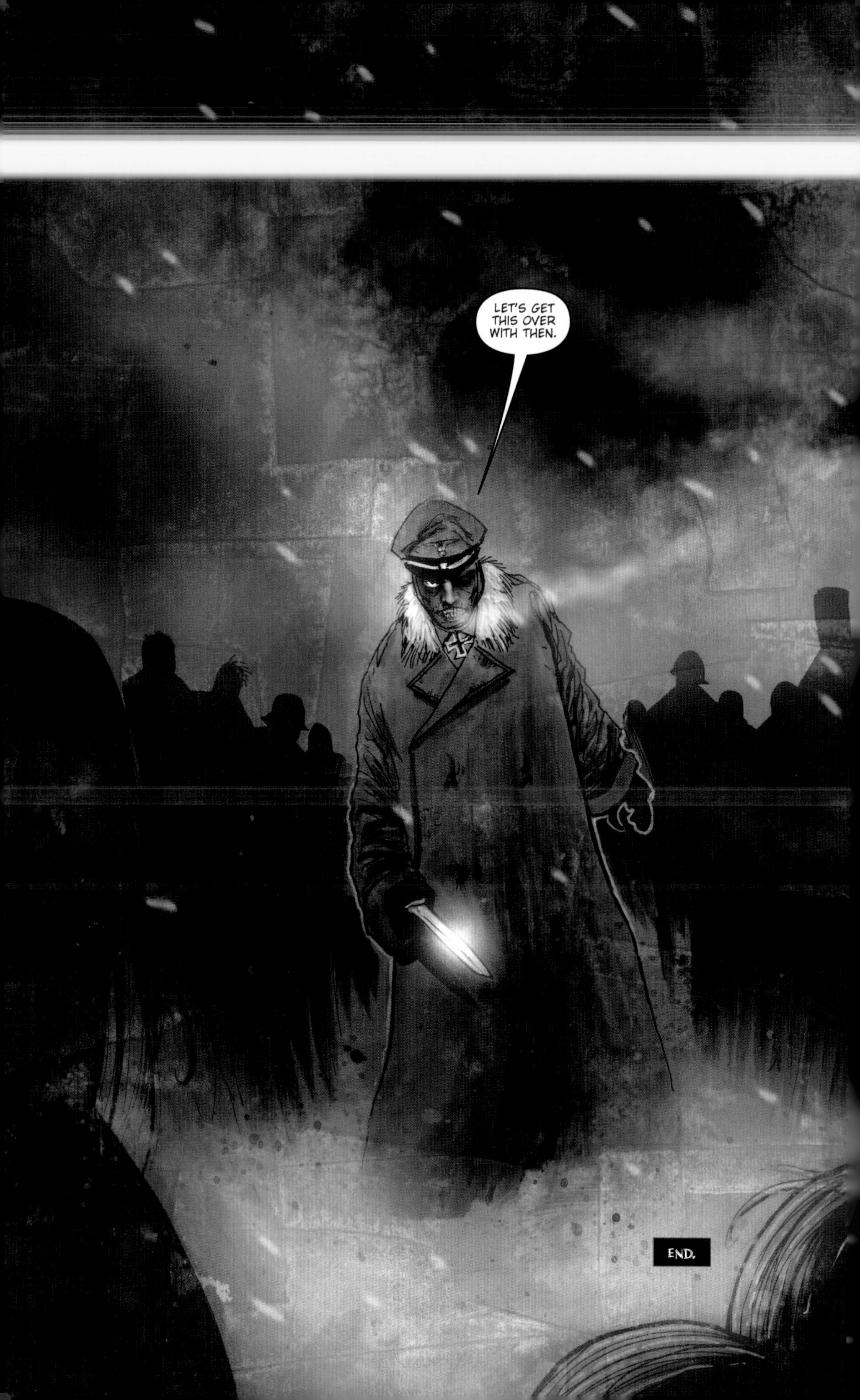
LET'S GET THIS OVER WITH THEN.
END.

ART GALLERY

The following is a gallery of Ben Templesmith's artwork for the 30 Days of Night: Red Snow series.

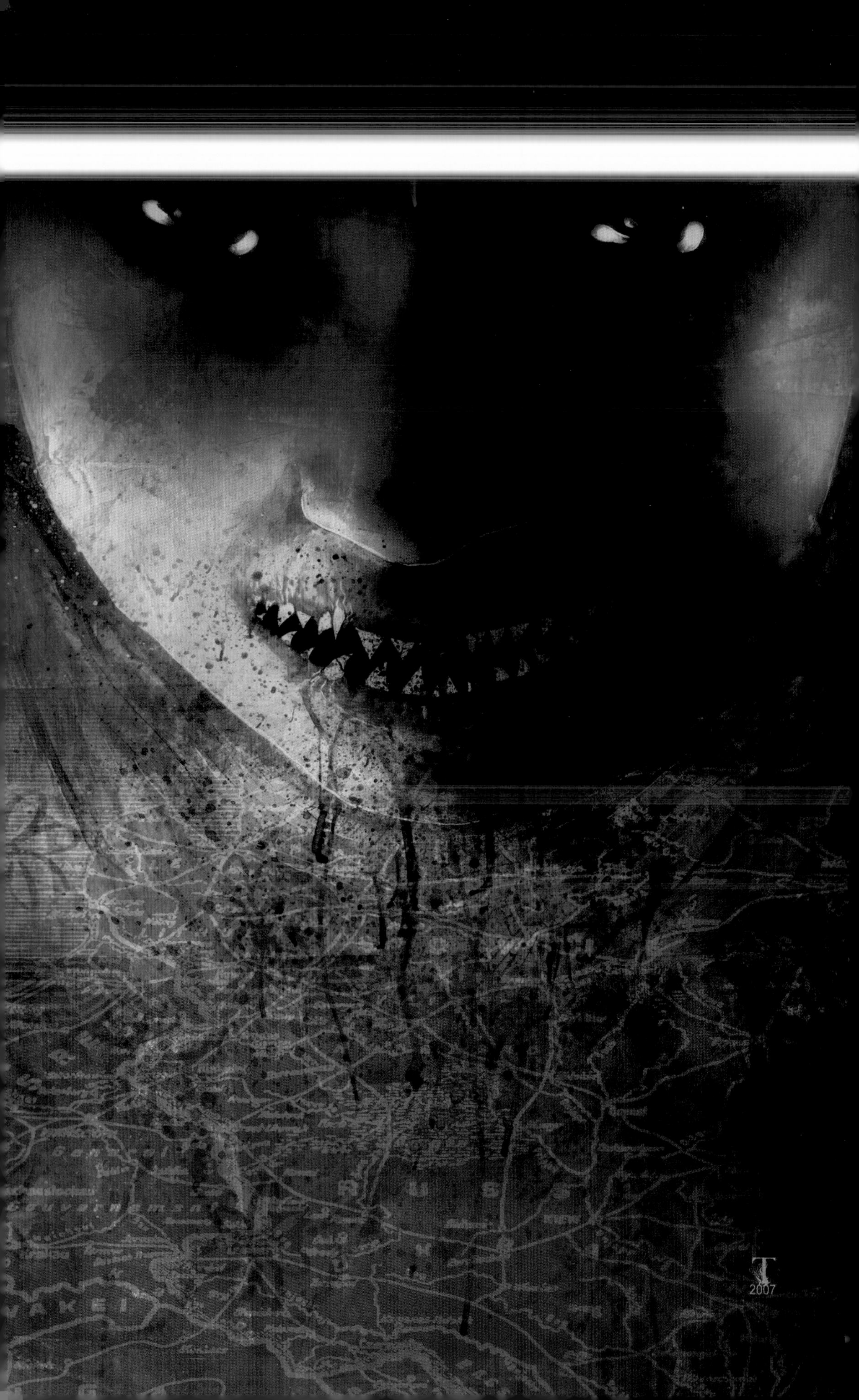
2007

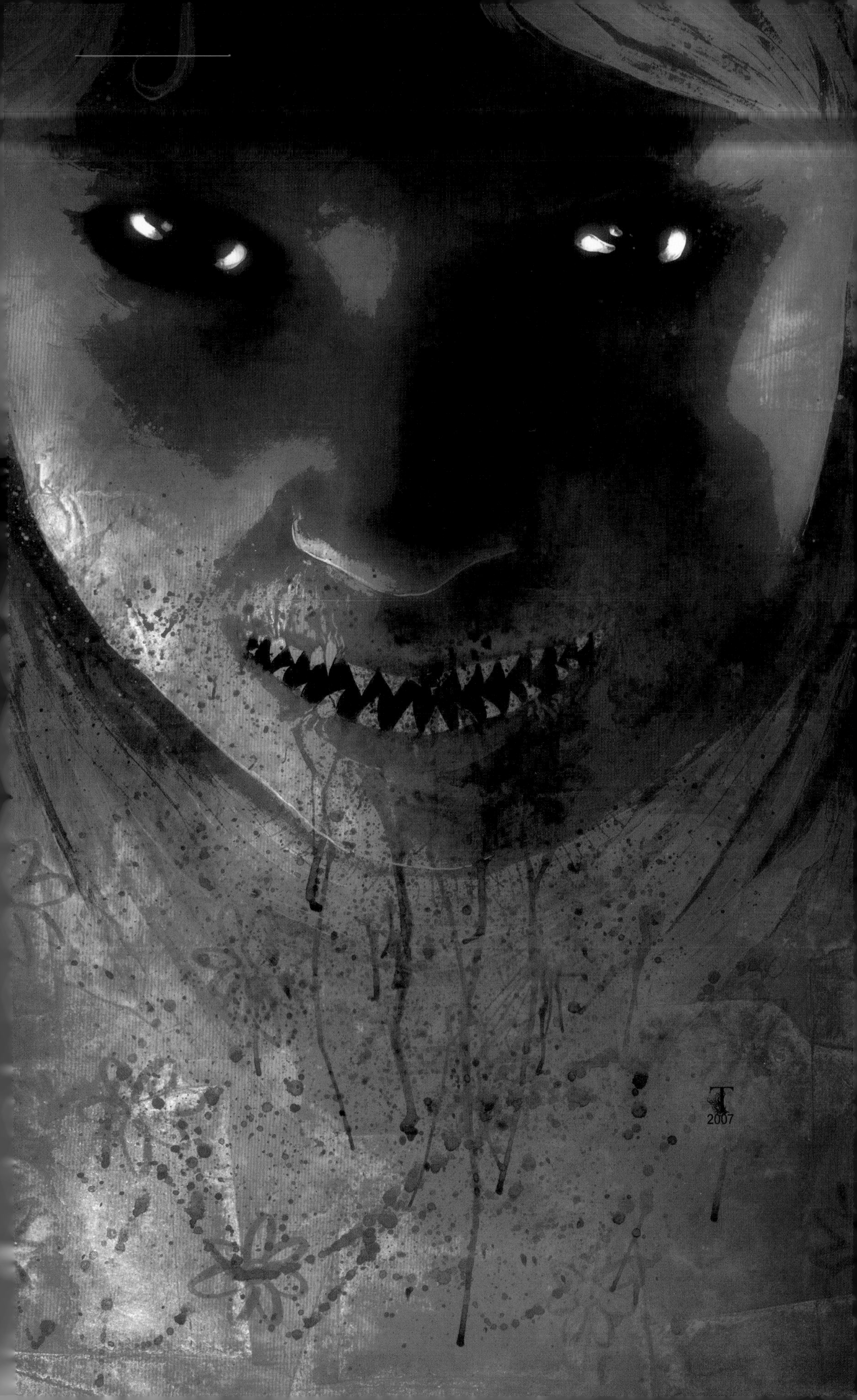

2007

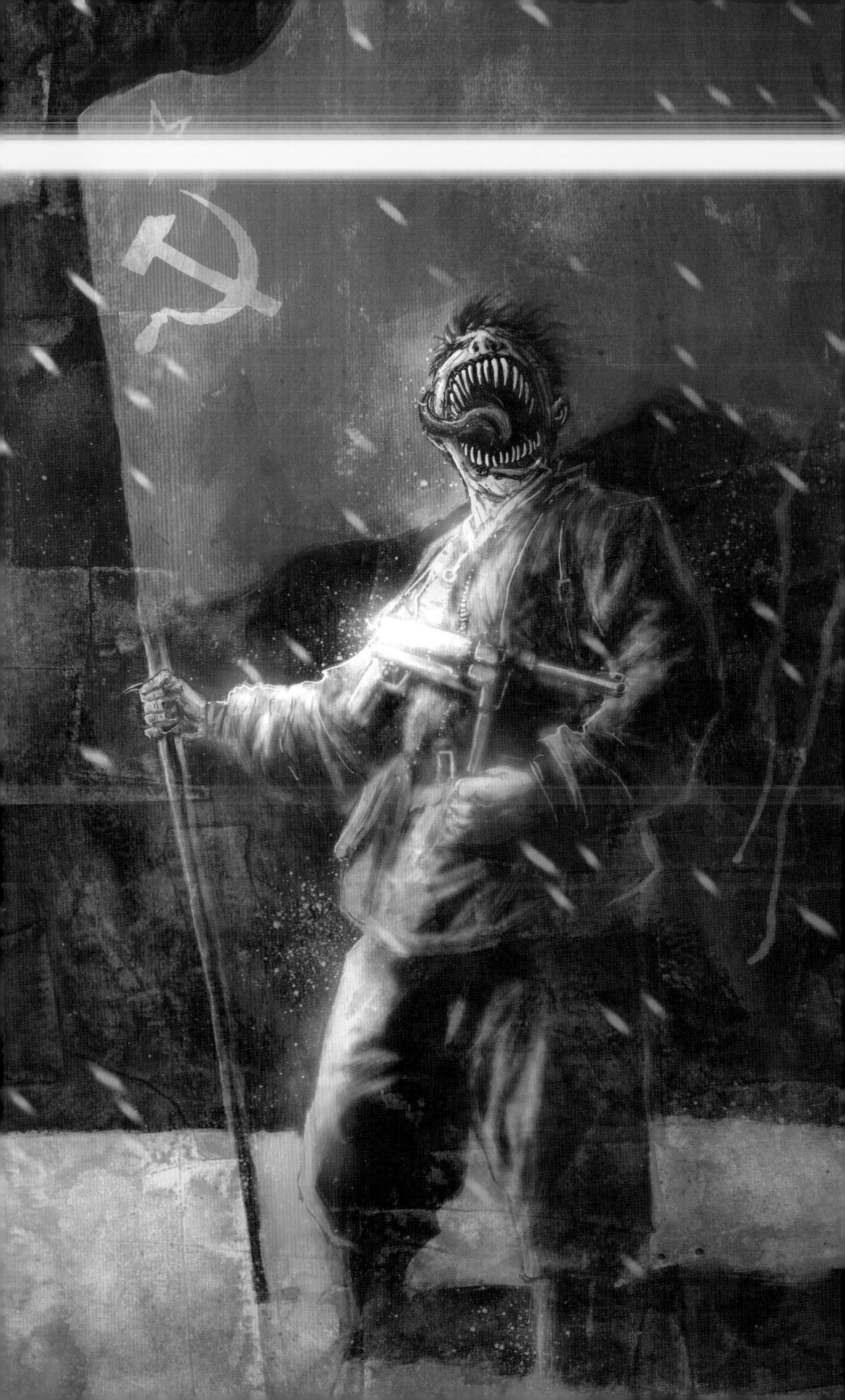

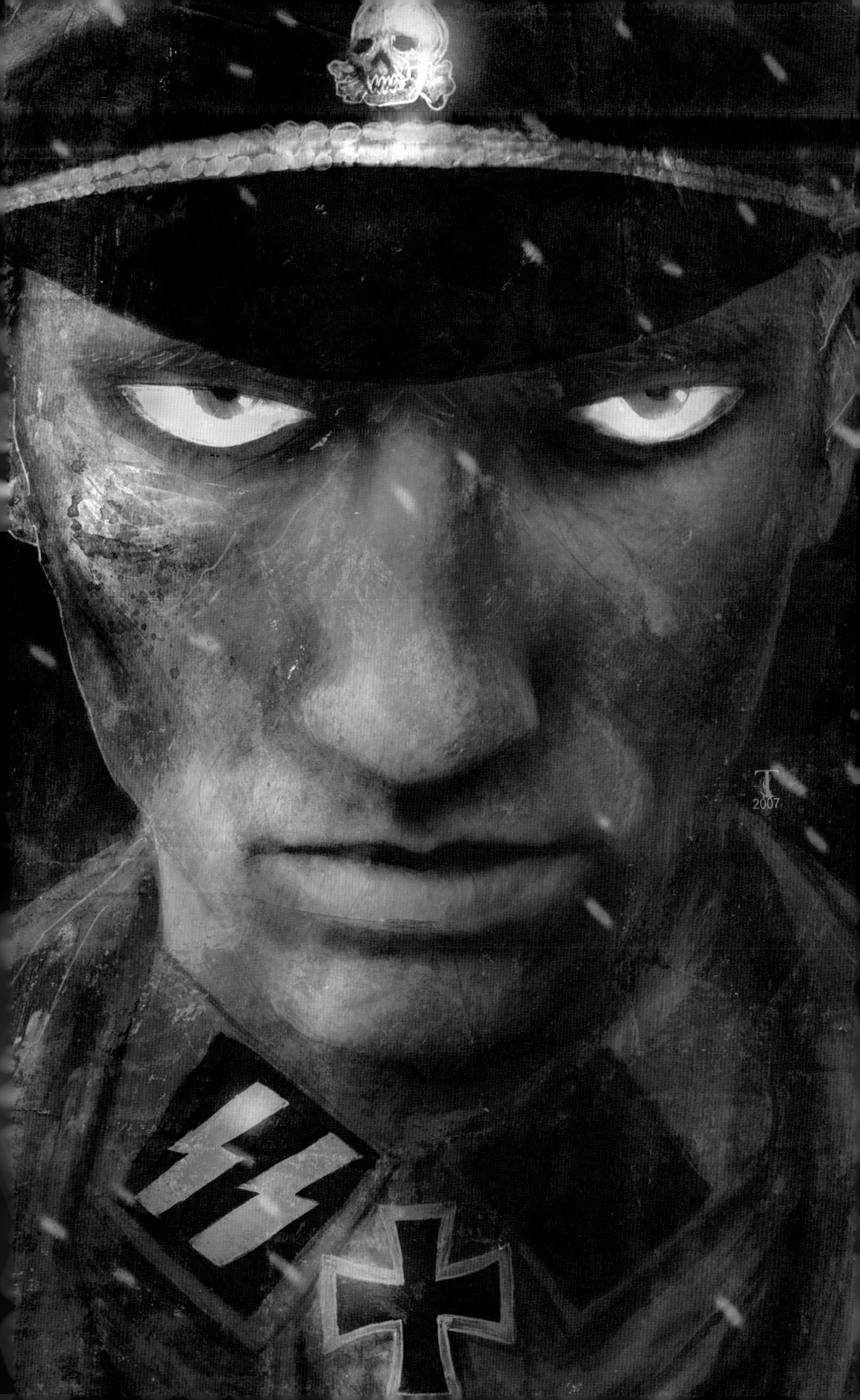
T
2007

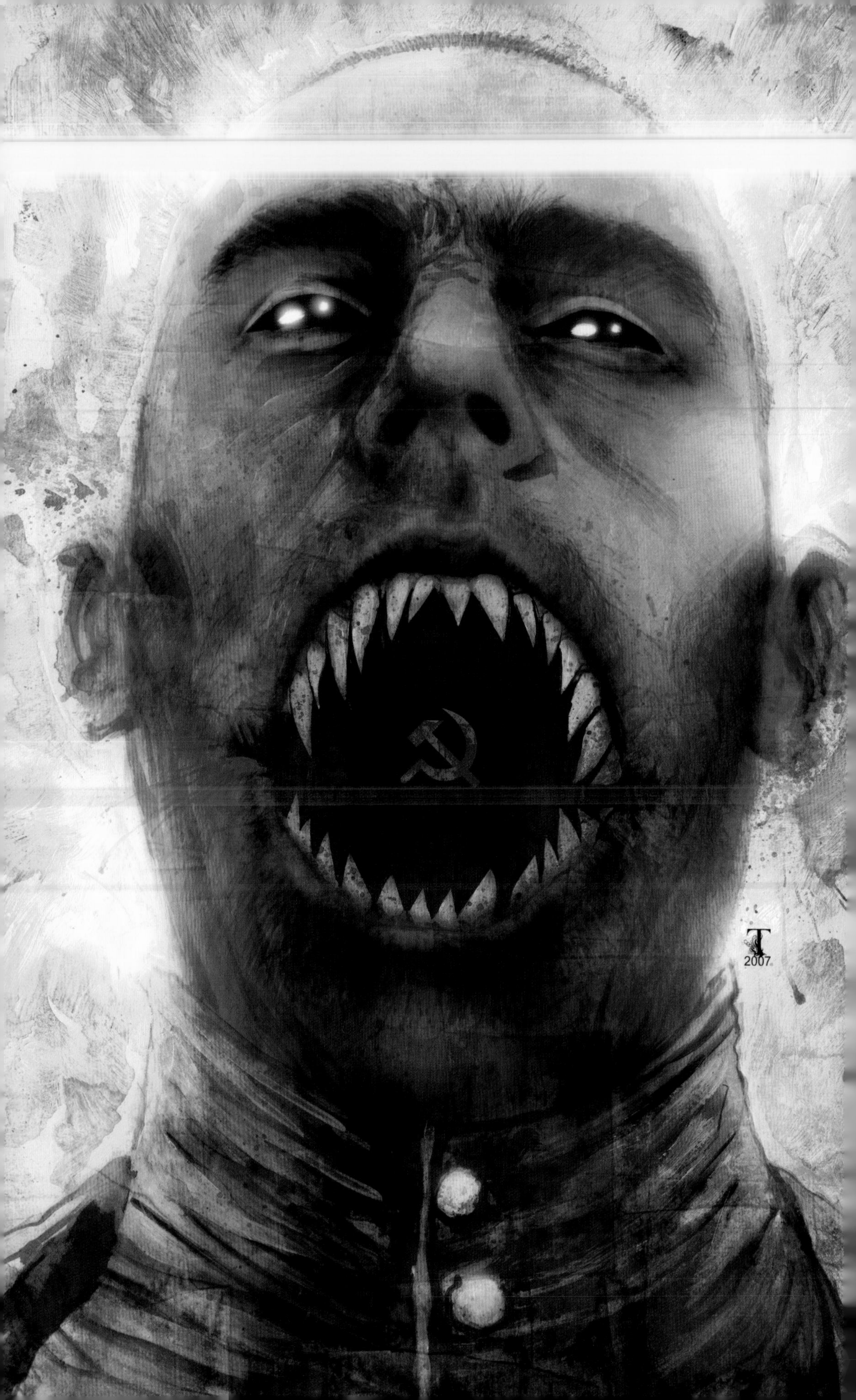
2007

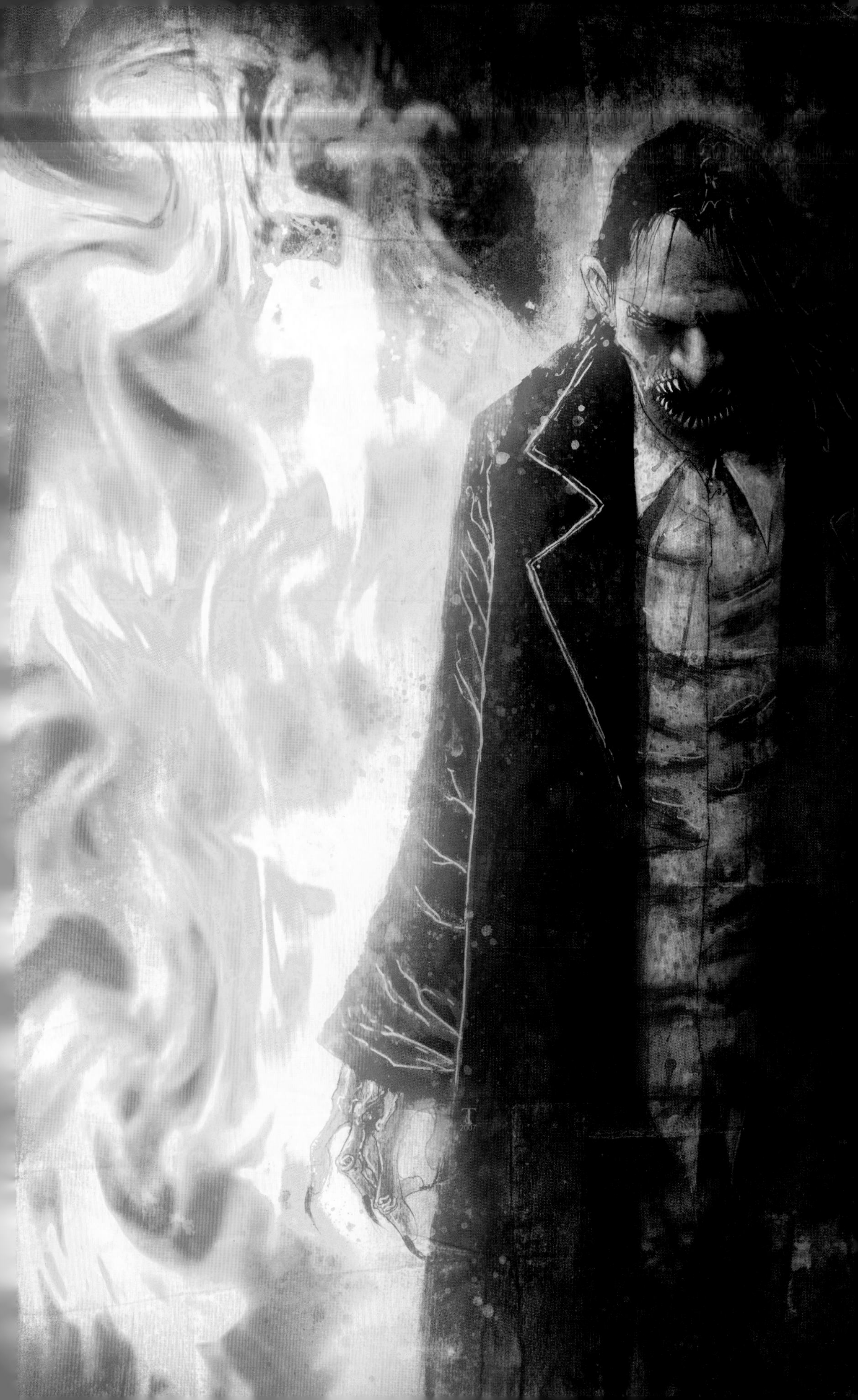

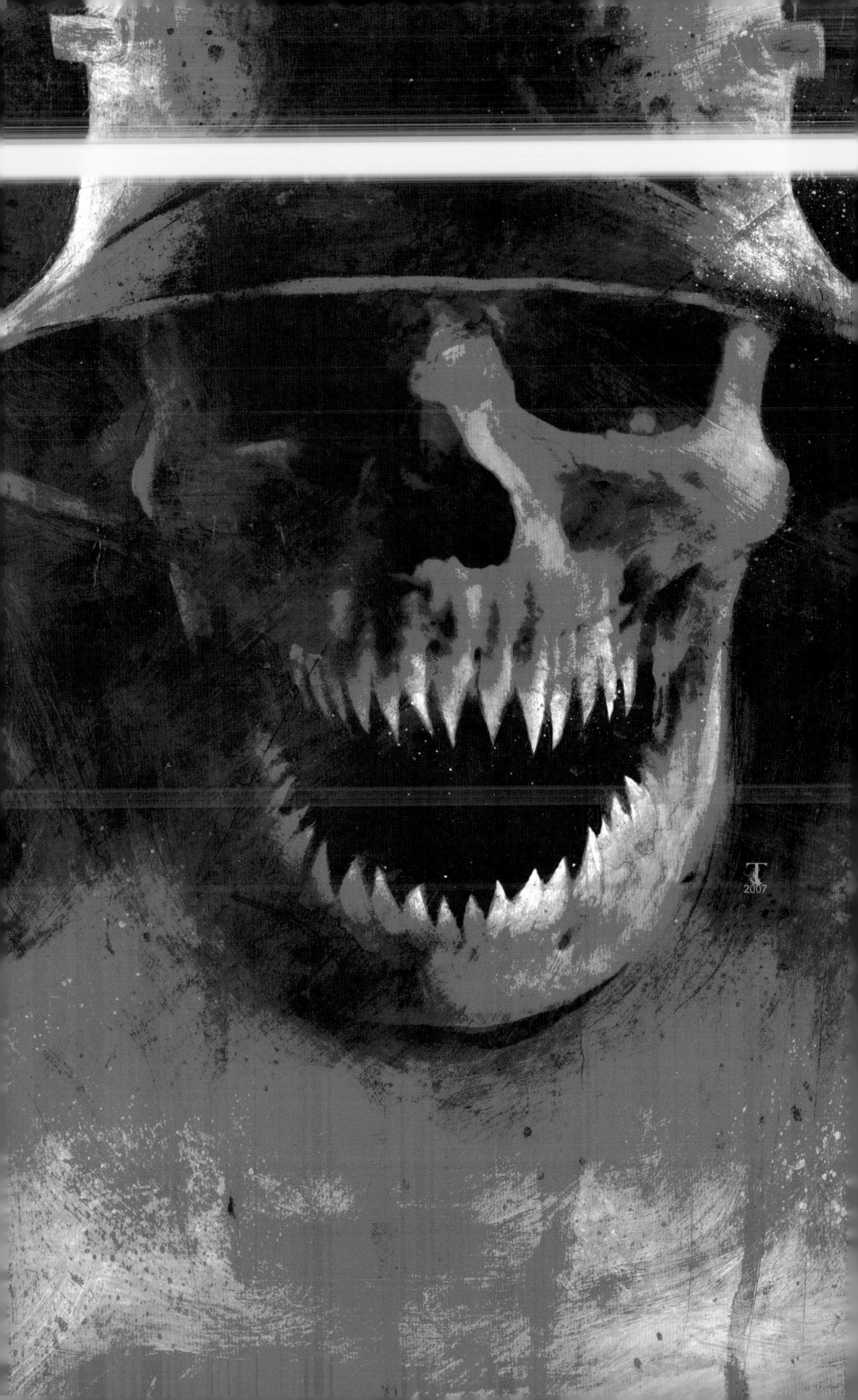
2007

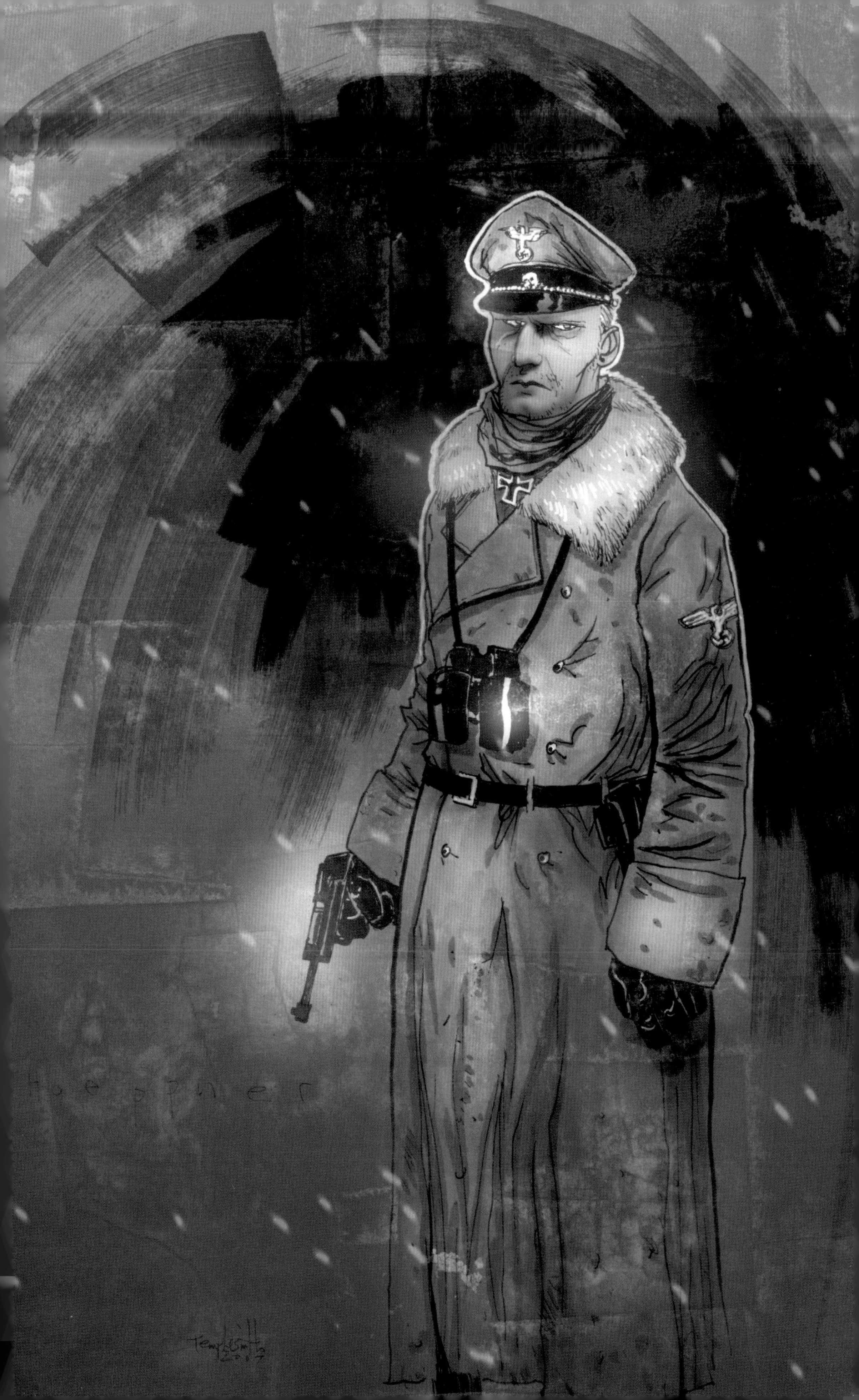
hoeppner

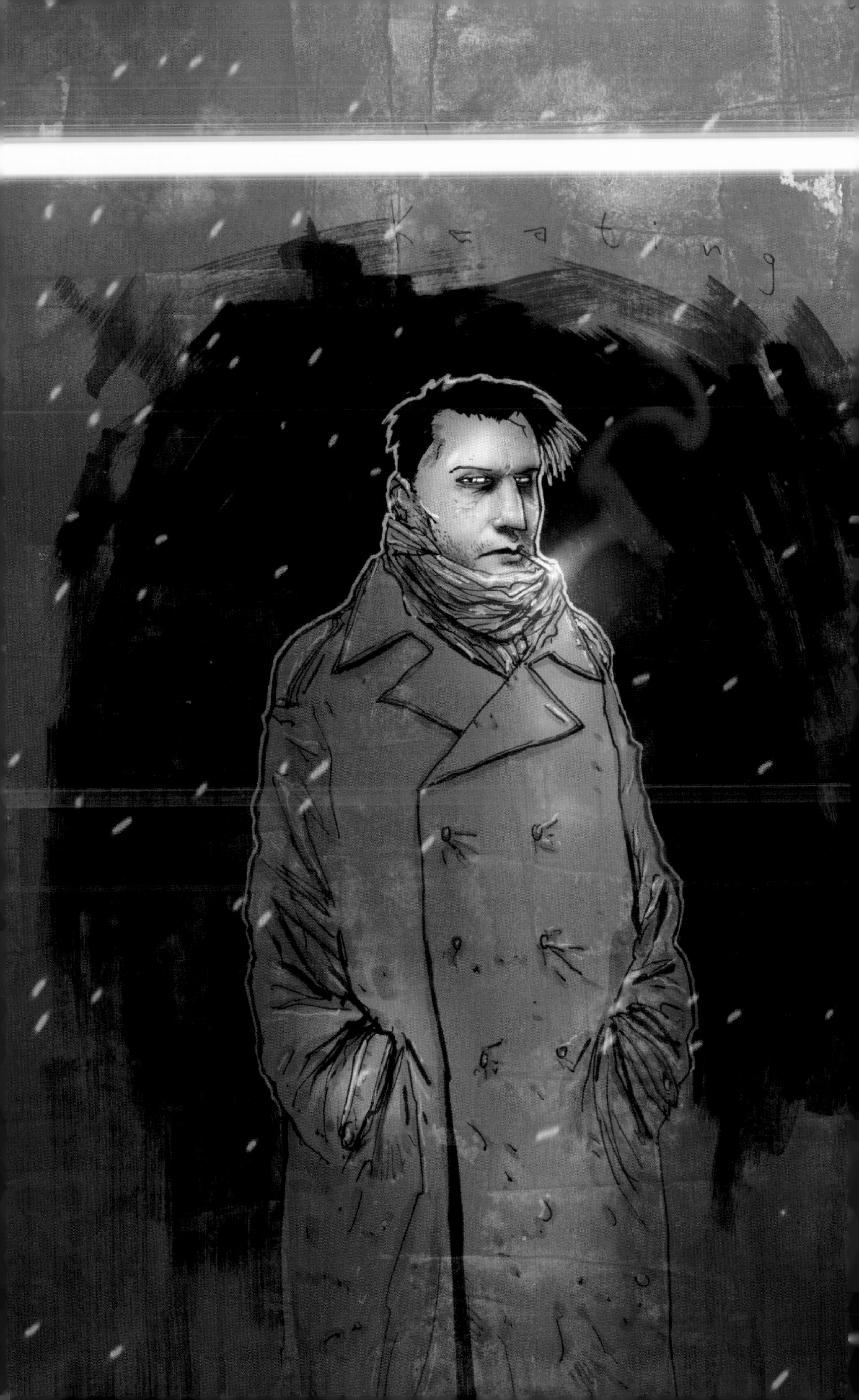
Keating

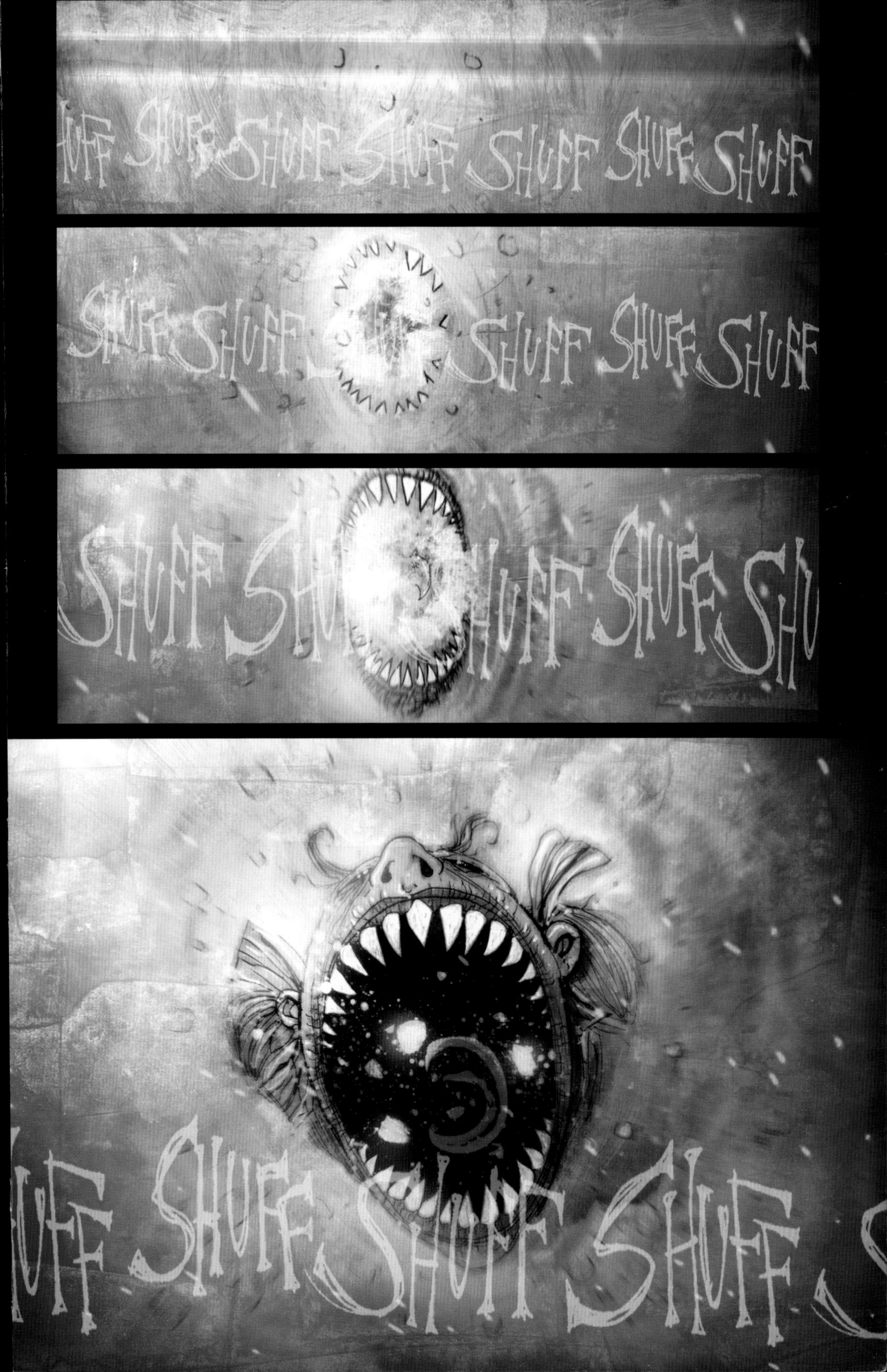
HUFF SHUFF SHUFF SHUFF SHUFF SHUFF SHUFF
SHUFF SHUFF SHUFF SHUFF SHUFF
SHUFF SHU SHUFF SHUFF SHU
HUFF SHUFF SHUFF SHUFF

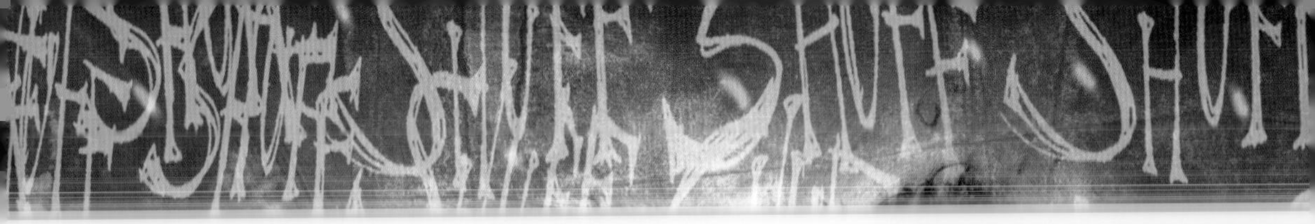
SHUFF SHUFF SHUFF

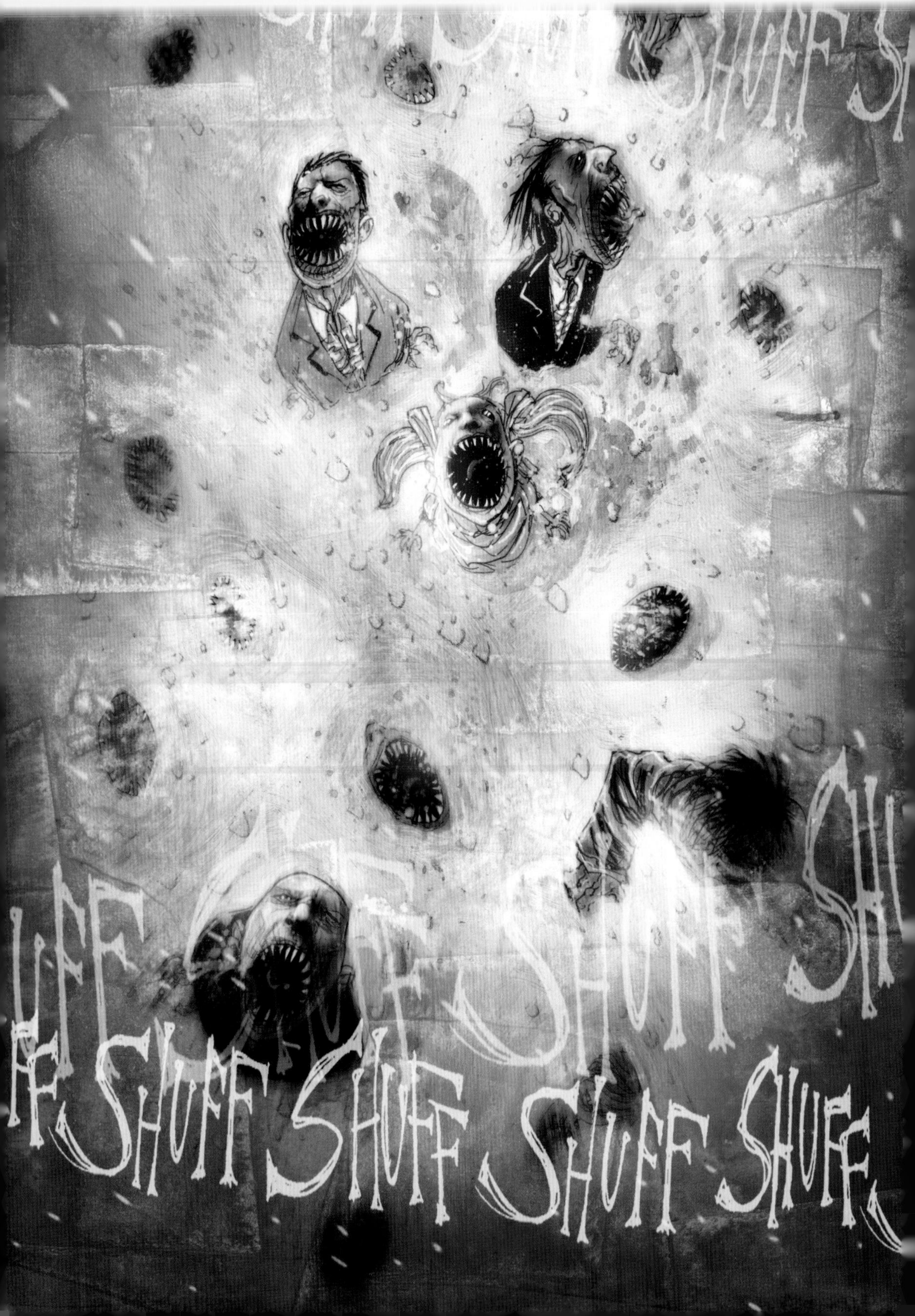
SHUFF SHUFF SHUFF SHUFF

BEN TEMPLESMITH
INTERVIEW

The following interview was first published
in IDW's Focus On: 30 Days of Night, printed
in September of 2007.

In 2001, artist Ben Templesmith was illustrating Todd McFarlane's *Spawn* spin-off, *Hellspawn*, written

as that little 2002 comic, *30 Days of Night*, has exploded in popularity and is on the cusp of being released as a big-screen movie by Sony Pictures, we talked to Ben about that early time, and what it's meant to his career in the interceding years.

IDW: In 2001, "30 Days of Night" was one of a dozen or so paragraph-long proposals that Steve Niles had developed as possible comic book series/screenplays. Did you think at the time that this one had any more potential than the others? How did you get involved with 30 Days of Night?

Ben Templesmith: I just thought it was the most interesting one of the group. I saw it as a chance to do some cool visuals. If it's fun to draw, it's probably fun for an audience to read, I guess. I got a very strong vibe of "The Thing," which is a favourite movie of mine, so it was really an obvious choice. We did it as another project we were jointly working on at the time left us with plenty of time to kill, so figured we'd do something else at the same time.

IDW: Did you always have a specific art style and color palette in mind for the series?

BT: Yes. Blues for the world of **30 Days** (it's the Arctic at night, after all) and splashes of red… for the, uh… red stuff events. You know, the nasty stuff. That kind of only works on the actual location for the original series, of course. Seems it worked well enough for the art to be quite memorable with some! So hopefully that means it worked.

IDW: When the comic became the subject of a bidding war between movie studios, did you feel like your career was about to change, or was it all too sudden for you to really reflect on what it meant at the time?

BT: Not really. It was all unexpected and just viewed as icing on the cake. This was all before the really big "comics-to-film" explosion, really. I'm happy that what happened with the book led to enough recognition for me to continue having a career up to now of course! I was a young punk nobody at the time. I really just thought "Great! I guess I get some money! " which is nice, as I was still freshly living my dream of doing comics. I didn't need anything more than that. My God, the Internet itself was still pretty new to me back then. I had little idea of anything. Never really understood much about Hollywood until much later. I was a sheltered child, yes, and my ambitions were (and still are) quite small!

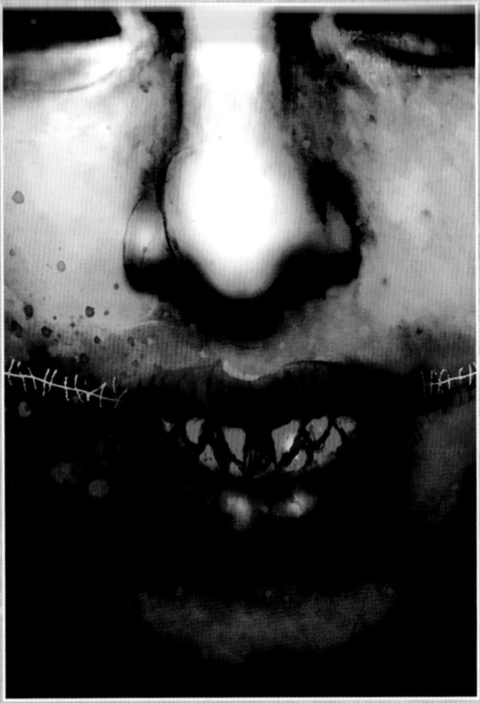

IDW: Now that you do have the luxury of time passed to look back at that exciting time, have things gone as you planned, for both the book (now franchise) itself and for you personally?

BT: Well, I never planned anything, so it really just happened the way it did thanks to people other than me deciding anything. I can't take any credit nor blame in that regard, I'd say. It simply is what it all is to me. I personally am not the type who likes endless sequels and such, but if a story is worth telling, then why not? It all depends. Looking back, I'm happy it seems to be one of the things that kicked off horror in comics again, and that I'm remembered for my art on it, as well as the fact I've been able to build on that initial success. Hopefully people don't see me only as "the vampire-drawing guy" now, either. It's always good to be considered more than a musician with a single note. Is that a phrase? So in many ways I'm most happy that I've been able to build a career around the initial success of ***30 Days***, but to also be able to have moved beyond it, so as not to only rely on that now. Of course, most things in my life currently are the end result of doing that one little book at the beginning of my career. Including my wife, who of course I met through IDW.

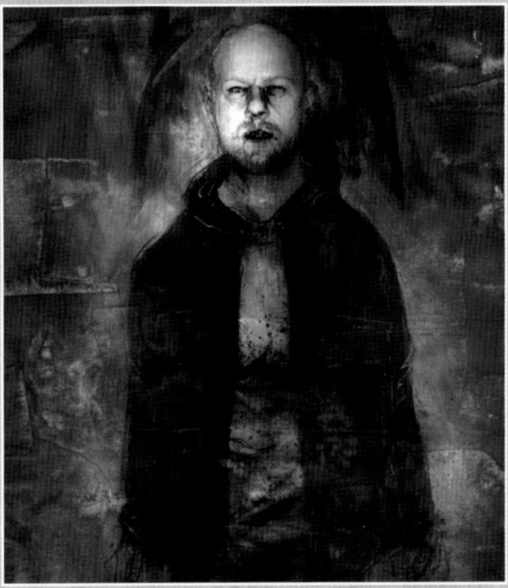

IDW: You recently spent some weeks on the set of the movie based on your original graphic novel. Did it feel like the culmination of a long career? What should fans of the graphic novel expect when they see it?

BT: Yes, I did, and it was, of course, amazing. Apart from being a bit of a trip down memory lane in a way, revisiting the book, it felt somewhat like the beginning of the end of a chapter of my life, yes, though *hopefully* not career! It's been a long, long time going from "we are going to option and make a film" through to "we are making the film" to shortly having the film out, and over with. After that, who knows? We'll wait and find out. I'm glad it's finally reaching a culmination. Fans of the book should, from my perspective as the visual guy, hopefully find an amazingly beautiful and nasty film that echoes all that made the book experience what it was art wise. David Slade did a wonderful job. Can't say enough about the level of detail and work he put into getting "the look."

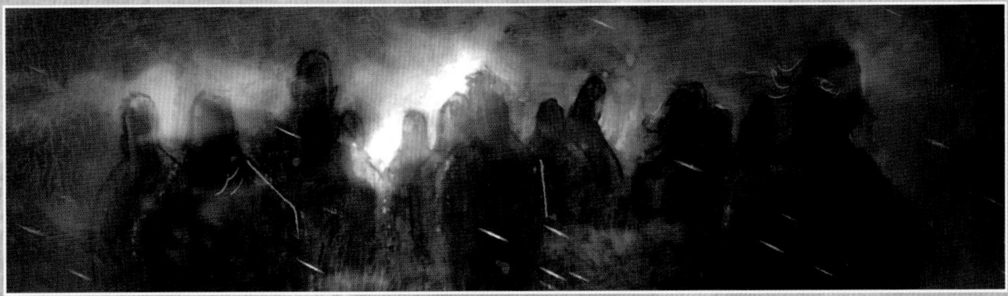

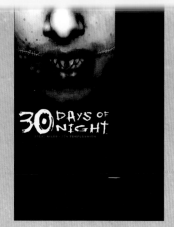
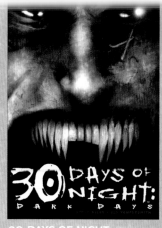
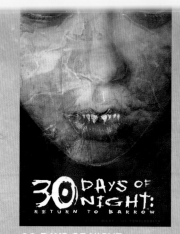

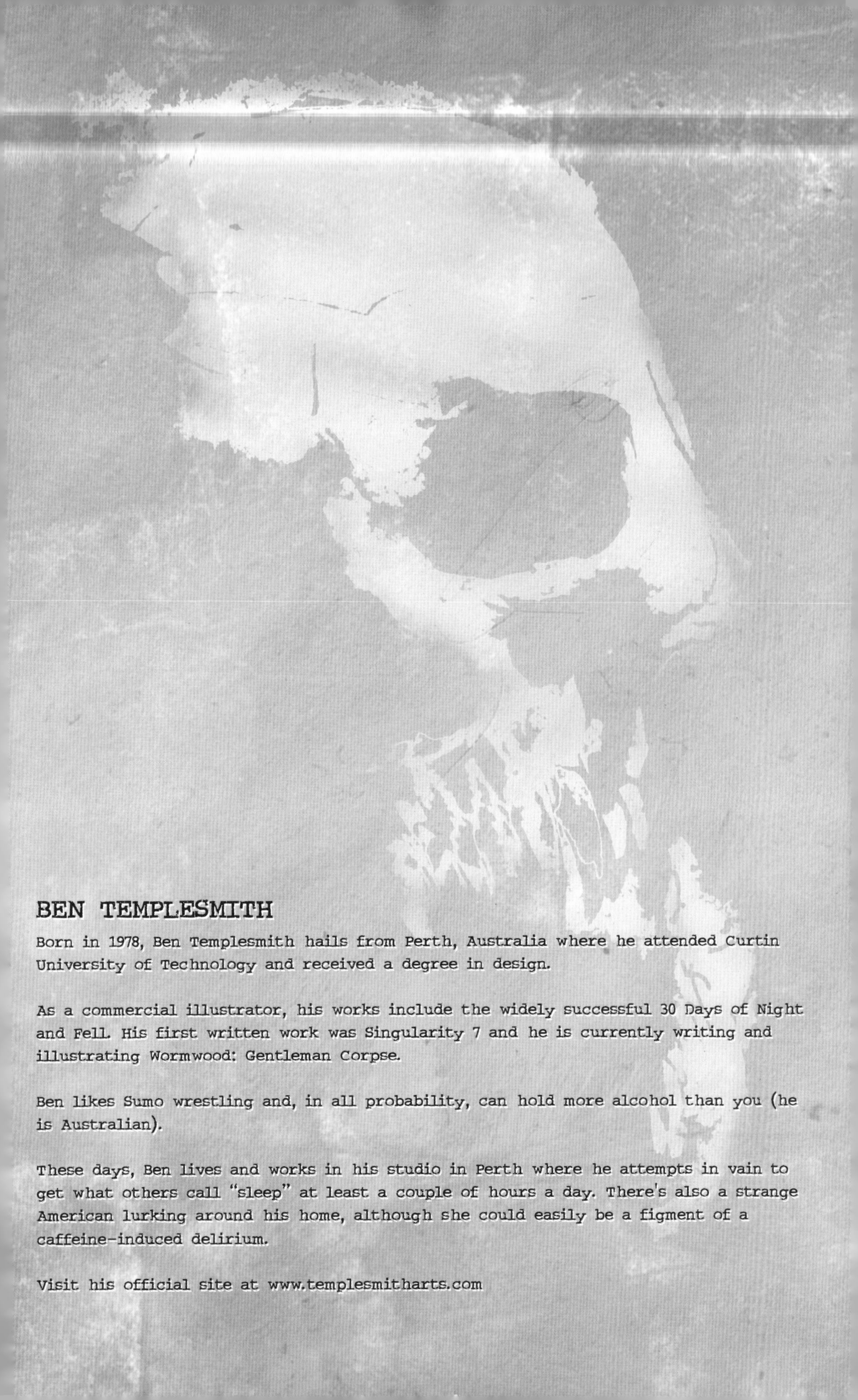

BEN TEMPLESMITH

Born in 1978, Ben Templesmith hails from Perth, Australia where he attended Curtin University of Technology and received a degree in design.

As a commercial illustrator, his works include the widely successful 30 Days of Night and Fell. His first written work was Singularity 7 and he is currently writing and illustrating Wormwood: Gentleman Corpse.

Ben likes Sumo wrestling and, in all probability, can hold more alcohol than you (he is Australian).

These days, Ben lives and works in his studio in Perth where he attempts in vain to get what others call "sleep" at least a couple of hours a day. There's also a strange American lurking around his home, although she could easily be a figment of a caffeine-induced delirium.

Visit his official site at www.templesmitharts.com

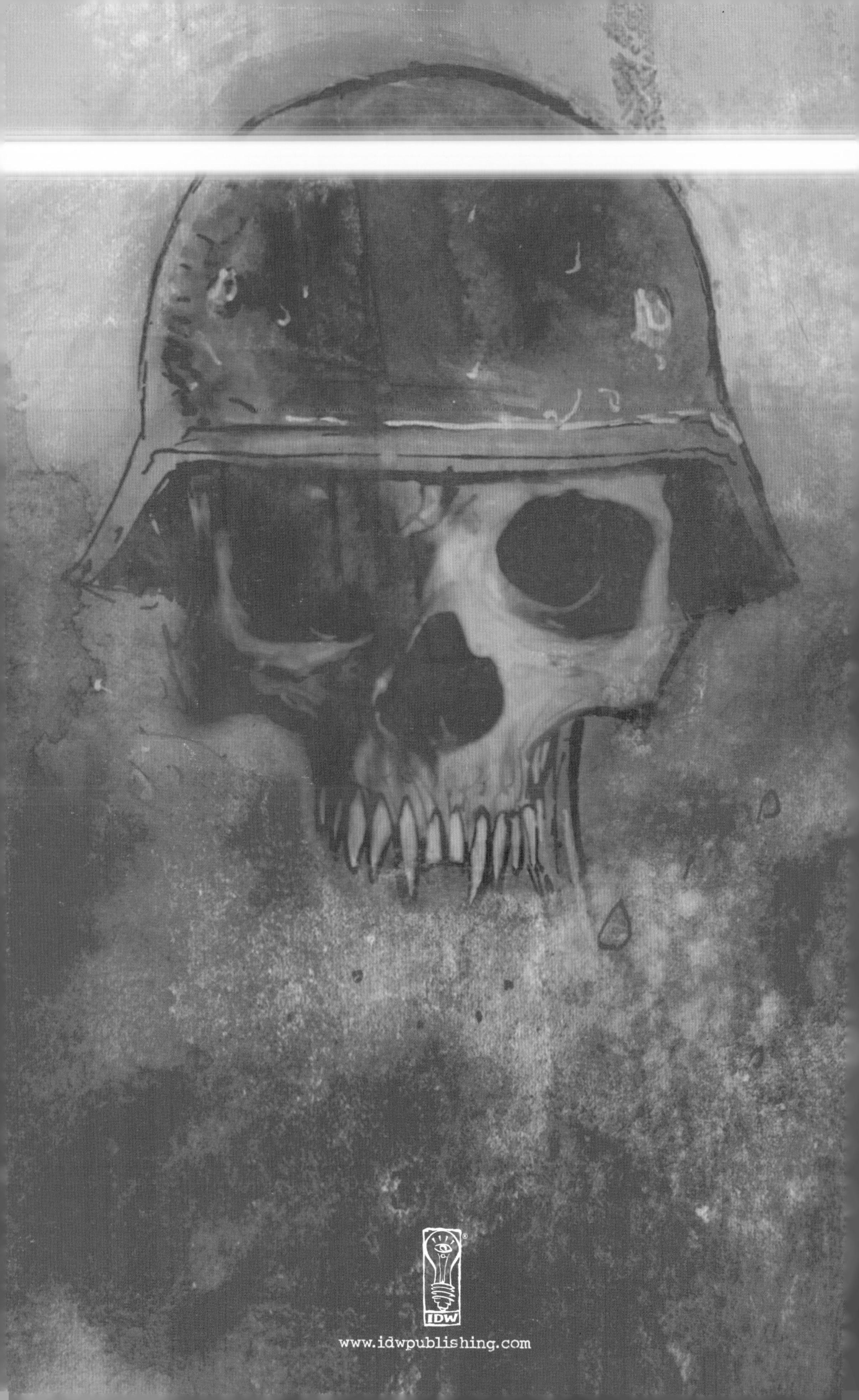

www.idwpublishing.com